THE
ROMANOVS

About the Author

Andrew Cook is a critically acclaimed historian and the author of five books. He has also been presenter and historical consultant on a number of hugely successful Channel 5, Channel 4 and BBC documentaries including *Jack the Ripper – Tabloid Myth*, *Prince Eddy*, *Three Kings at War* and *Who Killed Rasputin?* He lives in Bedfordshire.

PRAISE FOR ANDREW COOK:

Ace of Spies
'A myth-shattering *tour de force*' SIMON SEBAG MONTEFIORE
'Makes poor 007 look like a bit of a wuss' THE MAIL ON SUNDAY
'Successfully deconstructs many of the myths which have gathered around the remarkable life of Sidney Reilly' CHRISTOPHER M. ANDREW
'Brilliantly cuts through the webs of lies that Reilly spun'
BBC HISTORY MAGAZINE
'The absolute last word on the subject' NIGEL WEST

M: MI5's First Spymaster
'A brilliantly researched biography' STELLA RIMINGTON
'Serious spook-history' ANDREW ROBERTS
'Ground-breaking' THE SUNDAY TELEGRAPH
'One of the great espionage mysteries has finally been solved'
THE INDEPENDENT ON SUNDAY

To Kill Rasputin
'If you thought you knew how Rasputin met his end and who was responsible, think again' ANDREW ROBERTS
'A tale of blood, ice and thunderous politics, and Cook tells it both vividly and carefully' ROBERT SERVICE, AUTHOR OF STALIN: A BIOGRAPHY
'Astonishing' THE DAILY MAIL

Jack the Ripper
'Totally fascinating' SIMON SEBAG MONTEFIORE
'A triumph of research' ANDREW ROBERTS
'Exposes the hidden hand behind the Ripper myth' KELVIN MACKENZIE

The Murder of the
ROMANOVS

ANDREW COOK

AMBERLEY

This edition first published 2017

British Library Cataloguing in Publication Data.
A catalogue record for this book is available from the British Library.

ISBN 978 1 4456 6627 3

Typesetting and Origination by Amberley Publishing.
Printed in Great Britain.

Contents

Acknowlegements

I would like to thank the following people for their invaluable help: In particular I am indebted to Sandra Noble (Stephen Alley's granddaughter); Michael Alley (Stephen Alley's second cousin); Dr John Alley (from the American branch of the Alley family); Charles Alley (from the South African branch of the Alley family); Gordon Rayner (Oswald Rayner's nephew); Caroline Rayner (Oswald Rayner's daughter); Myra Welch (Oswald Rayner's first cousin once removed; Michael Winwood (Oswald Rayner's first cousin twice removed); Dimitri Kennaway (stepson of Joyce Frankel, Oswald Rayner's sister); Laurence Huot-Soloviev (great-granddaughter of Grigori Rasputin); 3rd Earl Lloyd George of Dwyfor (grandson of David Lloyd George); Mark Lane (grandson of William Compton); Svetlana Hodakovskaya (Senior Scientist, Museum of Political History, St Petersburg); Professor Derrick Pounder (Senior Home Office Forensic Pathologist and Head of Forensic Medicine, University of Dundee); Professor Vladimir V. Zharov (Senior Forensic Pathologist, Ministry of Health of the Russian Federation, Moscow) and to HM Government. As a result of an approach to the Cabinet Office, the Government agreed to provide me with a briefing on the British Intelligence Mission in Petrograd for the purpose of this book.

I am also grateful to Bill Adams; Professor Christopher Andrew (Corpus Christi College, Cambridge); Jordan Auslander; Dmitri Belanovski; Vanessa Bell (Assistant Archivist, News International Ltd); Gill Bennett (former Chief Historian, Foreign & Commonwealth Office); Robin Darwall-Smith (University College Archivist, Oxford); Howard Davies (The National Archives); Corinne Fawcett (University of Nottingham Archives); Dr Nicholas

Hiley (University of Kent); Rachel Hosker (Archivist, University of Glasgow); Professor A.V. Hoffbrand (Royal Free Hospital, London); Igor Kozyrin (Military Medical Archive, St Petersburg); Professor Christine Lee (Royal Free Hospital, London); Alexi Litvin (State Archive of the Russian Federation, GARF, Moscow); Natasha Nikolaeva; David Penn FSA (Keeper of the Department of Exhibits & Firearms, Imperial War Museum, London); Sarah Prescott (Archives Assistant, King's College, London); Kevin Proffitt (Senior Archivist, American Jewish Archives); Clare Rider (Inner Temple Archives); Michael Rosetti (Archives of the New York State Court); Graham Salt; Laura Scannel; Simon Sebag Montefiore; Professor Robert Service (St Antony's College, Oxford); Oleg Shishkin; Galina Sveshnikova (Yusupov Palace, St Petersburg); Mari Takayangi (Archivist, House of Lords Record Office); Phil Tomaselli and John Wells (Department of Manuscripts, Cambridge University Library).

Furthermore I would like to thank Bill Locke at Lion Television (Executive Producer of the Channel 4 documentary film *Three Kings at War*) whose unstinting support and encouragement enabled me to take this project forward.

A special thank you goes to Daksha Chauhan; Alison Clark; David Cook; Sonia Dipaolo; Julia Dvinskaya; Tami Elliott; Helen Kaltio; Nina Kalyan; Hannah Renier; Caroline Zahen; Chris Williamson and to RP Translate who facilitated the translation of source material into English. Finally my thanks go to my publisher Jonathan Reeve for his support throughout this project.

Preface

On 1 October 2008 Russia's Supreme Court ruled that Tsar Nicolas II be recognized as a victim of Soviet repression. The previous year a Supreme Court panel ruled that Nicolas and his family could not be rehabilitated because of a legal technicality: they had never been accused of a crime, so it was therefore impossible to rescind the accusation. However, an appeal was lodged by lawyers acting for Grand Duchess Maria Vladimirovna Romanov, who had brought the initial case, and the court agreed that the 2007 ruling was based on insufficient grounds.

The overthrow and subsequent murder of Tsar Nicolas II and the Russian Imperial family has long been attributed almost solely to the First World War. Without the war, seen as an inevitable cataclysm, many have argued that Nicolas would have survived and a Romanov might still today sit on the Russian throne, albeit as a constitutional monarch.

However, a growing number of historians not only disagree with this view but have argued that the fault-lines of the Romanovs' inevitable demise were already in evidence at least a decade before the war. Far from being an unavoidable tragedy, the war was, according to this theory, the indirect result of Nicolas's inability to control the course of events in his own sphere of influence, particularly in respect to Russia's critical relationship with Germany. As with the turmoil in Ireland, the war may even have delayed the moment of ultimate revolutionary eruption.

The Romanov demise was also in many ways more symptomatic of the growing tensions between the social classes that lived within the nation states. Europe at the turn of the twentieth century was a continent of two very different worlds. While economies and empires were growing, the majority of the 408 million population was still living in abject poverty. In Europe's largest country, Russia, peasants worked an average fourteen-hour day, six days a week. Theirs was a world of toil and struggle.

By contrast, in the world of state occasions, opulence and grandeur, rulers and landowners lived an apparently detached and carefree life. Queen Victoria was very much the lynchpin that held together the European monarchical club. Her sixty-four-year-long reign was one of perpetual dynastic expansion as she spread the influence of her kin to nearly all the palaces of Europe. When she died in 1901, Victoria left an extended family network that spanned nine European thrones. From London to Berlin, Oslo to Madrid, Victoria's offspring and their spouses were at the very top of high society. Not only were her grandsons George and Wilhelm to be monarchs of two of the most powerful empires in the world, she had also brought Nicolas, the Emperor of Russia, into the fold with the marriage of her granddaughter Alexandra in 1894.

My own interest in Nicolas and his family was rekindled when a friend working at GARF (the National Archive of the Russian Federation) stumbled across the complete correspondence between George V and Nicolas II, which began in 1890 and continued right up to the critical events of 1917. As a result of an invitation to visit Moscow and view the correspondence first hand, I became intrigued by Nicolas's contradictory character and by the extent to which he had effectively signed his own death warrant.

The subject of the murder of the Romanov family has been open to speculation for many decades and has given rise to a host of conspiracy theories and claims of escape and survival. During my own Romanov research, undertaken over the past decade, I came across a variety of source material, some of which later made valuable contributions to my books on William Melville (*MI5's First Spymaster*, 2004) and Rasputin (*To Kill Rasputin*, 2005).

When Channel 4 commissioned the *Three Kings at War* project in 2006, additional substantive research was undertaken, both here in the UK and more particularly with the co-operation and assistance of GARF and Moscow State University in Russia. Through this exclusive access, critical new evidence was unearthed which would cast new light on the circumstances surrounding the fate of the Imperial family and the myriad of myths that have surfaced over the best part of a century. A year after the broadcast of *Three Kings at War* the missing bodies of Alexei and his sister Maria were discovered in Russia and the results of the scientific investigation that followed are included in this book for the first time. Perhaps now the family can finally rest in peace.

1

La Grande Illusion

At 9 p.m. in the dark, cold night of 17 February 1920, less than six months after Lenin's assertion that the entire Russian Imperial Family were now dead, an ordinary working woman, in a black shawl, black skirt and boots, stood on the Bendlerbrücke in Berlin. Gloomily she stared down into the waters of the Landwehrkanal. Alongside the bridge rose the Bendlerblock, the Ministry of Defence, with its private apartments for senior officers in the German Army and Navy. Lamps glowed behind their curtains and reflections danced and flickered on the black water beneath.

The murdered corpse of Rosa Luxembourg, the well-known revolutionary, had been dragged out of the Landwehrkanal only last summer. This other, anonymous young woman was very much alive when she fell in, and she was seen. The Landwehrkanal is no more than seven feet deep, but in February's freezing temperatures she might not survive. A helpful police sergeant hauled her to safety and she was taken to hospital.

She was an odd girl. As she said almost nothing and was incapable of caring for herself she was dispatched – by someone with a black sense of humour – twelve kilometres away to a state-run mental hospital called Dalldorf. (The town of Dalldorf near Hamburg happens to be situated next to a much bigger, deeper canal.) There she stayed for two years, never once revealing her name. The nurses called her Fräulein Unbekannt, 'Miss Unknown'. The doctors reported that she had, at some time, been scarred by a bayonet and bullets; that to judge from her accent, she was probably from eastern Europe.

She was silent and her depression manifested itself in apathy. One day, an inmate called Clara spotted a resemblance between Miss

Unknown and a picture of the Grand Duchess Anastasia in the *Berliner Illustrierte*. She looked, looked again, and was convinced that they were one and the same. Clara had a connection with some monarchists, who had a connection with a journalist, who heard the story and, in October 1921, raised the question in print: Was one of the Tsar's daughters alive? Speculation snowballed. Miss Unknown was released from the institution and hunted down – with some difficulty, as she seemed frightened of what she was saying.

What she finally revealed caused a sensation that rippled out to news agencies all over the world. She said she was Anastasia, the fourth daughter of the Tsar, now aged twenty-one and the lone escapee from the firing squad. Questions came thick and fast. It emerged that she had been shot with the rest of the family, but one of the executioners – a young man called Tchaikowsky – had found her unconscious and secretly nursed her back to life. They had fled Russia for Romania; Tchaikowsky raped her; she had taken the resulting baby to an orphanage in or near Bucharest, and Tchaikowsky himself had been killed in a brawl. She had fled across Europe by train hoping to find her Aunt Irina, the sister of the Tsar, in Berlin. Overwhelmed by shame at having borne a child and fear of what Grand Duchess Irina would say, she had leapt into the Landwehrkanal.

Or alternatively, she had been drugged and stripped and thrown into 'a lake' near the Berlin Zoo by people who wanted to get rid of her. She told several stories and the details changed as time passed. That didn't seem to matter. Nor did her scant resemblance to the Grand Duchess Anastasia, nor the fact that she knew neither French nor English (languages spoken by the Tsar's children from their earliest years). She understood Russian, but did not speak it. She had an explanation for everything and there were people who wanted to believe her. Some of them hoped to make money out of her.

The economic imperative was a projected claim on the missing millions of the Romanov dynasty. The Romanovs had been among the most fabulously wealthy individuals in the world. It seemed the Tsar had made a secret deposit – a fortune for his children in the event of his death – at the Bank of England (Anastasia, or Anna

Anderson, as her followers came to call her, also said sometimes 'a bank in England') and there would be a claim.

In 1925 this was privately investigated, apparently by Mr Zahle, who was the former President of Denmark, possibly on behalf of the Tsar's mother, who had found refuge in Denmark, her natal land. The Zahle report was confidential and will not be released for public scrutiny until 2025. Another reliable source stated that an OTMA account (Olga, Tatiana, Maria, Anastasia – the Grand Duchesses) had indeed been set up in London years ago by the Tsar, but it had been taken back to help pay for Russia's war effort.

The Grand Duchess Anastasia was born in 1901. People who had known her well, her tutor, her nanny, some surviving relatives – people who had seen her regularly before and during the First World War – said that this young woman in Berlin was nothing like her. Others, mostly distant relations who had known her only slightly or not at all, seemed convinced that Anna Anderson was really the Grand Duchess. If she wasn't Anastasia, who was she? Nobody rushed forward to say 'she is my child' or 'she is my wife'.

The Tsarina's brother, Prince Ernst of Hesse, employed a private detective who cleverly identified her as a factory worker from the Gdansk region, born in 1896 and named Franziska Schankowska. Schankowska's landlady confirmed that this was who she was, as did an incident in 1916 at the factory where Schankowska had worked. It was an arms factory, and Schankowska had dropped a hand-grenade. The foreman had been torn apart before her eyes and she had suffered serious shrapnel wounds.

Anna Anderson and her supporters vehemently denied that she was this Schankowska person. There were odd details that confirmed the Anastasia story, and rather more that contradicted it, but nothing could be proved. Members of the Schankowska family, confronted by Anna Anderson, recognized her immediately but refused to claim her, in writing or in court, as their own. Newspaper articles continued to sell. Books were written. Two other Anastasias appeared, one in Russia, the other in Bulgaria.

Gleb Botkin, whose father had been the Tsar's doctor, insisted in 1927 that Anna Anderson should leave Europe for America, where he lived. She feared for her life, for dark reasons connected to the Tsar's alleged fortune. She flew to New York where wealthy supporters offered accommodation on Park Avenue and a glittering social life. In white satin and fur, her hair fashionably shingled, her gaping gums supplied with false teeth, Anna Anderson was, for a season, the person to meet. Rachmaninov paid her living expenses for several months. Here in New York, she revealed that her claim to the Romanov fortune must be made before the tenth anniversary of the Tsar's death on 17 July 1928. She said that if she stayed in Europe, rival claimants might have her done away with.

Any claim on anything required legal proof of identity, and this was not forthcoming. She moved in with a couple of supporters who had a house on Long Island. They had invited the house guest from hell: obstructive, passive-aggressive, avoidant, pathologically selfish. Eventually she ran out of friends and money and was returned to Germany, in 1931, to a mental institution near Hanover.

The Prince of Hesse (the Tsarina's brother) died at about this time, and the next head of the House of Hesse would have opposed her claim on anything from the estate. She saw him as the enemy. In no time a new set of distant-Romanov backers was assembled, and a lawsuit focused on proving her identity began soon afterwards. It would last – on and off, stopping and starting depending on the funds and witnesses available, wartime bombs and Germany's defeat, occupation and economic recovery – for nearly forty years. People from all over Europe came to testify for one side or another. One of them claimed to have been part of the firing squad, but was unmasked as an impostor.

Anastasia was kept in the Hanover asylum until the late thirties; when, in 1938, she was out, the German police tried to mount an investigation into her identity. True to type, she locked herself into her flat for a week and refused to say anything. The Second World War intervened to save her from further harassment. She spent most of it hiding in a German castle at the owner's expense. Afterwards, fussed over by a group of charitably disposed women, she was invited to live in a colony set up on anthroposophical lines approved by Rudolf Steiner at Unterlegenhardt, in the Black Forest. She was a trying resident who made long international phone calls in the middle of the night at the expense of the colony.

Post-war, the court case stopped and started as before. Graphologists, psychiatrists, historians, linguists, genealogists and forensic dentists were called in. Decades passed. Other Anastasias appeared, in Italy, Canada and elsewhere. The first Tsareviches turned up, and girls claiming to be her older sisters Olga, Tatiana and Maria. Oddly enough none of these people was particularly enthusiastic about re-uniting with any of the others.

In middle age Anna Anderson moved out of the main building at Unterlegenhardt to a wooden hut in the woods, where she lived for about fifteen years in fractious squalor with big dogs, disturbed very occasionally by a passing reporter or a photographer with a long lens. A play was produced in 1954, and a film called *Anastasia* was an international hit in 1956. Ingrid Bergman got an Oscar. The screenwriter (who had not even known 'Anastasia' was still alive) was persuaded to give Anderson a cut of the royalties. She got a new house, and some of her legal fees were paid. Her new accommodation quickly became as squalid as the old. Coachloads of rubberneckers turned up hoping to catch sight of her.

There she remained until the late 1960s, when she was forced back into a mental home by the local council, appalled by a starving feline population and general filth. For the two decades of her stay at Unterlegenhardt, her lady supporters had worked tirelessly to increase donations towards her upkeep and had arranged two re-mortgages; yet she had kept, and often failed to feed, over sixty cats and lived surrounded by heaps of unopened letters, mostly containing banknotes and cheques years old.

In 1968 her fare back to America was paid by Jack Manahan, a wealthy fifty-year-old genealogist friend of Gleb Botkin. After all that time in cold smelly accommodation, she looked much older than sixty-seven, the age that Grand Duchess Anastasia would be if she were alive. The authorities would not permit her to stay in the hotel room Manahan paid for in Charlottesville, Virginia, as her visa would run out in six months, so Manahan married her. She got a meal ticket, and he, in return, got a Grand Duchess for a wife – albeit one who was about to lose in court.

The German court which had first debated her identity in the 1930s gave its verdict in 1970. 'Anastasia' did not win. An old woman now, still intermittently institutionalized for mental instability, Anna Anderson was officially judged a fake. She had unwittingly founded a small industry. New Anastasias had never ceased to turn up, in Chicago, in England… But she, whose identity was unproveable, continued to insist that she was the one and only Anastasia and so did her supporters. Their incontrovertible argument was that nobody could prove the Grand Duchess had died.

Anderson died in 1984. If she was Anastasia, she was eighty-three; if she was Franziska Schankowska, she was eighty-nine. Photographs show that in her youth she looked nothing like Grand Duchess Anastasia. Her dental records were different, she spoke a different language and she had no knowledge of the rites of the Orthodox Church. Yet the desire to believe in a resurrection myth can be irresistible when a legendary figure suddenly disappears, and it was strongest of all with the Romanovs because there were no bodies.

What, people said, if all or some of them had been assisted to escape, either after a botched execution or even before? The British, with their year-round access, at Murmansk, to the open sea, would have made perfect rescuers. The King of England could have offered the Tsar's family new identities in some quiet corner of the British Empire. Surely they must have lived out the remaining months of the war in a castle in remotest Scotland, before sailing for Canada under new names, to wait until Russia would permit them to return?

In the late 1980s, several years after Anderson died, Russia's Communist economic and social system was essentially the one that had been founded in 1918. If any monarchists had survived Stalin's purges on Russian soil, they were poor, their lives a long struggle relieved only by dreams. They had plenty of time to argue over unsolved mysteries.

And what of the few, the very few, well-informed investigators? There were no bodies and the more one thought about it, the more likely it seemed that some, at least, of the Romanovs might have been assisted to escape from Ekaterinburg. Tsar Nicolas II had been close to two powerful men: the King of England and the Kaiser. The Germans had no access to Siberia but the British could have done it. At one time in the civil war that went on until 1921, British agents had been with the White Armies in the Urals. And everyone knew the British security services had worked in cahoots with the Okhrana (their Russian counterparts) on and off for thirty years, to protect the Russian royal family. The last time had been in the summer of 1909.

2

Georgie & Nicky

'Counterparts' they may have been, but members of the Okhrana, in 1909, operated in a different universe from the detectives who guarded the English king. The Tsar's reign to date had been fifteen years of protest and mild rebellion, quelled by vicious pogroms and massacres, which were answered with assassinations, followed by arrests and executions, resulting in uprisings and mutinies: a tit-for-tat war between the Romanovs and the minority among their citizens. By 1909 this minority, in Russia and in exile abroad, split into several factions, most important of which were the trigger-happy Bolsheviks or the equally angry, but less violent and more numerous, Social Revolutionaries. The Okhrana were constantly engaged in putting out forest fires.

To be a British Special Branch officer a man must have distinguished himself in the Metropolitan Police and the University of Life. To be an officer in the Okhrana a man must be a member of the Corps of Gendarmes. And to get into that, he had to be of the nobility, to have passed out well from a military college, to be Orthodox, to have no debts and to have been in a good regiment for six years at least. The Corps of Gendarmes had been formed as a police anti-corruption squad, but its Okhrana sections in Moscow, St Petersburg and Warsaw (which was within the Russian Empire) were tasked with spying upon and arresting members of revolutionary and dissident organizations. In practice, 'revolutionary' and 'dissident' meant pretty much the same thing to the Okhrana. Fiercely dedicated to protecting the status quo, it had developed an impetus of its own.

General Alexander Spiridovich, who was the senior Okhrana officer in the Russian protection squad in 1909, complained that the Tsar and his family had never taken their personal danger seriously enough. He blamed Stolypin, the former Prime Minister. Stolypin, he said, had insisted on telling the Tsar that these 'local risings' were nothing to worry about.

When King Edward VII invited the Tsar to England, a visit to London was considered out of the question. Spiridovich saw London as a hotbed of violent agitators. Russian political exiles from all over Europe (including Lenin and the young Stalin) had convened at a pub in Stoke Newington only two years before, to plot the downfall of Tsardom. But the annual regatta at Cowes on the Isle of Wight, like Glorious Goodwood and Derby Day, was a delightful fixture of the English summer season, an event to which it was a compliment to be invited. A secure one too, for on an island, would-be attackers would be trapped.

So in the summer of 1909 the Okhrana men surrounding the Tsar looked forward to sailing there. The Imperial annual diary generally consisted of a holiday in the warm Crimea in March and April, the bracing Baltic seaside in May, sailing off the Finnish coast in June and July, a brief stay at Peterhof before hunting in Polish forests in August, Crimean sunshine again in September and October, and four months of snow at Tsarskoe Selo, their home outside St Petersburg, between November and February.

This year in July they were at Peterhof, the vast complex of gilded palaces, fountains and gardens on the coast near St Petersburg, so that the Tsar and Tsarina might receive in gracious splendour his uncle and aunt the King and Queen of Denmark. Only after the guests' departure could the Imperial attendants complete preparations for the visit to England. The logistics of the journey, via the Kiel Canal with a brief stopover at Cherbourg before the Channel crossing, were terrifying, largely because of the security required. Spiridovich commanded two officers and 160 men, most of whom would be going with him.

The Kiel Canal was German territory. This summer Kaiser Wilhelm was at pains to mend fences between Germany and Russia; their relationship, key to his international strategy, had cooled. He instructed his aide, Captain Hintze, to do all the Okhrana asked and more. Hintze made sure that while Tsar Nicolas, his family and entourage travelled along the Kiel Canal, all maintenance work would be stopped and the workmen would be kept three kilometres from the banks.

On 15 July the party left Kronstadt in the enormous 401-foot Imperial yacht *Standart*. Only this year, Monsieur Fabergé had made, within a glass egg about twenty centimetres long, a perfect miniature of the *Standart*, omitting of necessity the sparkling chandeliers, mahogany panelling and deep carpets within. Now the real-life ship was accompanied by the *Polar Star*, a yacht that belonged to the Tsar's mother, the cruisers *Admiral Makharov* and *Rurik*, and a division of torpedo boats.

The Kaiser himself, Her Majesty the Kaiserin and their eldest son made a quick visit to the *Standart* at the canal approach, bringing flowers and words of welcome. A guard of honour on the banks sang in Russian 'God Save the Tsar'. Two detachments of cavalry accompanied the *Standart*'s stately progress through the canal, one on either side. Halfway along, another guard of honour appeared and another choir sang the anthem. The entire anthem-and-guard ceremony took place for a third time as the Russians entered the North Sea. Spiridovich and his fellow officers were particularly impressed by the height of the guards of honour, who all looked as tall as giants. And the German cavalry had Cossack horses! No detail had been missed. The Kaiser had made his admiration clear. Could he woo the Tsar? No one knew.

Between Kiel and Cherbourg there was rough sea and fog, and Spiridovich noted that the women and children – not, of course, the men, heaven forbid – were sea-sick. At last, through fog, ships of the French navy fired cannons to welcome the Russians to Normandy; Cherbourg lay ahead. The President of the Republic came aboard and took the Tsar away to inspect the French Mediterranean and North squadrons in the harbour. There was dinner aboard a French ship for the Tsar, and aboard a different French ship for the Russian officers; and an exchange visit with the Tsarina as hostess; and gifts from the President – Gobelins tapestries for the Tsarina, carefully chosen toys and trinkets for each child and two nights of fireworks.

The proximity of Paris was of concern to the Okhrana. Paris was a hotbed of revolution, as relaxed as London in its treatment of dissent. Some of the Russians had Parisian ladies come to meet them ashore and on other boats but no doubt this was entirely in the course of duty.

On 1 August at 8 a.m., the British squadron arrived accompanied by French ships and the Russian guests passed into the Royal Navy's care. They would be escorted to Cowes by three British cruisers, *Indomitable*, *Implacable* and *Invincible*, and outlying torpedo boats. On their arrival at Cowes that afternoon in a leaden sea with a cold wind, the fat English King wheezed aboard the *Standart* from his yacht the *Victoria and Albert* and took the Imperial couple back with him. At 3 p.m. the Tsar, who had been made an honorary Admiral of the Fleet, was to inspect the entire British navy, and by that time the sun was out.

Spiridovich was awestruck. 'At that moment I understood at last why our royals have always been so keen on the Fleet. The Fleet expresses a state's military power.' You couldn't see a whole army, it was simply too big, but a navy could be drawn up before you in all its formidable glory. He saw three rows of big warships and many others right across Spithead – 153 ships, not counting torpedo boats and dinghies, with twenty-eight admirals in command. British hurrahs and the Russian anthem drifted across on a strong wind. Dreadnoughts were the latest thing in warships, rendering obsolete all that had gone before. The Russian navy only had one, but here were several, looking to Spiridovich like monstrous smoothing irons.

Up and down the lines ploughed the *Standart*, and the Russians were astonished to see ladies waving hankies from many of the dinghies and even some of the ships. Years later, Spiridovich said that they had been jealous of it all: the impressive navy, the spontaneity and relaxed goodwill. Aboard the *Polar Star* was a liberal Francophile, pro-European party (as opposed to the more Slavophile leanings of many) led by the Minister of Foreign Affairs, Isvolsky, with a monocle, and his advisor Savinski, derided by the Okhrana officers as a fashion-plate. Isvolsky in particular delighted in the impression the British were making. He had talked with the King at length in London before they brought the Anglo-Russian entente into being in 1907, and again on the Baltic coast during the King's visit to Russia's Estonian coast in 1908, and it was only thanks to Edward VII's personal intervention that Isvolsky had recently been excused a diplomatic gaffe in the Balkans that had nearly resulted in war with Germany.

Cowes was crowded with chaps in sailing togs and ladies in picture hats and many Russians went ashore, having fun trying to make themselves understood. The Russian officers, used to military costume, never could get civilian dress quite right. Their trousers were crumpled; Spiridovich was understandably preoccupied by smoothing irons. But on that first evening, he had to attend the Tsar and Tsarina at dinner on the *Victoria and Albert*. No two individuals could have been more different in outlook than Tsar Nicolas II and King Edward VII, and conversation focused safely upon sentimental recollections of the yacht in Queen Victoria's time.

The following morning, delegations were received aboard the *Standart* and the Lord Mayor of London presented a magnificent gold coffret. Before lunch the Tsar, having been made a member of the Royal Yacht Club, went off with the Prince of Wales to race in the King's yacht *Britannia*. The children were driven to Osborne, the royal estate, by car. Its home farm, Barton Manor, had been placed at the Tsar's disposal and they played on the beach. The Tsarevich was delicate and must not swim or even paddle. He was kept well clear of the King's grandson Bertie, the future King George VI, who had suddenly got whooping cough.

In the early evening the older girls, Olga, Tatiana and Maria, aged fourteen, twelve and ten, went unrecognized into the town to shop, with their people. (One wonders what shopkeepers made of their Scottish accents, learned from Palace staff since babyhood; a new tutor, Mr Gibbes, had been hired last year to teach them Received Pronunciation.) Word got out about the girls in grey dresses, and police had to clear a way through the crowds. The Okhrana officers had no intelligence to indicate assassination attempts, but the situation made them uneasy. Although they were fully armed, they kept their authoritarian impulses in check. They had been told to show sensitivity to local conditions. In England in the 1890s, the then head of the British royal protection squad had remarked: 'The Russian police had to be taught that they could not shoot at sight and that suspects could not be carried off into the unknown without certain formalities.'

Protected by apparently benevolent British policemen, these children had never had such freedom before, and pleaded to stay ashore longer. In two carriages, with attendants, they set off to visit a church, where the vicar showed them items of interest such as a seat sat upon by Queen Victoria. A tame choice of entertainment, but at least something of which Mama would approve. The Tsarina was as usual lying down for the day.

The Russians were in England for only three days, but there was fraternization. English officers came aboard with young wives in white organdie dresses, and journalists were shown around the *Standart* in the absence of the Imperial family. Some of the Russians even spent a few hours in London. Only the Tsar and the two Russian admirals were never allowed ashore; the Okhrana could not take that risk.

Cowes Week was an annual event of which King Edward VII, exhaling cigar smoke towards the sky over the English Channel, was extremely fond. A pretty little town only a few miles from the south coast, it offered a refuge from the gutter press and London's tired millions. Thirty years ago, as Prince of Wales he had indulged a passion for Lily Langtry, his actress friend, on a yacht here. Now the King was sixty-eight-years-old, vastly overweight with a drinker's complexion, breath like a cork and baggy eyes. The sea air, he hoped, would do him good; but he could not ignore the ominous drumbeat of war. It could be heard behind every event like this now: an insistent threat from Germany. Everyone knew why the navy had been so triumphantly shown off. The Triple Entente between France and Russia and England must hold. The British army was not all it should be, despite recent improvements, and the Germans scorned it. The Russians, technologically backward as they still were, must stay on side; a strong British navy, and Russia's limitless supply of cannon fodder, seemed the only available deterrent.

Temperamentally Edward VII had nothing in common with his Russian guest. Where the King was old, self-indulgent, worldly and gregarious, the Tsar was only forty-one, slightly built and passive, with few close friends. Edward despaired of Nicolas as a weak character, easily influenced and averse to confrontation, and Nicolas knew it. He was more comfortable with Edward's son, his cousin George, Prince of Wales, who was forty-four. While some physical resemblance between cousins is to be expected, Nicolas and George looked like twins. Everyone noticed it, though as the French President had observed, George's 'colour was not so pale, his expression less dreamy, his smile less melancholy and his gestures less timid'.

Cowes rejoiced in the Russian visit. By day rich men raced fast cutters and yachts, and by night their wives entertained high society at splendid dinners and dances. All the hotels were full. Dwarfing most of the other yachts in the harbour, the royal pair – the *Standart* bigger by twenty feet, and heavily armed – made an impressive sight.

Both had been built bigger and faster and grander to compete with the *Hohenzollern II*, owned by the Kaiser. Older cousin to the Tsar and the Prince of Wales, and nephew to the King, Kaiser Wilhelm was one foreign monarch whom the King preferred to avoid; the man was a bully, two-faced, personally insulting and beyond reason in his views. In England, people thought that King Edward had pulled out of a visit to Berlin the previous year because of his Danish wife's hostility to all things German. In fact it was the prospect of having to spend more than an hour in Wilhelm's company. By avoidance one slighted him, and caused further petulance, but so be it.

By inviting the Tsar to Cowes the English quietly scored a diplomatic triumph. Points were being subtly made: that the institution of monarchy was alive and kicking here despite British democracy, that English people generally were pretty much content and ill-disposed to rebel, and that this branch of the Royal clan was altogether nicer – and nationally, imperially, culturally more advantageous to know – than pushy Wilhelm.

British politicians, working behind the scenes with Isvolsky and his team, had no visible part to play on the stage that was Cowes. The Tsar would never understand that Edward VII wielded nothing like the autocratic power that he himself insisted upon as ruler of

Russia. The King was too canny not to keep the Foreign Office's position in mind at all times and knew how to play a convincing role as diplomatic figurehead. He had been doing so, working with backstage politicians and civil servants, when he helped negotiate the *Entente Cordiale* with the French in 1904.

In 1905, Nicolas had been bewildered and humiliated to discover the limits to his own decision-making skill. A yacht had been involved then, too, but much less happily – for it had been aboard *Seiner Majestät Yacht Hohenzollern II*, rocking in calm water north of Stockholm in 1905, that Wilhelm II, his moustachios twitching riskily, had asked dear Nicolas – the morning after a lavish dinner – to sign a tripartite treaty of friendship which France would join later. Nicolas had been only too delighted. The English were cross with him about the war with Japan but now – an ally! Dear cousin Willy, godfather to the baby Tsarevich! Willy had always understood his – Russia's – need for a friend.

Russian diplomats had been appalled. They had already put in place an understanding with France, and it was the cornerstone of their entire foreign policy. The Tsar's consent to Wilhelm's treaty was hastily withdrawn. Nicolas was chastened. In foreign policy, though in nothing else, he had listened to advisors ever since. Russia, he had been made to understand, did not want a treaty with Germany in 1905. Four years later, at Cowes, it still did not want one. Friendly advances from the British, on the other hand, were looked upon with perfect equanimity.

Defiance from politicians and civil servants had been new to the Tsar in 1905. He had only just, smarting from the ignominy of a disastrously lost war with Japan and a revolution, conceded that a Duma, a lower house of Parliament, would have a constitutional right to participate in decision-making. He grumbled about it still, four years later.

His wife would never understand the need for a Duma at all. She was the Tsarina Alexandra, 'Alicky', a niece of King Edward VII. She had been beautiful in her early youth, but she had always cultivated a martyred air and her tight little mouth was now set in an expression of affliction. To unkind eyes she had become, at thirty-seven, a whining depressive with religious mania, but Nicolas adored her. She flattered him and believed it her duty to direct him in the correct path. It was one of those marriages with several people in it, the others being the mystic peasant Rasputin, and Alexandra's ever-present companion Anna Vyrubova. Alexandra hung on Rasputin's every word. Rasputin had treated her sick son Alexei, the Tsarevich, when doctors could do nothing. It had been a miracle; and ever since, she had been convinced that Rasputin's utterances came straight from God. Rasputin represented 'Russia' or 'the Russian soul' or an idealized Russian serf, a messenger sent by God with holy commands to be implemented by the Tsar and Tsarina. Ideas and policies had a way of originating with Rasputin, and passing through Alexandra to Nicolas, whose autocratic power remained potent enough to put most of them into action. Rasputin's insights were, after all, God-given. Nicolas affected to believe this because his wife did; to challenge it would cause her too much distress. It would imply that there was no hope for little Alexei at all.

Nicolas and Alexandra were flawed, but they were family. When, like the Kaiser, the Tsar or the King, one could speak intimately with the Kings and Queens of Belgium, Norway, Greece, Denmark, Romania and several others and know that they were all close blood relatives, there was an understandable tendency to personify a country's political will in its head of state and make diplomatic alliances in an informal, personal way. King Edward VII knew better, but the constitutional framework of Germany gave more power to Wilhelm, and Wilhelm did not doubt that Germany's destiny was his own. As for Nicolas, Alexandra never allowed him to doubt that he ruled by divine right. He could and did dissolve the Duma when he felt like it and his regime was brutal, yet many millions of peasants saw divinity in him. Cruelty and starvation, they thought, would be alleviated by the gentle Tsar at once, if only he knew; but his wicked advisors did not tell him how they suffered.

Disability ran in the families descended from Queen Victoria. Nicolas and Alexandra had four daughters and the little Tsarevich. He had inherited haemophilia, the rare disease in which the blood lacks coagulant, through the female line. George, Prince of Wales, and his wife, Princess May of Teck, had five sons and a daughter and their own youngest son, Prince John, suffered epileptic fits and learning difficulties.

Nicolas and George – Nicky and Georgie, as they addressed one another above the wind, as *Britannia* sped across the Solent – had other things in common. They were both second sons. Nicky's parents' firstborn son had died while Prince 'Eddy', George's sleepy-eyed, good-natured older brother, had lived to be twenty-eight before dying of influenza. Eddy, that earlier Prince of Wales, had made a play for Alexandra when she was still Princess Alix of Hesse, but she had not been interested; Nicolas was always her favourite. Eddy had subsequently become engaged, six weeks before he died, to Princess May of Teck, who had long been a favourite of Queen Victoria at court. When the period of mourning for Eddy was over, May had married his brother George. No one was much surprised; this is how such matters were arranged, in royal circles.

May was a shy, intelligent, aesthetically sensitive woman married to a philistine, sometimes irascible, essentially good-hearted man. Alexandra and Nicolas, not to mention Wilhelm, felt slightly superior to May of Teck. There was a morganatic marriage in her background, and in Alexandra's company she may have been conscious of it. Bloodlines mattered less to the British, who were, with some exceptions, more secular in outlook. For Wilhelm and the Romanovs, one's unsullied pedigree was proof of superiority. Science had not figured noticeably in their early education.

Not that George had ever been other than intellectually lazy. He saw himself as a bluff, no-nonsense sailor, and had spent much of his life in the navy. He was the only monolinguist among this royal crowd. All the rest, including the absent Wilhelm, had learned English, French and German and often a fourth language from tutors and governesses, their parents and travel; indeed German had been the King's first language, and he still spoke English with a guttural accent. Years of tuition had failed to din German or French into George.

He had little interest in European culture generally. The Pacific, where he had sailed as a naval cadet in his youth, and India, of which he would one day be the emperor, captured his imagination more. He held his father's and grandmother's anti-racist views, foresaw Indian independence and abhorred the brutal attitudes of some of the British occupiers. In England he was happiest living quietly with his family, his sporting guns and his stamp collection in York Lodge, an adjunct to the main house on the Sandringham Estate.

Nicolas and Alexandra were similarly uxorious and adored cosy domesticity. They had palaces by the score, and did indeed live in one at Tsarskoe, but as Russian palaces went, it was understated and modest. The faux-bourgeois habit of life, and mistrust of fashionable metropolitan society, was something instilled in Georgie, Nicky and Alicky by their grandmother, Queen Victoria. Thankfully for the sake of colour and life, it had skipped a generation in Edward VII.

Wilhelm, sulking in Berlin while Nicky cosied up to the English, was less uxorious and home-centred than Nicky and Georgie. Fifteen years younger and much fitter than his uncle Edward VII, people said that his hectoring personal style had developed to compensate for his own disability. His left arm was withered, but by force of will he had taught himself to ride, shoot and swim and dominate other people. He was suspicious of the motives of others, and afraid that Germany would one day be encircled and overwhelmed by an alliance between Russia, France and England. Worse still, as he never failed to believe and to impress upon Nicolas, Russia was threatened with invasion from the east by what he called the Yellow Peril (Japan and China), and from within by the insidious influence of the Hidden Hand: the Jews. Both the Tsar and the Kaiser believed in a worldwide Jewish conspiracy. They were always suspicious of King Edward, who had close Jewish friends and was an 'arch intriguer and mischief maker', according to Kaiser Wilhelm.

Georgie got on better with both of them. He was temperamentally indulgent, inclined to be ill-tempered sometimes, but lacking his father's capacity for dislike. In his eyes, Wilhelm was socially a blunderer, but George found what good there was – the Kaiser had learned to shoot rather well, for instance, despite the withered arm. He made Wilhelm godfather to one of his sons. What George absolutely hated was unpleasantness, and if there was any, he might choose to ignore it. After attending the wedding of Nicolas and Alexandra in 1894, he wrote to his grandmother: 'When they drove from the Winter Palace after the wedding they got a tremendous reception and ovation from the large crowds in the streets, the cheering was most hearty and reminded me of England.' There could be no higher praise. Nicolas was a 'dear boy', 'very popular' and 'kindness itself to me'. That this had been the day when Grand Duke Serge botched the organization of a wedding feast for members of the public, over a thousand of whom were trampled to death – and that the Imperial couple had been so insensitive as to go to a ball that night anyway – he omitted to mention.

Somehow contentious issues were avoided throughout the three or four days at Cowes. At a banquet on the last night, the British agreed that it had been just long enough, had conveyed goodwill, and had shown off British naval power. Job done: the Russians were on side. That evening the whole immobile British fleet was lit up in outline – 'like a fairy story' gasped Spiridovich; and the next morning, it was gone.

They sailed back to Russia at a snail's pace through dense fog and Nicolas arrived at Kiel too late to inspect the German Fleet. The Kaiser came aboard loudly complaining about God, who constantly visited such misfortunes upon him. This got an icy reception from the pious Romanovs. 'One could see that there was not much cordiality in the conversation that took place between himself and the Tsar,' noted wry Spiridovich.

They were back at Tsarskoe Selo before the middle of August. Tsarskoe, 'the Tsar's village', was an 800-acre private estate with a small town, mansions, gardens, follies and grace-and-favour lodges and lakes scattered over two parks. It contained also the baroque Catherine Palace. The Alexander Palace was the one they lived in. This was a two-storey neo-classical mansion that occupied three sides of a courtyard, with tall windows and a colonnade, statues, wide staircases, acres of parquet flooring, a picture gallery and lustrous chandeliers. It occupied a delightful park of its own, with a lake, private gardens, woods and so on, patrolled by Cossacks on horseback. It made York Lodge, where the Prince of Wales lived, look like a beach hut, but by Romanov standards it was a rather ordinary house.

There had been a railway station at Tsarskoe since 1837, but in the summer of 1909 a long-awaited improvement was complete. A private railway line now brought visitors direct from a special platform at St Petersburg to the Alexander Palace. It is those little details that make all the difference.

The Tsarina returned from England in a poor state of health. Her medical advisor, Dr Botkin, could not say what the matter was but by tacit consensus the Okhrana officers decided – before she even left the ship – that it was nothing serious. She was a sickly woman. At various times she suffered from oedema, sciatica, and heart pain, and she was afflicted by neurosis; it ran in the Hesse family, they said, as haemophilia did. Privately, her staff said she had never learned Russian as well as a Tsarina should. The children all spoke English with her but everyone outside the family thought of her as German. A Russian professor of medicine once spoke to Spiridovich about her 'hystero-neurasthenic problems and psychological trouble'. He saw depression, mysticism, impressionability, anxiety and a lack of capacity for logical thought. Nobody would argue with any of that, except the Tsar.

3

The Problem

Russia had not one problem, but many, in the years before the First World War. 'Russia needs peace,' Nicky had written to King Edward in 1908, 'more than any other country at the present moment.' Russia needed peace because Russia needed time to develop an industrial base and skill-based industries such as chemicals, mining, engineering and banking. Foreign investment was pouring in, but with industry came a working class, and educated technocrats and managers. As the urban proletariat gained self-respect and confidence, there was social unrest. Russia in the twentieth century struggled with a feudal system that had last been effective in the thirteenth; the population could see it, the foreign diplomats could see it, but the autocrats themselves, the Tsar and Tsarina, were, as Haldane remarked of Kings generally, 'carefully protected against disagreeable realities'. They refused to countenance change.

International political alliances could also produce unintended consequences. When King Edward died in 1910, and the Prince of Wales became King George V, Britain and France and Russia were in one alliance, and Germany and Austro-Hungary in the other. Each member of the alliance agreed to defend the rest against all comers. This might have worked, had these been self-contained countries, but they were not; for the most part they were empires. They had grabbed bits of land when they needed them, and now the passage of goods and services to the home country was, or could be, everywhere confronted by obstacles. As a result no single empire was satisfied to leave the world's political geography alone.

Russia was huge; it sprawled from sea to sea across Europe and Asia with enormous mineral reserves in the east. Its only warm-water port was on the Black Sea, and despite Isvolsky's best efforts Turkey still controlled access to the Mediterranean via the Dardanelles. At the moment, Russia wanted peace in which to develop, but was nervous about Germany which was increasingly meddling in Turkish affairs.

Germany had already spread all the way along the south Baltic coastline and into Silesia. An upstart country, which like Italy had not existed as a constitutional entity until the nineteenth century, Germany had come late to empire-building and found that all the choicest places had been taken. At home, German governments were dependent on support from the farmers. The farmers insisted that tariffs must protect German food and grain production. This was all very well for them, but it increased the cost of living, which pushed up wages, and meant that German industrial exports were over-priced abroad. Industry languished and the government invested in armaments to kick-start it; but that raised taxes. Another enterprise enthusiastically embarked upon was the Berlin to Baghdad railway, an overland route to East Africa via Iraq. Goods in and out of Germany would have to travel overland because the British controlled the quicker route through the Suez Canal. Wilhelm did not trust the British.

For their part, the British needed a clear defensible route to India and the Persian oilfields. They could not trust the Germans now, because overland access to both Persia (in which they had agreed spheres of influence with Russia), and India, might be obstructed by the Berlin to Baghdad line. Besides, when Britain produced the first Dreadnought in 1906, the Germans (still seeking to compensate industry for its lost exports) had belligerently started producing Dreadnoughts of their own, stepping up their arms production and enlarging the Kiel Canal so that Dreadnoughts could patrol it. Seven eighths of everything the British ate and used was imported; if Germany ever succeeded in blocking access to British ports, more than fifty million people could go hungry. Britain was soon spending more on its own navy than ever before, somewhat to the detriment of its army.

Thanks to the alliances between empires, there were flashpoints all over the world. Turkey, for instance; should Serbia make a move against it, Germany would come to Turkey's aid, but Serbia was a Slav nation and therefore supported by Russia. In this eventuality Germany could find itself attacking Russia from the south, an opportunity it would be only too happy to take. On the other hand, were a French colony to be attacked by Germans, the Russians and British were bound by their entente to pitch in alongside France and repel the invader. A German gunboat did indeed provoke an 'incident' at Agadir, in Morocco, a French possession, in 1911. It was the second time the Kaiser had done something like this in North Africa and hot words were exchanged. Wilhelm, by testing reaction to aggression, had got his answer, and it was: the Triple Entente is solid.

'In the final battle between the Germans and Slavs, the Anglo-Saxons find themselves on the side of the Slavs and the Gauls,' he sneered. International relations, like much else, he interpreted along racial lines. But all he wanted, he said, was peace, and he was building a powerful navy simply 'to protect our trade'. 'There is no denying that they are intriguing and girding against us from every hole and corner,' he wrote furiously of the British.

In one sense, he was right: his paranoia, by contributing to the build-up of German military and naval strength, demanded 'girding against' so it became a self-fulfilling prophecy, and as war loomed ever closer it was not unusual for the competing Great Powers to spend five per cent of their national income preparing for it. In another sense, he was wrong – about the British. Britain had a Liberal government and it was not belligerent. It was not pacifist, either. The pacifist appeasers tended to be socialists, who argued that working men of all nations should not be manipulated into fighting each other for the benefit of international capital. The government's Liberal position was to regard war as a distraction, wasteful in every possible respect, which would only reluctantly be undertaken in defence of British territory, culture and values.

Wilhelm was disingenuous in presenting himself as a victim of British aggression. In fact he saw war as a solution to the growth of socialism at home. Socialism unnerved him. The combined costs of high food prices (to protect German farmers) and high taxes (to pay for defence spending) meant that the working class in German cities were labouring under an unfair burden, and their anger meant socialist ideas were spreading.

The British Foreign Secretary, Sir Edward Grey, actively pursued peace with Germany, but in the years before war broke out, squabbles between the two sets of allied countries happened so frequently, and so poisoned the atmosphere, that all parties knew the day must come when an argument could not be settled. In 1912 Russia encouraged a tripartite pact between Serbia, Bulgaria and Greece which nearly started a war with Turkey. That was averted at the last minute in London, although the Balkans remained a flashpoint. Internal relationships between the allies were often awkward. The Russians, who had a sphere of influence in northern Persia by agreement with the British, interfered in its constitution and tried to introduce a Shah of their own choice. In 1913, they went too far. Nicolas had never been able to rebuff German overtures, and now it seemed that Russia was likely to conclude an agreement on a branch line from the Berlin to Baghdad railway towards the Caspian. George V despaired. It would be India next, he thought. His father had been right; Nicolas was simply too weak.

But he remained an ally. When the Kaiser's brother Prince Henry visited King George in 1912 and asked him whether, if Germany went to war with France or Russia, the British would leap to their defence. 'Undoubtedly, yes – under certain circumstances,' the King replied, and recorded the conversation for the benefit of Sir Edward Grey. Grey, thanking him, agreed that:

... if Austria attacked Serbia aggressively, and Germany attacked Russia if she came to the assistance of Serbia, and France were then involved, it might become necessary for England to fight (as the German Chancellor said that Germany would fight) for the defence of her position in Europe, and for the protection of her own future and security.

He could not have been more prescient.

Against this ominous political background, at the head of the Russian political pyramid was Nicolas II, the complacent autocrat who believed that God was in charge and it was one's duty to go with the flow of history. His most powerful subjects, next to him at the top of the pyramid, simply despised him. They despised his fatalism, his claustrophobic marriage, and the unwashed Rasputin whining and babbling in the background. Many aristocrats of unimaginable wealth and thousand-year pedigree had never shared in the general kow-towing and adulation of the Romanovs, dismissing them as a bunch of seventeenth-century parvenus. Ironically it was these same people who now began to accuse him (behind his back) of living in the past.

Nicolas understood pride of birth, but underestimated the significance of the liberal opinions these people held. For him, they were the ones who did not understand Russia. The Tsarina, and his own education, told him that only the 'people', the peasants as numerous as grains of sand between here and Vladivostok, mattered. It was their 'soul' and their faith which supported him. He seemed unaware that change was gathering pace. 'Had a long and satisfactory talk with dear Nicky,' wrote King George, equally placid, after they met at a royal wedding in Berlin in 1913, '... he was just the same as always.'

The Tsar conferred with important politicians and travelled abroad occasionally. The Tsarina Alexandra remained mostly within the private sphere, with her ladies, her obedient daughters and her spoiled invalid son. In her mauve boudoir, surrounded by a clutter of embroideries, fringes, wax flowers, twiddly little boxes and ornaments and some of her collection of 600 icons, she prayed with Rasputin and exchanged confidences with Anna Vyrubova. Nicolas kept her informed of the affairs of the nation and at this stage she was not widely suspected of influencing her husband politically. Nor was Rasputin, although the Okhrana kept a close watch upon his contacts, movements and louche lifestyle in and out of Petrograd. Although as the years passed the views of 'Our Friend' were alluded to more frequently in Alexandra's correspondence with her husband, in these pre-war years his behaviour, inside and outside the court, caused more scandal than anger.

In London, George and May of Teck had no taste for the racy, gossipy life of a court, but they carried out their official duties graciously, they saw people, they held banquets and garden parties, opened hospitals, attended the theatre and the galleries and invited interesting people to luncheon at Buckingham Palace. When the London season was over, they invited guests to shoot and fish at Balmoral or Sandringham. As a constitutional monarch, the King saw it as his duty to be socially visible, to assist and advise career diplomats wherever necessary, and to promote worthy causes.

The Tsarina did not feel called upon to do anything for Russia except exist. Her duty was to her family. Since she was largely absent from St Petersburg and it remained a sociable city full of diplomats, wealthy aristocrats and moneyed bankers, the vacuum must be filled. So a lively alternative court sprang up, led by worldly men and women who came into contact with new currents of thought from Europe. They were as impatient as anyone with the pathological conservatism and superstition of Alexandra. As the years passed, as she took no exercise, her health declined and eventually, sometimes pushed about in a wheelchair, she was isolated entirely. Not that she was not part of a social circle; she was; but it was a circle of ladies devoted to Rasputin.

She had always been a difficult person. She said very little to those of whom she disapproved, who included most of her husband's relations, but occasionally bestowed a brief, frozen smile and a superior inclination of the head. This made people feel they had said something stupid or predictable, so they avoided her company. She was interested only in finding a cure for her son's haemophilia. She listened to doctors but they did not have a cure. Rasputin, the wild prophet, had so far been the only effective doctor and Rasputin caused talk. Dirty and straggle-haired, glittering of eye and incoherent of speech, he was widely derided as the drunk and womanizer that he was. The Tsarina, and her côterie, thought that anyone who dared peddle 'lies' about Our saintly Friend was poisoned by the Devil. The Okhrana, had they taken her on a mission to observe Rasputin's private life, could perhaps have convinced her otherwise but even that is uncertain. Delusions were her central problem in engaging with the world. She believed in God and the Devil, that Rasputin was inspired by God and that the Tsar ruled by divine right and that they could be challenged only by those of evil intent.

At the time, when secular and rational thinking was slowly eroding religion, delusions fascinated most people. Spiritualism was fashionable in Europe. It was the era of Aleister Crowley, Madame Blavatsky and, within a decade or two, Aimée Semple MacPherson, mystic exhibitionists all. All over Europe and America, some of the adults who saw Houdini escape from padlocked boxes underwater believed he had done it by magic. It never occurred to them that he might be a contortionist with phenomenal control of mind and muscle, and a lock-pick.

Primitive habits of mind held sway, terrifyingly, at the head of a pyramid which, by 1914, consisted of 175 million Russians. There was an indescribable difference between the splendid, pampered existence of the Tsar and the hard lives of the superstitious peasants, at the very bottom of the heap, who challenged neither his right to rule nor the priests. To them, he was their Little Father.

Nearly every peasant was a serf, as in the Middle Ages in Europe but with added vodka (vodka sales provided a third of the Tsar's tax revenue). The serf's bleary outlook was informed by a rich Slavic mythology involving spirits and devils, along with an old, authoritarian brand of Orthodoxy. The land worked by serfs belonged to some noble family. Some of the nobility, like the Romanovs and the Yusupovs, owned enormous swathes of countryside and were absentee landlords. Others lived in the country as feudal seigneurs.

The cities had moved forward into the twentieth century. The working class lived close to the factories, docks and railway yards. As their peasant forebears had done, they tended to spend their money on vodka, leaving little for pots and pans, good food and new clothes, so this was far from being a nation of shopkeepers. But there were post office officials and academics, skilled craftsmen of property, managers and technocrats and lawyers, a kind of middle class, lacking a strong commercial sector but among whom angry ideas were fermenting. They were educated and politically aware and, at the very least, doubtful of the Tsar's capacity to maintain the feudal pyramid forever. Revolutionary talk was everywhere and nowhere; strictly clandestine, not publicly expressed for fear of the Okhrana and a knock on the door at four in the morning. People disappeared. It was a relief to the routinely anti-Semitic populace that most who did were Jews.

In earlier centuries, the first stirrings of rebellion had come from the Jews. The Orthodox Church taught that Jews were, and always had been, inspired by the Devil and carried out ritual murder. To kill them was an act of Christian faith. Successive Tsars supported this view. Its outcome was murder, cruel persecution, restrictions on means of livelihood, and confinement, since the eighteenth century, beyond the Pale of Settlement. Most of all it meant that ordinary people expressed a deep-rooted suspicion and paranoia about anything new or original because it might be 'Jewish'.

The result was mass Jewish migration south and west to the edges of Empire, Galicia, Odessa on the Black Sea, the Baltic ports and East Prussia and beyond. And serious study. Jews had to think their way out of this. Jewish individuals were prominent in the early anarcho-socialist movements since the obvious solution to the tyranny of the Tsars was to wrest power from them. Ideally this would happen by democratic means; but as Alexanders I, II and III were succeeded in 1894 by Nicolas II, that hope came to seem ludicrous. Nicolas II was a tyrant like his predecessors, who married a woman, Alexandra, whose sister Elisabeth actively promoted belief in the *Protocols of the Elders of Zion*, the forgery about world domination by a Jewish conspiracy. This Tsar would never be a constitutional monarch, just as he would never disbelieve the *Protocols*.

An enormous, rich land like this needed railways and ships, dockyards and mines, roads and a telegraph system but it was backward. The expertise to set up and manufacture these resources was European, and so long as the political situation remained stable, Russian industries attracted European capital. Well before 1914, banks from Paris, London and Berlin were active in Moscow and St Petersburg. With them came European thinking, and a wonderful flowering of Russian culture: these were the great years of Nijinsky, Stravinsky and Pavlova, Diaghilev and Chaliapin, when Russian composers and performers, and painters like Malevich, were acclaimed in Europe and America as they were at home. The *beau monde* of St Petersburg, whose lives during the season were a round of theatre visits, gossipy teas and night clubs, were fabulously wealthy and spoke English or French. To be comfortably off you needed about a thousand roubles a year; some of these people got hundreds of thousands in unearned income from their estates, even millions. They spent lavishly on jewels, furs, gambling and travel. In their citified world of fashion, most young men became Army officers. They were educated, disillusioned with the Tsar's régime and 'liberal'.

These were the people whose 'decadence' the Tsarina loathed. In this she reflected a wider backlash against liberal thought. Conservative members of the bourgeoisie and the army, suspicious of anything new and difficult as possibly inspired by Freemasons or Jews, led gangs of thugs like the Black Hundreds which promoted pan-Slavism and conducted pogroms. Pan-Slavism meant that Mother Russia must turn her back on Europe, and embrace – indeed, swallow up – those countries where the population thought of themselves as Slavs. This included much of Russian Poland and the Czech Republic and Bosnia-Herzegovina, Slovakia, Serbia and two thirds of the Austro-Hungarian Empire. The stage was set for conflict.

4

The Family Goes to War

Sarajevo was the capital of the Balkan state of Bosnia-Herzegovina. Austro-Hungary had controlled the country for forty years, but had only formally annexed it in 1907; it was in manoeuvring over Bosnia-Herzegovina that Isvolsky had nearly lost his job. Serbia claimed it.

In 1914, Serbian National Day, 28 June, was provocatively chosen for the official visit to Sarajevo of Archduke Franz Ferdinand, nephew of the Austrian Emperor and Inspector General of the Imperial Army. Having recovered from a bomb scare earlier in the day, he and his wife stepped into an open landaulet to be driven away to safety. Seated high behind their chauffeur they were a conspicuous target; the Archduke in a plumed hat and green uniform, his beloved wife Sophie in a white boater. Both, as the world knows, were assassinated by pistol shots from a young Serb nationalist called Gavrilo Princip. He had been trained in terrorism by a Belgrade underground group called the Black Hand. With the arrest of Princip, the house of cards tumbled.

The Russian Imperial family was cruising in the *Standart* off the Finnish coast, as they habitually did in June. Far away on the other side of Europe, Archduke Ferdinand was assassinated. On the same day, in Russia, there took place an act of violence which caused them far more distress: an attempt on the life of Rasputin.

Rasputin had embarrassed them that spring. His presence at Livadia, in the Crimea, in attendance upon the Imperial Family had become known. Crowds followed him everywhere so Nicolas had insisted he leave. He had returned to St Petersburg to collect his wife and daughter and take them home to Pokrovskoye, his natal village in Siberia. Pokrovskoye was a remote place – a big village on the Tura river, where Rasputin owned the single two-storey house and was the only local man of national importance. It was a collection of dirt roads and wooden cottages where motor cars were unknown and life went on much as it had done a hundred years before, except for the steamers that glided by along the river.

Here Rasputin could find peace and quiet and retrieve his bruised self-importance. He thought he was safe in Pokrovskoye, away from his enemies, but he was wrong. A former prostitute called Goussyeva, her looks wrecked by disease, travelled all the way from St Petersburg, and entered the town disguised as a beggar.

On 28 June, as Rasputin walked down a quiet street, a beggar woman came close. He looked up and was gazing into her ravaged face as she surreptitiously withdrew a knife from her rags and stabbed him viciously in the midriff. Rasputin, with what was apparently a mortal wound, collapsed into the dust. Goussyeva was hustled away shrieking about having killed the Anti-Christ.

It was twelve hours before Rasputin arrived, by cart on a stretcher, at a hospital. When Nicolas and Alexandra heard they immediately arranged for the best medical attention to be sent. The Tsarina telegraphed daily for news. Rasputin would recover, she learned, much to the disgust of the Okhrana officers on the *Standart* and the relief of the ladies of the court.

In warm sunny weather, the Finnish holiday went on. A tennis net was set up ashore; there was happiness, bathing and beach games for the Tsar and the girls. Olga was eighteen now. There was tentative exploration of the idea of marriage. One whose prospects were being considered was Prince Alexander of Serbia; another was Edward Prince of Wales. Olga, though, insisted that she must marry a Russian. In any case she was not ready to fly the security of the family. Tatiana, at seventeen, was the tallest and prettiest, the most reserved but the one who naturally took charge; custom and etiquette demanded that Olga must be engaged to be married before Tatiana, but she was not without suitors. Maria and Anastasia were fifteen and thirteen. All four were thought of as 'children' and had led such sheltered lives that a courtier who overheard Tatiana and Olga talking together when they were over twenty said they seemed about ten or twelve.

The little Tsarevich, ten years old and appropriately dressed in a sailor suit, watched the swimming and beach games from a safe distance, supervised by his tutor Pierre Gilliard. He was not allowed to participate for fear of injury. A calamity occurred nonetheless when he hurt himself boarding a dinghy. He twisted an ankle, it haemorrhaged, and he was confined to bed in great pain. Dr Botkin attended him but could do little, and Rasputin was not available to help. The Tsarina catastrophized. Disaster befell Rasputin, disaster befell the Tsarevich; she was being tested by God.

In St Petersburg, indeed in every city across Russia, the working poor were sick of poverty and exploitation. There were riots that summer. The dockers and factory workers paraded under the red flag of socialism. The Tsar hardly noticed. The German ambassador did; he shook his head, and gravely reported the state of Russia to Berlin.

In the third week of July the Imperial Family must leave the fjords for a brief stay at Peterhof, and the visit of the French President. The Tsar gave orders that the tennis nets should be left on site, ready for their return. The Tsarina knew better. 'I shall never see the fjords again!' she said, her face a mask of affliction. With time, her son recovered.

The German Chancellor, preoccupied by Sarajevo, thought Nicolas 'did not understand the issues'. It was true that the Tsar, as he sailed back to Peterhof on the *Standart*, was convinced that a crisis could be averted. Once Poincaré's official visit was over he and the family would be able to resume their vacation. He was not alone in his complacency. Cries of 'Wolf!' had been heard in the Balkans so often. In London, hearing about the Sarajevo disaster, King George had noted: 'Terrible shock for the dear old Emperor,' in his diary. He had been sincerely fond of the dead Archduke, a rather good shot, and called upon the Austrian Ambassador himself to offer his condolences. He felt it as a personal loss, and did not understand the political implications. In Paris, Le Figaro pronounced the assassination regrettable but 'nothing to cause anxiety'.

In Berlin, Kaiser Wilhelm received a furious letter from the old Emperor Franz Josef in Vienna. The Archduke's assassination was, Franz Josef wrote, not the work of a lone assassin but a Serbian outrage, a hostile act from Belgrade that could not be ignored.

Proving it would be difficult, but there was no doubt in his mind. Wilhelm assured him of German support.

Diplomatic activity in the capitals of Europe failed to resolve the Austro-Serbian squabble and attitudes became entrenched. In the third and fourth week of July, messages were flashing between Austria and Serbia, Serbia and Russia, Germany and Austria, France and England.

On 20 July, the new French Ambassador Maurice Paléologue lunched with the Tsar as they awaited the arrival of the President of the Republic at Peterhof. Paléologue expressed concerns about the implications of Sarajevo but the Tsar dismissed them. 'I can't believe the Emperor [Wilhelm II] wants war… If you knew him as I do! If you knew how much theatricality there is in his posing!' Poincaré arrived in a magnificent warship, with three other warships in attendance. The Russians could not match that yet, but they produced a force of 60,000 troops for review, and everyone understood that this was just a small complement of the army that could be assembled if required. Everyone was satisfied. It was theatre; posturing, not real life.

In the evening of 24 July, towards the end of the official visit, the Tsar was as sanguine as he had been at the start. Having discussed the Austro-Serbian argument with Poincaré, he told Paléologue: 'Notwithstanding appearances, the Emperor William is too cautious to launch his country on some wild adventure and the Emperor Franz Josef's only wish is to die in peace.'

So they could all sleep easy in their beds. What the Tsar did not know was that on the day before Poincaré's arrival, the Austrians had composed, but not sent, an ultimatum to Serbia that was so truculent, and so demanding, that the Serbs would be too proud to comply. The Austrians were sure of it; there would be war, and they would defeat Serbia with the backing of Germany, if necessary. 'I am behind you and ready to draw the sword wherever your action requires,' Wilhelm had barked only last year. He was convinced that the Russians would not risk intervention on behalf of Serbia.

Austria delayed dispatch of this ultimatum so that the powerful political élites of France and Russia, together at Peterhof for four days, would not have the chance to come up with a co-ordinated response. Only as Poincaré's visit drew to a close had the Austrian ultimatum reached Belgrade. The Serbs had forty-eight hours in which to answer, or Austria would mobilize.

Serbia turned to Russia for help. On 25 July the Tsar suddenly grasped the nature of his predicament, and was appalled. This was a situation he had long dreaded. Russia could not retreat from its obligations a second time. Seven years before, in 1907, Isvolsky's gaffe, which had resulted in Austrian annexation of Bosnia-Herzogovina without a reciprocal seizure of the Dardanelles by Russia, had been enormously humiliating. Nicolas did not want war in July 1914, any more than he had then. Russia was not yet unready for war. But national pride would not permit it to slink away a second time.

Everything had been tried: mediation, delaying tactics. The Russian Foreign Minister now was Sazonov. He asked Austria to prolong the forty-eight-hour deadline. Vienna refused. He asked Germany to mediate. The German government refused. He implored Sir Edward Grey to convene a conference of ambassadors in London. Sazonov himself agreed to participate, but Germany declined.

Finally he told Serbia to comply with everything the Austrians wanted. They gritted their teeth, sent their concessions to Vienna, and heard nothing. Seeing that Serbia had simply rolled over, the Austrian Chancellor was nonplussed. He had expected defiance, not this. He did not act on the document he had received for two days. When the German ambassador in Vienna asked to see it, he was told it was caught up in a backlog of paperwork.

In London and Paris, nobody knew whether Austria was going to declare war or not; if it did, they would all have to take sides. The consensus was that war, if it came, would be short and decisive. The British retained their naval supremacy and had belatedly built up their army with Territorial units. But preparations were piecemeal as they were in France, where conscription had been extended to three years. A short war meant massive firepower, a show of strength, a willingness to hurl everything against the enemy as soon as possible. As one crossed St James's Park to the Foreign Office, or the Alexandre III to the Quai d'Orsay, on those warm summer mornings, the roar of cannon seemed impossible, like lightning from an azure sky.

Finally, on 28 July, the Austrians decided to take what they really wanted. They rejected the humble and conciliatory Serbian response and declared war. On the 29th, Austrian troops began shelling Belgrade from across the Danube, disregarding white flags hanging from the buildings. Wilhelm was convinced that the Tsar would wring his hands and do nothing. The German Ambassador in St Petersburg had told him that Russia's morale was at its lowest, that the population had the 'mood of a sick tom-cat'. Wilhelm had observed the slow extension of Russia's railways and the slow build-up of Russia's navy and concluded that the Tsar would not be in a position to make war until 1916. Until then, he would back away from aggression as he had in a similar situation in 1907.

The only possible exception would be if the British stepped in with a promise of assistance. It was important to establish the precise position. That very week his brother Prince Henry had popped into Buckingham Palace after Cowes, to say goodbye, and King George assured him that Britain would avoid involvement. 'We shall try all we can to keep out of this and remain neutral,' he had said. Prince Henry reported this conversation by letter at once, and Wilhelm took it most seriously. The British, he told President Wilson, would not go to war in support of Russia over Sarajevo. He imagined that King George had ultimate authority over foreign policy as he did himself. As to the French, he was dismissive. They had extended their conscription term, certainly, but by comparison with his own their army was undermanned, ill-equipped and unready for war. Thanks to the Schlieffen plan his troops could roll through Belgium and devour the French in a few weeks.

The British Navy mobilized on 29 July and the Russian on the 30th. 'Then I must also mobilize,' announced Wilhelm. 'The Russian Tsar assumes the guilt.' On 31 July he sent the same dramatic wire to both King and Tsar. 'It is not I who bears the responsibility for the disaster which now threatens the entire civilised world. Even at this moment the decision to stave it off lies with you.' He expected Russia to back down.

Rasputin, recovering from his wounds in a distant hospital, was an instinctive pacifist with an equally instinctive insight that the

Tsar's régime, and Russia's economy, could never survive a war. He telegraphed one of his messages from God. 'Let Papa not plan war, for with the war will come the end of Russia and yourselves and you will lose to the last man.' Anna Vyrubova received this telegram, took it to the Tsar and saw it torn to pieces in anger before she had left the room. Nicolas dared not order the man to cease all contact. Alexandra was a depressive already. If he banished Rasputin from Tsarskoe, and anything happened to Alexei – the consequences did not bear thinking about.

In the last few days of July, personal telegrams flew between Nicolas and Wilhelm but achieved nothing. The steamroller of war had begun its inexorable journey. Wilhelm thought furiously that he had never been able to trust Nicolas. In the late 1890s the Tsar had wanted to unite with France, a Republic! against the Anglo-Japanese 'threat'. In 1905 he had not been able to deal with Bloody Sunday in St Petersburg without conceding a constitution. It was all weakness, weakness; Wilhelm would have none of it. A constitution indeed! A betrayal of monarchist principles. No moral fibre... He thought bitterly of the way Nicolas had backed away from the treaty they had signed on the *Hohenzollern* that same year – proof in itself that one did not have to rely on 'pygmies and handmaidens' to make foreign policy, but could come to an arrangement between sovereigns. Nicolas had 'embraced me... and kept on gazing at me with grateful, beaming eyes' on that occasion. But he was not to be trusted. He had seen them, at the wedding in Berlin last year, Nicolas and George, plotting behind his back. And now look what it had all come to.

'Personal rancours and dislikes seem to play a considerable part in policy, and that appears to me very dangerous,' observed one of the few Jews to whom Wilhelm had ever been cordial, the shipping magnate Albert Ballin. Ballin had expressed these misgivings to the Chancellor at the time. It was, indeed, a crucial weakness of the monarchist ideal.

By midnight on 1 August, Russia and Germany had effectively, though not yet publicly, declared war. At the last moment Wilhelm was rattled by a sudden fear of the force he had unleashed. The prospect of that enormous Russian army advancing through East

Prussia was enough to make anyone quail. He wired the Tsar: 'I must ask most earnestly that you, without delay, give your troops an immediate order under no circumstances to make even the smallest violation of our frontiers.' The telegram arrived at two in the morning – too late; hundreds of thousands of Russian soldiers were already on the move. Nicky had given up on Willy he told Paléologue later. 'All was over forever between me and William,' he wrote. 'I slept extremely well... I felt as if a weight had fallen from my mind.'

The following afternoon, he made public the declaration of war. The German Ambassador, Pourtalès, had told Berlin that if the Tsar ever did this, it would be the end of his reign. The incensed population would finally turn upon him. Pourtalès had been entirely mistaken, at least in the immediate term. All talk of socialism was swept away in a wave of patriotic euphoria. Crowds swept through the streets – or as Robert Massie described it,

> ... workmen exchanged their red flags of revolution for the icons of Holy Russia and portraits of the Tsar. Students rushed from the universities to enlist. Army officers, caught in the street, were happily tossed in the air. 'Vive la France!' yelled the mob, and wrecked the German Embassy.

Even smart young army officers who frequented the liberal society of St Petersburg (now considered too German sounding and henceforth re-named Petrograd) had been delighted to gossip and laugh at the Imperial family, were overwhelmed by the prevailing fervour and competed for a chance to be first to march in triumph along Unter den Linden. They would be in Berlin, they told each other, within weeks.

5

A Kind of Happiness

War was declared and Alexandra exulted in Nicolas as a knight of old, galloping to victory before his men with lance at the ready. There was a romantic identification with the warlord in Tsar, Kaiser and King. They loved dressing up, playing soldiers and sailors. In the years of cordiality, all three monarchs had presented one another with uniforms at the drop of a plumed helmet. Wilhelm had two roomfuls of them, and was rarely seen in anything else. George took an obsessive interest throughout his life in the minutiae of ceremonial dress. As to the Tsar, his country had produced some of the most dashing uniformed men in the world: the magnificent Cossacks in fur hats, high boots and waisted, flared coats. It stirred the soul to watch them. Even the Tsar's chauffeur wore gold braid half an inch thick.

To announce the start of war, on 2 August 1914, Nicolas had appeared on a balcony outside the Winter Palace in the simple khaki battledress of an infantry regiment next to Alexandra in white. It was a sartorial statement of intent. From now on, men would fight and women would make sacrifices. 'Liberal' opinions were no longer voiced. In the euphoria of action, rich young officers wore their uniforms with pride. At last they had stature and credibility. They were engaged in public service. Young Romanovs and Yusupovs, the spoiled rich boys whose lives had seemed meaningless before, would be chivalric heroes in the service of Russia, the Tsar and whatever it was that made them Russian. Most defined this as a Slavic identity. Suddenly, Petrograd was all for the Tsar, and for defending Slav Russia against Teuton Germany. In villages all over Russia, patriotism and adoration of the Tsar did not waver, but conscription was dreaded. Able-bodied men must leave the farmland that required their labour. There was much prayer and no illusions. Few expected to return.

Alexandra intended Nicolas to be Commander-in-Chief. This was his destiny as Tsar. Only Nicolas had the God-given right to lead the standing army plus the newly conscripted one – which together came to four and a half million men – into battle. She disregarded his uncle, Grand Duke Nikolai Nikolaievich, but no one else could. Russian squaddies worshipped 'Nikolasha' because he had been a career soldier for forty years, and because he was six feet six, fit, brave, intelligent and trustworthy with the well-being of his men at heart.

Government ministers were appalled when Tsar Nicolas made plain his intention to command the army. They knew who the soldiers wanted, and knew as Alexandra never could the importance of trust to a body of fighting men. They persuaded Nicolas that he must put his uncle Nikolai in charge of operations. It was some consolation that command would be shared between Nikolai and the Minister of War, Sukhomlinov, whom the Tsar liked. Alexandra was bitter about it, but Nicolas saw reason.

Alexandra did not trust politicians or statesmen generally. She was silent in their presence, but confided to her circle that she found them 'citified' and out of touch with the 'real Russia'. Whether she meant this, or was simply defending her self-conceit from a sneaking suspicion that she was out of her depth, we cannot know. She swallowed her resentment and moved on. The invalid – for years, she had suffered from swollen legs and sciatica, and had put her feet up, rising late, lying whole days on a couch or being wheeled about in a chair – suddenly got up, got herself trained as a Red Cross nurse and sponsored hospitals. Workmen were called in to transform the sumptuous reception rooms of the Catherine Palace into wards.

That August, everyone was a monarchist. In September, the major strategic battles of the war were won and lost and Russia struggled desperately not to fall back from the west. This was not the fault of Nikolai Nikolaievich, but of decades of outdated military thinking, and above all of the criminally negligent Minister of War, Sukhomlinov. As short and round as the Commander-in-Chief was tall and spare, he was a pomaded dandy with an expensive wife, an engaging personality and a fondness for riding the Trans-Siberian railway back and forth to Vladivostok, on expenses. He had charmed the Tsar, who was always susceptible to a friendly face.

For the first ten months of the war, it was Sukhomlinov's job to organize Russia's military logistics. The challenge would have taxed the cleverest procurement officer, but Sukhomlinov had not the faintest idea what was required, indeed did not appear to think his duties mattered. Supply and sustenance alike were ignored. Millions of men blundered forth to war half-starved, in leaky boots, with scant ammunition, too few guns, too few tanks. Requests to speed up the production and transport of shells were dismissed with a shrug. As to mobilization itself, it was elephantine, in a country where the railway lines were half-built or non-existent and divisions were expected to race to a front which might be a thousand miles away.

Nikolai Nikolaievich set up his HQ at a railway junction in Baranavichy in today's Belarus. From there he had a 550-mile western border to defend, roughly from the Baltic to the Crimea, and two separate objectives. He must deploy his force on two fronts.

The first, and more important, war aim was to divert Germany from invading France. Kaiser Wilhelm had seized the initiative by implementing the Schlieffen Plan in the first forty-eight hours of war. The Plan was based on the correct assumption that Russia would take a while to mobilize, so Germany must send a million men in a breakneck surge westwards through the Low Countries, wheeling round south of Paris to cut it off. With France in the bag, Germany could then turn its attention to the lumbering Russian army in the East.

Nikolai's second objective was to keep the Austro-Hungarian army from breaking into Russia through what is now the Ukraine. He maintained control of this southern army himself. In the north he sent two forces to attack East Prussia (now Poland): General Rennenkampf's army, roughly 200,000 strong, would be transported down the Baltic coast to pierce the border from the north-east, while Samsonov's army of 170,000 men would attack it from the south-east and cut off the German defenders. With the German attack contained, they would head for Berlin, only 150 miles away.

It was an excellent strategy but senior officers in the field had not fought for a while, nor trained in modern weaponry, attitudes and techniques. They were in the habit of telegraphing tomorrow's battle orders *en clair*, so the enemy was well briefed. Rennenkampf sent young cavalry officers with swords to confront German cannon. They had learned about the honour of the regiment and gentlemanly behaviour at military college. The carnage of men and horses was horrifying. Behind them rushed a massive, armed body of Russian infantrymen who succeeded in breaking the German line. It was a hard-won victory, but was not pressed. The stand-off that followed gave time for the German commanders in the field to be replaced by Generals Hindenberg and Ludendorff.

General Samsonov, struggling up from the south-east without benefit of railway or paved road, urged his troops and horse-drawn gun-carriages over miles of stony pot-holed lanes, forests and uncultivated land. Men and animals had nothing to eat yet battled on, covering at best twelve miles a day. When they finally reached East Prussia, they met almost the entire German force which had been removed from the stand-off with dozy Rennenkampf and transported by train to meet them. 80,000 Russians were killed or wounded, 90,000 taken prisoner, and 500 guns forfeited. This was the Battle of Tannenberg, and in abject distress Samsonov, a conscientious man, shot himself.

Days earlier the Germans, hit hard by Rennenkampf's force, had telegraphed for assistance. Seven divisions had been detached from the line near Paris and sent to East Prussia. By the time they turned up they were no longer required. But because Von Moltke, commanding the western front, had broken with the Schlieffen Plan at a crucial moment, the Germans in France fell back under a fierce French assault. The Battle of the Marne, in September 1914, began the stalemate that would characterize the western front from then on.

Nikolai Nikolaievich's southern army attacked the Austro-Hungarian army in Galicia (today's western Ukraine) and drove all before it. In no time the Russians were charging towards Vienna. The Austrians panicked, and begged for German reinforcements; but by the time they arrived the Russian advance had been stopped – on orders from the Tsar. France, once again, had implored him for more troops to attack Germany's eastern edge.

In the first month of war, the Tsar had made two other decisive moves. First, he banned the sale of vodka. Second, he decreed that St Petersburg was hence to be known by its Slavic name, Petrograd. Having achieved these things he left for the Stavka, Nikolai Nikolaievich's HQ in Baranavichy. There, amid serious men, including a few British observers, he was happy. He sat by as Nikolai developed a military strategy. Otherwise, the Tsar was unable to make a difference; as he complained to the British General Hanbury-Williams, who was stationed at Baranavichy, he gave orders but they were not always carried out.

By the end of 1914, all sides were desperate, but none so desperate as the Russians. Grand Duke Nikolai Nikolaievich was frustrated. He was already trying to work without tools. For many reasons, the military supply chain was breaking down disastrously. A million men had been lost. There were more, of course, pouring in daily, but if nothing were done to provide guns and food they would be led unarmed and hungry into battle. Ordinary soldiers had faith, because they had nothing else. They would go to their death singing hymns. At Tsarskoe Selo, Alexandra worked heroically as a nurse at the Catherine Palace, never flinching as she was called upon to treat hideous wounds, and her two oldest girls assisted her. She was too busy to see Rasputin, too fulfilled to worry about her sciatica.

Dr Alexander Helphand, an important exporter in Constantinople, was in a position to make a shrewd assessment of Russia's shaky infrastructure; and he saw that there would soon be an opportunity to launch and win what John Buchan called 'the return match for the pogroms'. In February 1915 Helphand returned to Germany, no longer an academic with suspect socialist friends but a wealthy man with a clear aim: to get rid of the Romanovs.

Armed with the introduction from the German Embassy in Constantinople, he visited the foreign Ministry in Berlin and talked to people who mattered. He put it to them that Russia could be defeated from within. As was well known, it was rotten at the core. Its underfed masses would suffer horribly from the ineptitude of their leaders and could, if subtly provoked, be driven to rebel. He knew that the German informants kept an eye on Russian Bolsheviks in exile. He was in a position to ensnare some of those Bolsheviks into causing insurrection when the time came. The demagogue Lenin, for instance, was chronically under-funded. If he and Trotsky were offered backing to make trouble in Russia, they would take it.

First, the ground in Russia must be thoroughly prepared by propaganda and a well-financed network of revolutionary cells. The Bolsheviks could then be induced to return to Petrograd where they would engineer a general strike, which would lead to revolution. At that point Russia would have to sue for peace. There was nothing to fear from the Bolsheviks in the longer term; they were a tiny group, who would inevitably be overshadowed by more numerous, malleable and politically sophisticated Social Democrats. There were many Social Democrats in Russia, and in its armed forces, who would be happy to promote insurrection in advance if they had any money to exploit such media of communication as there were.

He had thought out his proposal in detail. There was no point in trying to interest Germans in what might happen to the Tsar, because all they were interested in was Russia's surrender. He focused on the need to create the kind of social breakdown and mutiny that had taken place in 1905. He put it to them that the money required would pay for propaganda and a press campaign to undermine Russia's ruling class and its war aims, and destroy morale. None of the Bolsheviks need know where it was coming from.

The German Foreign Ministry did not like the sound of promoting 'social democrats' and had no intention of dethroning Nicolas II, but the potential for a Russian surrender was too good to miss. The threat of revolution alone, they thought, would be enough to make the Tsar sue for peace. Among the exiles they knew about from informants, Lenin was in Switzerland and Trotsky in Paris. They made available a first installment of a million marks. The operation was handled with the strictest secrecy.

Dr Alexander Helphand, a Russian academic who had made his home in Germany, made his way to Zurich, found Lenin and got nowhere. Lenin simply didn't trust or respect his old friend any more since Helphand had become, quite literally, a fat capitalist. No matter; part B of the plan, namely the promotion of discontent from within Russia, was adroitly handled. Helphand set up an import-export agency in Copenhagen and was able to channel funds quietly into Russia through his network of Russian and Scandinavian agents. Perhaps he flaunted his wealth too conspicuously. The Allies suspected him of exploiting Russia and raking in profits for Germany, and launched a press campaign saying so. The Russian political exiles concluded that he was a German agent. This didn't matter much to him. As long as money was made available for their cause, they could believe what they liked about where it was coming from. Lenin's own subsistence money was very probably drip-fed from a Swiss in Zurich called Karl Moor. Moor, whether Lenin knew it or not, was a German agent.

In the first months of the war Rasputin's influence at Tsarskoe Selo had been almost non-existent. The Tsarina was busy nursing and the Tsar usually absent. But in January 1915, Anna Vyrubova was gravely injured in a railway accident. At the hospital to which she was sent, nothing could be done for her. Rasputin, fifteen miles away in Petrograd leading his usual chaotic life, did not even hear about her condition until the following day. As soon as he did he rushed to the hospital and was admitted. Nicolas and Alexandra sat at her bedside believing she would die. Dramatically, he called her back to consciousness from delirium. 'Now wake up and rise!' he is said to have cried, and she did try. He turned to the Imperial couple. 'She will recover, but she will always be a cripple,' he said, and staggered out.

He proved right, and Anna Vyrubova, walking with a stick, became an even more devoted acolyte. The Tsarina was immensely pleased with him, and his influence was restored. Within months she had begun to write subtly prodding letters to the Tsar, who did have a tendency to fraternize with the troops. 'You are too kind and gentle... Be more autocratic, my very own sweetheart... Be the master and lord, you are the autocrat.'

Nikolai Nikolaievich had an enormous army again by the spring of 1915. With four million men and too few guns, he recommenced the campaign against Austro-Hungary. Once again the Russians were racing unchallenged towards Vienna. This time, Hindenberg and Ludendorff unleashed a major offensive against them. Heavy artillery drove the Russians right back all the way along the line; 1.4 million of them were lost or wounded and nearly a million taken prisoner. Russia's border was pushed east about 200 miles, and Poland was occupied by Germans.

At the same time, Helphand's campaign of subversion was thriving on fertile ground. Many of the dead soldiers had been unarmed. Even Nicolas was appalled, and mentioned this state of affairs to Georgie – they maintained a desultory correspondence throughout the war; platitudinous congratulations, pious hopes, stilted commiserations that, on Georgie's side at least, sounded like a school essay:

> I feel most deeply for you in the most anxious days through which you are now passing, when your army has been compelled to retire on account of the lack of ammunition and rifles, in spite of the splendid and most gallant way they are fighting against our most powerful enemy.

The dead bodies were real, though. A Guns for Russia movement gained ground in Britain.

As the soldiers' predicament became common knowledge in the cities, in the summer of 1915, there was a surge of anti-Tsarist feeling which focused largely on Alexandra. She, whom Russians had always thought of as German, was suspected of influencing the Tsar and undermining Russia on purpose. Rasputin was said to be a German agent.

Alexandra disliked Nikolai Nikolaievich, probably because she was jealous of his popularity and a little fearful. Rasputin had no cause to be fond of him either. When he had offered to come to the Stavka and provide spiritual succour, Nikolai had replied: 'Do come. I'll hang you.' Now Nikolai Nikolaievich had failed. Together they exploited the Tsar's weakness and vanity until he conceded, at the end of the summer in 1915, that Uncle Nikolai must go. He would do the job himself. Ministers, aghast, threatened to resign. They protested that the army's morale would suffer. He did not change his mind.

In Moscow that September of 1915, the British Attaché Robert Bruce Lockhart noted in his journal:

> During the last few days it has become clear that the Duma is to be dissolved. This afternoon it is now an accomplished fact. It is felt, however, that the change in the supreme command and the dissolution of the Duma are all part of the same intrigue and that the Court is responsible for it.
>
> Some say that it is a pro-German movement to provoke a revolution and thus make peace. Others say that it is simply a move of the reactionaries to gain time, and to put off the evil day as far as possible.

The 'court', now, was Alexandra, her small circle of followers, and Rasputin; their sole supporter in government was the Prime Minister, an old man of traditionalist views called Goremykin. Day after day in the cities, there were wildcat strikes, skirmishes, rumours of Rasputin influencing the Tsar in favour of Germany, drunken crowd violence, and ever-less-effective maintenance of order.

The Tsar took no notice. On his way to take command at the Stavka (which in retreat had been relocated east of Baranavichy, at Mogilev) he read a letter from his wife:

> My very own beloved one, I cannot find words to express all I want to – my heart is too full... You have fought this great fight for your country and throne – alone and with bravery and decision... Sleep well, my Sunshine, Russia's Saviour.

The Tsar rejected a peace proposal from Germany and set to work.

Rasputin, once again a valued advisor at Tsarskoe, was a fervent monarchist, for he was dependent on 'the Tsars', as he called them, for a living, probably for his life itself. His pacifism did not go down well with Nicolas, who made his opposition to Germany clear, but his influence was nonetheless strong. There is no evidence that Rasputin knowingly took German money but his venality was notorious; he was effectively the Imperial gatekeeper, the fixer if you wanted the ear of the Tsar. His influence was not all bad. He did, for instance, keep reminding Alexandra that the state of the railways was such that no food was getting through to the cities. This was a detail apparently beyond her capacity to improve, and nothing happened.

How the Allies must have groaned. Later Lloyd George would compare the Russian Empire to:

> ... an unseaworthy Ark. The timbers were rotten and most of the crew not much better. The Captain was suited for a pleasure yacht in still waters, and his sailing master had been chosen by his wife, reclining in the cabin below.

Helphand had perhaps been away from dissident thinkers for too long, or maybe despite his brilliance he had always underestimated the intelligence of working people. In Berlin in the autumn of 1915 he launched a paper called *Die Glocke* (The Bell). It was a call to international solidarity with the oppressed in Russia. The immediate target audience were German socialists. In its pages he set out to convince them that the German High Command were entirely supportive of their wish to stand side by side with the Russian workers. His readers, try as they might, somehow couldn't quite envisage a bunch of haughty Prussians in spiked helmets as protectors of the proletariat. They scoffed at his proposition and he forfeited even more credibility.

His relationship with the Foreign Office and the networks inside Russia remained unchanged. There was a second promoter of the revolution now, an Estonian called Keskula, who had concluded pretty much as Helphand did that Lenin was the one who could make it happen. Keskula also talked to the Germans, but failed to raise money from them. The question being asked in Berlin was when exactly the foreseen revolution might happen. Helphand reported in November that morale was low, both in the army and in the factories and streets; but Russians were not ready to rise and overthrow their masters just yet.

At Mogilev, no longer (as at Baranavichy) lodged in railway carriages, but now in a house, Nicolas appointed General Alexeiev as commander in all but name. Alexeiev, a safe pair of hands, succeeded in stabilizing the front with Germany. Nicolas loved the life at headquarters and decided that it would be good for Alexei, the Tsarevich, to join him. Somehow he managed to persuade the anxious Tsarina that the boy should do so. Together, away from the overwhelmingly female presence at Tsarskoe, they were both happy. Gilliard, the tutor, and Derevenko, the big sailor who carried Alexei when necessary, were there too. The boy was curious, intelligent and spoiled, but always brave, and he loved it. He played soldiers and, in a sense, Nicolas did too. It was a holiday for him; he who all his life had simply given orders now had simply to observe. He sat in on meetings of the High Command as policy was made and orders issued by others.

Nicolas had knowingly left behind a gap in the civil administration. With his consent, as the war progressed Alexandra would learn to fill it. To quote Massie again: 'It was not a formal regency; rather, it was an almost domestic division of family duties. As such, it was wholly within the tradition of the Russian autocracy.' Rather different from tradition was the fact that the nation was on its knees and the Empress, in charge, was doing the bidding of a peasant from Pokrovskoye who took cash for favours.

In November 1915, the Tsar took his son away from HQ on a railway journey to visit the troops in the south. He was not required to administer the operational workings of the war; that was left to Alexeiev. As the sumptuously appointed ten-coach Imperial train rolled sedately back towards the Stavka, Alexei hurt himself and his nose began to bleed. Alarmed, the Tsar had the train diverted to Tsarskoe to find immediate medical attention. Alexei's condition worsened. His usual two doctors had no idea what they could do. The Tsarina, despairing, sent for Rasputin. He arrived and knelt at the bedside. Maintaining his gaze upon the little boy's face, he murmured to Nicolas and Alexandra: 'Don't be alarmed. Nothing will happen.' And then he left. And Alexei got better from that day on. The doctors could not explain it.

That, at any rate, was Vyrubova's version; Gilliard the tutor, who was also there, gave the doctors some of the credit. But like Vyrubova,

Alexandra was convinced that Rasputin had worked a miracle again. She kept her son at home for the next six months. Rasputin began to have dreams about the disposition of troops – about military strategy. These insights he passed on to Alexandra, who wrote them down and sent them to Nicolas. Nicolas told General Alexeiev, who smiled and said nothing. Alexeiev was naturally worried about security; the map of his tactical aims was always made in two copies, one for him and one for the Tsar. He suspected, correctly, that the Tsarina saw this second copy, and that Rasputin was also perfectly well aware of its contents.

In January 1916, Bruce Lockhart noted in his diary that the Mayor of Moscow had had a private audience with the Tsar. And how were things in Moscow? Nicolas asked. There was, he was told, no fuel and not enough to eat since the railways were run so badly; there would probably be riots. 'Well, one must not be too severe with them,' said the Emperor. Was he not exaggerating? No. 'Everything I can do will be done,' said the Emperor.

Evidently he could do nothing, and Petrograd was in an equally dreadful situation that winter, the coldest for years. Transport was disorganized, there was no coal, no bread and no produce from the countryside. (Bread and produce were important as they had never been before, because nobody had vodka to obliterate the pangs of hunger or even potatoes to make moonshine with.) Very little meat was to be had because there were 'not enough refrigerators' (this in the depths of winter with sub-zero temperatures) – yet Meriel Buchanan reported that 'tons of rotting carcasses could be seen conveyed through the streets on their way to the soap factories'. The 1,000-kilometre railroad from Petrograd to Murmansk, Russia's new port on an unfrozen sea, was not yet complete. At Archangel provisions, ammunition and stores of every kind were piled up in confusion, the one narrow-gauge railway being quite incapable of dealing with the enormous mass of material. Hundreds were dying of cold at the front.

In February, while Nicolas was at the Stavka, Alexandra was confident enough in her newly adopted powers to have Prime Minister Goremykin, with whom the Duma defiantly refused to work, replaced with the obscure Stürmer. A nonentity in his late sixties and not very bright, Stürmer had been recommended to Rasputin by the religious authorities. He was not up to the job; he didn't seem to know what was going on in meetings; he had no known policies. Paléologue was appalled. 'The most that can be said for him is that he has a pretty talent for cunning and flattery.' From then on, Alexandra and Rasputin would make decisions, and Stürmer would tell the Duma what to do. Polivanov, the Minister of War who had replaced the idle Sukhomlinov last year, was energetic and decisive. For the first time, food and munitions had begun to get through to the Russian armies. He was no friend of Rasputin, though, so he had to go. Alexandra promoted a less effective crony.

In the cities, inflation soared. The Tsar's coffers were drastically depleted by lack of the income from vodka sales. Sober and cold, the population demanded more bread, more vegetables and more coal. Millstones had stopped turning, fields lay unharvested and mines no longer worked at full capacity; the endless demand for more soldiers was robbing Russia of its labour force. And of course, there was the transport breakdown. Sir George Buchanan was not alone in thinking that people would not stand for this much longer. 'I repeatedly warned the Emperor of his danger.'

The Tsarina had other things on her mind. The foreign minister, Sazonov, had annoyed her. For years Sazonov had been someone the French and British Ambassadors, Maurice Paléologue and Sir George Buchanan, could work with. He had overseas experience and had obtained Allied consent for a push to open up the Dardanelles Straits to Russian shipping. In the spring of 1916 he suggested to the Tsar that Poland might at last be granted its promised autonomy, and the Tsar agreed. Alexandra was horrified. 'Baby's future rights' (her son's claim to Poland) were to be given away. Sazonov's reputation at Tsarskoe nosedived. Under pressure from his wife the Tsar backed away from his promise about Poland and Sazonov, who was on holiday at the time, was sacked.

Sir George Buchanan, hearing that Sazonov must go, had no time to contact London before the deed was done. He must see the Tsar at once. His daughter Meriel later described how he had requested an urgent meeting on his own initiative. He told Nicolas earnestly:

I cannot exaggerate the services which Monsieur Sazonov has rendered the cause of the Allied governments, by the tact and ability he has shown in the very difficult negotiations which we have conducted since the war began. Nor can I conceal from your Majesty the apprehensions which I feel at losing him as a collaborator...

It was no use. The replacement was the dunderheaded Prime Minister Stürmer, who could not handle one job, far less two. 'Low, intriguing and treacherous' was Paléologue's assessment.

The Tsar and usually his son were away at the Stavka throughout most of 1916. In June and July the Russian army in the south had a great victory in Galicia. It came at enormous cost to both German and Russian life. Because of the bloodshed, Rasputin insisted that the attack be stopped. It was, but the border further south remained porous and it was not until August that Romania entered the war on the Allied side.

In Petrograd, government ministers succeeded one another like figures on a fairground ride. The next placeman of Rasputin to whirl into view, in October 1916, was Protopopov, a sick man, but an intimate of Rasputin for several years.

Protopopov had led a parliamentary delegation to Great Britain, France and Italy and held talks with a German agent in Stockholm on the way back. Soon afterwards he became Minister of the Interior, the person in charge of civil order and (taking over from the Ministry of Agriculture) maintenance of food supplies to the civilian population.

By now Russia's predicament was incurable. The one efficient War Minister had long gone, and the munitions supply had dried up; guns were either imported, to remain crated in the snow at Archangel, or unmade, there being insufficient metal for their manufacture. The Tsar understood, and was overwhelmed with anxiety. Gilliard observed him on a visit to Kiev: 'He had never seemed to me so worried before. He was usually very self-controlled, but on this occasion he showed himself nervous and irritable, and once or twice he spoke roughly to Alexis Nicolaievich.' General Alexeiev had told him that ordinary people thought Rasputin was the Tsarina's lover.

That much was evident from the letters seen by military censors. Derided as a cuckold, he had lost the respect of the people, something he had always taken for granted.

If Alexandra did not comprehend the situation, she certainly knew how much she was hated. On hospital wards she was often treated with surly disregard. In November 1916 Miliukov, the leader of the liberals in the Duma, virtually accused the triumvirate of Rasputin, Stürmer and the Tsarina of treachery. Stürmer's private secretary, another constant visitor to Rasputin's flat in Petrograd, had been charged with blackmailing banks, and Stürmer himself was suspected of treason. The protesting Duma and other voices, including Buchanan's, eventually forced the Tsar to demand Stürmer's resignation from public life; this he did despite Alexandra's chiding voice – 'such a devoted, honest, sure man' she wrote of the hopeless, hapless politician.

The word on the street was: 'Rasputin is a German spy and so is his mistress, Alexandra.' In Moscow, Meriel Buchanan noted that the Tsarina was thought to be communicating with the Kaiser by radio from the roof of the Alexander Palace. An intercepted letter from her brother Prince Ernst of Hesse, who happened to be a German army officer, and several other German attempts to communicate with the Tsar, were dragged in to back up these stories.

The damage was done. The more sophisticated 'liberals' in society had begun to talk about direct action against the Romanovs: possibly beginning with the murder of Rasputin, certainly ending in the deposition of the Tsars. The war was no closer to ending, the people could barely afford fuel or food even if they could find them, and the army had deployed, and largely lost, over twelve million men.

6

The End & the Beginning

As 1916 drew to a close the Tsarina was frantic. Trepov, Stürmer's replacement as Prime Minister, had accepted the job only on condition that Protopopov, Minister of the Interior, must go. No! She was horrified. Letters, metaphorically tearstained in her distress, were ineffectual. She arrived at the Mogilev and argued with the Tsar. Raised voices were heard. She had the influence, but he alone had ultimate power. She won. Protopopov would stay.

The tone of Nicolas's letters to Alexandra, immediately after this clash of the Titans, indicates contrition. He admired her strength. Weeks later, he seemed to take a step back, to become detached for the first time, to perhaps see her pig-headedness for the monstrous obstacle it was. Yet he remained trapped within her orbit. His political problems were distant; more proximate, his army's lack of leadership was the despair of the British allies and he knew it.

Trepov, exasperated, tried to resign. The Tsar ordered him to stay. Desperately Trepov got his brother to offer Rasputin an enormous bribe and professional advancement if he would only engineer Protopopov's downfall. Rasputin had no use for either; he was perfectly happy as he was. But the offer, proof of his influence, delighted him.

At the start of December, the Duma cheered a rousing speech from the monarchist deputy Purishkevich. Rasputin must be overthrown. 'Revolution threatens and an obscure moujik shall govern Russia no longer!' Within weeks the Tsar and Tsarina had also been urged, one way or another, to change their position on autocracy, and/ or Rasputin, by two Grand Dukes and the Tsarina's elder sister Elisabeth. Elisabeth – Ella – had once been the bride Kaiser Wilhelm most desired. She had instead married Grand Duke Serge, the inept

Governor of Moscow who had been murdered during the 1905 revolution. Since his death she had been a Mother Superior, in an expensively designed habit, with her own order of Orthodox nuns. She was the one person Alexandra might have been expected to listen to, and she had no more luck than anyone else.

Rich, fashionable Russians were plotting, but not in secret. They talked about the plots they had fabricated. You were nobody in a nightclub unless you were part of a band of would-be assassins, or at the very least, an officer in a corps that intended to kidnap the Imperial Family and hold them under house arrest while the politicians sorted things out.

Several British Intelligence officers, and a number of young Russian officers, had become involved in something only slightly more sophisticated. The British were Oswald Rayner, Stephen Alley and John Scale. Scale, the senior man, knew what was afoot before he left for Romania on a mission to blow up oilfields, burn grain stores and thereby hinder the German advance. He kept in touch from afar. Stephen Alley was an engineer from a family of Victorian railway builders, educated in Russia and England, with years of experience in railways and the Caucasian oilfields, who could pass in any Russian company for a native. He had been born in a Moscow palace that belonged to the Yusupov family. The Yusupovs were much longer-established, and even richer, than the Romanovs.

The two key Russians, both young men, still in their early twenties, were Grand Duke Dmitri Pavlovich Romanov and Prince Felix Yusupov. Yusupov, a homosexual socialite and so far non-combatant member of the Corps des Pages, was married to Princess Irina, a famously beautiful Romanov. He was an old friend of Oswald Rayner, whom he had met at Oxford. Rayner was a brilliant linguist, fluent in French, German, Swedish and Russian, but his origins had been humble and it was only the support of wealthy patrons that had allowed him to blossom and had taken him to University College and the Bar. Like Alley, he had been recruited into the Intelligence service at the start of the war.

As Felix and Dmitri drank toasts and listened to the gipsy singers, as they took tea in drawing rooms, as they slid from their horses and hurried off the parade ground in whirling snow, they plotted to kill Rasputin. What remains unclear is whether British intelligence officers proactively approached them with the idea of carrying out the murder by proxy or whether they heard about their desire to kill Rasputin at an early stage and sought to exploit the opportunity for their own ends. Either way, the longstanding personal rapport between Yusupov, Alley, Scale and Rayner was key to the collaboration. Together they pondered on how to lure Rasputin to a place where he might be done away with. They cast about for some irresistible bait. In his vanity, and rapaciousness, Rasputin saw himself as the great seducer. Felix Yusupov would therefore get to know him, before casually inviting him to meet Irina his wife, the richest and most beautiful woman in Russia.

One afternoon in late December, Anna Vyrubova climbed down from her carriage into the snow-laden courtyard and stepped upstairs to Rasputin's flat as she often did. The living room was alive with people as usual. She saw Rasputin's regular two or three friends who dropped in or stayed from time to time, others who might not have met him at home before, but with the samovar steaming and the buzz of conversation this was like any other day. Rasputin, favouring her with his attention for a few minutes, confided that he was going to be introduced to Princess Irina that night at the Moika Palace. Vyrubova knew it, everyone did: a huge Yusupov mansion fronting a canal in the centre of town. When, later that day, Vyrubova was at Tsarskoe with the Tsarina, and happened to mention this appointment of his, Alexandra was puzzled. 'There must be some mistake. Irina is in the Crimea.'

The next morning was a Saturday. By midday the news had travelled by word of mouth all over Petrograd: Rasputin had been taken away or kidnapped. At Tsarskoe, only Vyrubova had heard anything. It had something to do with a disturbance at the Yusupov palace. Her friend Mounya Golovina had rung secretly, from outside Rasputin's flat, and said that he could not be found. Golovina had heard (and whether it was true or not nobody knew) that policemen and guards on night duty, muffled in thick uniforms and patrolling the other side of the canal, had heard shots from the Moika Palace before dawn. Shortly after daybreak a frantic search had been mounted.

Vyrubova, in trepidation, said nothing at first. The story was in the Petrograd evening papers. Some time that evening Alexandra herself heard it, and was distraught. Police were scanning the river routes to and around the islands on the Neva, expecting to find a body. They must suspect that ill had befallen Our Friend! Petrograd lay covered in a thick layer of snow; the Neva was frozen solid, the islands blanketed in white. Nothing had been found.

News of the mystery flashed through Russia. Many peasants, deep in the country, were devoted to Rasputin. They thought of him as the voice of the people who could speak directly into the ear of the Tsar. The aristocrats had killed him, they told one another, because he spoke wisely, and against their interests. In the cities nearly everyone of every class was jubilant. They had seen Rasputin as the single biggest obstacle to victory in this horrible war. It was as if, with the removal of one man, the sun would break through the clouds, railway trains would steam across Russia again, prices would fall and the shops would be full of fresh-baked pastries. Nicolas simply worried about the effect of Rasputin's death on Alexandra. Without Our Friend and his spiritual conviction, her hopes for the Tsarevich's future would crumble.

Within days, Rasputin's body was found in the Neva, frozen solid and clumsily tied with rope. It was fished out of the ice and a hasty post-mortem showed evidence of murder by shooting. In 2005 a review of the ballistics evidence by Home Office Pathologist Professor Derrick Pounder indicated that the bullet which caused the fatal wound in Rasputin's forehead came from a British officer's Webley hand gun.

Rasputin was buried with haste to avoid violent demonstrations. Nicolas and Alexandra were shocked and embittered. They had little doubt who the culprits were, and both Yusupov and Dmitri Pavlovich Romanov were exiled from Petrograd. Alexandra was particularly disgusted about Dmitri's involvement. At one time he had been considered a potential husband for Olga, her eldest daughter.

Alexandra grieved, then recovered her wits. She prided herself on her resilience and strength. Her husband appeared to be in a state of nervous collapse; it followed that the Lord, as a test, had burdened her with the responsibility of steering Russia on the correct path while her weak and vacillating husband carried out the executive role. With Rasputin gone, if anyone had been in any doubt that the Tsarina had held the reins all along, they were no longer. Resolutions became firmer by the minute. The sun did not break through the clouds.

She had a kind of Juliet balcony made above the receiving room in which Nicolas interviewed important visitors. It allowed her to eavesdrop, from behind a curtain, on the confidences of those who visited the Tsar: ambassadors and politicians, mostly. She reviewed these discussions with him, to remind him of the importance of backbone.

Anna Vyrubova received death threats. Alexandra insisted that Vyrubova move from her home in the village into the Alexander Palace for better protection. Trepov's obdurate refusal to play the part of Prime Minister having prevailed, he was allowed to resign in January in favour of her choice, Prince Nicolas Golytsin. Golytsin was seventy-six years old, had no idea how to do the job and emphatically didn't want it, but she insisted. Minister of the Interior Protopopov, meanwhile, was creepier than ever, flattering her and Anna Vyrubova and hinting that his advice was informed by the spirit of Rasputin.

This impressed nobody outside that closed circle. General Sir Henry Wilson was visiting Russia, briefly, as part of a mission with Lord Revelstoke and Lord Milner. He had known the Tsarina from her girlhood, but could not fail to hear the despair and anger in Petrograd and Moscow. Alexandra and her husband were 'riding for a fall. Everyone – officers, merchants, ladies – talks openly of the absolute necessity of doing away with them.'

Lenin, far away in Zürich and living from hand to mouth, heard nothing of this. From his vantage point, Russia seemed to be crumbling from within, but with a proletariat apparently willing to suffer endlessly for the maintenance of Tsarism, how could revolutionary ideas ever take hold? He was depressed. This was his darkest hour.

The Romanov families were furious at Alexandra's obduracy. The Imperial couple had fallen out with the Dowager Empress, Maria Feodorova, and with all the Tsar's uncles and cousins. They both refused to concede that Nicolas had not, constitutionally, been an absolute monarch since the revolution of 1905. Grand Duke Alexander even shouted at Alexandra: 'I realize that you are willing to perish and that your husband feels the same way, but what about us?... You have no right to drag your relatives with you down a precipice.' Nicolas ushered him from the room.

They refused to confront opposition. Alexandra, on the rare occasions when she encountered it, shut her mouth like a trap. Occasionally she pointed out that only the Devil inspired evil thoughts. When Nicolas was warned, or challenged, he thanked the advisor profusely and expressed his outrage afterwards in private. Sir George Buchanan, who independently of the Foreign Office delivered an informal opinion that the Tsar was in danger, wrote: 'The Grand Duke Serge remarked that had I been a Russian subject I should have been sent to Siberia.'

At the end of January, Rodzianko, the President of the Duma, made one last attempt to pierce Nicolas's thick hide; and for one shocking moment, he appeared to succeed. Nicolas said: 'Is it possible that for twenty-two years I tried to act for the best and that for twenty-two years it was all a mistake?' Rodzianko summoned up the courage to say 'Yes.' But it changed nothing. A month later, with street riots, flaring everywhere like tinder in a sunbaked forest, being put down by force on Protopopov's orders, revolution was imminent.

In London in 1917, *The Times* was the journal of record. Its reports were generally believed by the people who ran the country. On Thursday 8 March, having informed British readers that 600 men had been lost in Romania, it followed with a routine report that was meticulously dull:

On his arrival at Main Headquarters today the Tsar was greeted, among others, by General Alexeiev, Chief of the General Staff, to whom his Majesty expressed his satisfaction at seeing him restored to health after his illness, and again at his post.

In Petrograd that day yelling crowds broke into bakeries and looted the bread. A peaceful protest was held, and looting occurred on a larger scale the next day, Friday. Protopopov's orders were disregarded. On Saturday there were widespread demonstrations and the announcement of a general strike.

On the Sunday, Cossacks were called up to shoot protesters and two hundred people died in Petrograd alone. In the barracks other soldiers mutinied. The Tsar received a telegram from Rodzianko. He read it: street disorders, a plea for a constitutional government. Seen it all before. 'Some nonsense I shall not even bother to answer,' he said. That morning in church he appears to have had a minor heart attack.

At Tsarskoe, Alexandra took soothing phone calls from Protopopov. Everything was under control, he told her. She was more concerned about her children – she always called them children, although the two eldest were now young women – for two of the girls had measles. By mid-week, her husband had abdicated and she knew nothing about it.

As early as Friday 16 March, *The Times* announced:

REVOLUTION IN RUSSIA.
A 'WIN THE WAR' MOVEMENT
There has been a revolution in Russia. The Emperor Nicolas II has abdicated... The Parliamentary leaders, with the people and the Army at their back, have carried out a coup d'état.

While the bulk of the Petrograd garrison held the city for the Parliamentary cause, M. Rodzianko, the President of the Duma, demanded of the Tsar a new Government. Failing to receive satisfaction, M. Rodzianko placed himself at the head of a Provisional Government of 12 members.

In less than 200 words, three centuries of Romanov autocracy came to an end. An editorial reassured readers that the transition would proceed smoothly and war would be prosecuted with renewed vigour.

A great Revolution has been accomplished in Russia... The news will hardly come as a surprise to those acquainted with the internal situation in the Allied Empire as it has recently developed, and who have observed the ominous suspension of telegrams from Russia within the last few days... The great danger was that the Tsar might fail to realise the position with sufficient promptitude, and that he might either resist the Revolution or defer his decision. He has had enough of wisdom and of unselfish patriotism not to take either of these courses... To the Tsar, in particular, the highest credit is due. Had he chosen to resist the demands of the Duma there were, doubtless, plenty of troops ready to support him.

The ex-Tsar seemed to be quite the hero. The Allies could hope for a new Russia of 'united people, who are led by a constitutional Government of their own choosing under the auspices of their historic dynasty'.

Just like us, in fact. King George had heard the news from the Foreign Office. He was horrified. 'I am in despair,' he wrote. There had been 'practically a revolution'. But he comforted himself 'the rising is against the Government not against the Tsar.' One of Nicky's uncles or brothers would take over, then...? It was puzzling. Throughout the week after the abdication *The Times* was at pains to exonerate Nicolas from any blame at all. Everything, a reader like King George was allowed to think, would come right in the end.

Sir George Buchanan informed the Foreign Office that the Tsar was expected to retire to the Crimea, but to be quite sure of his safety the Provisional Government wanted the whole family to leave Russia as soon as possible. 'My thoughts are constantly with you and I shall always remain your true and devoted friend, as you know I have been in the past,' King George wrote in a sympathetic telegram that was sent to the Alexander Palace, but intercepted and never delivered. Despite his Foreign Office briefings and intermittent correspondence with Oliver Locker-Lampson, a British officer in Russia, he did not seem particularly well informed about the fury that had been mounting for months in Petrograd and Moscow. But then, rather like Nicky, he found it hard to see the big picture. Civil servants and politicians with death-delivering decisions to make had been exasperated to receive, many times since the outbreak of war, picayune royal frettings and admonitions over details of protocol.

Bonar Law reassured the House that the Tsar had abdicated at the demands of those who wanted, not peace, but more efficient prosecution of the war. A *Times* correspondent on the spot painted a more confused and far less cosy picture. He described the crowds, mutiny, the capture of the arsenal and loss of telephone contact that preceded the Tsar's overthrow. Buchanan and Paléologue were cheered on their way to the Foreign Ministry and:

A group of 22 members of the Upper House... yesterday addressed a telegram to the Tsar, in which, after reviewing the circumstances which have brought the people to a state of utter despair and led to the downfall of the Government in Petrograd, they say: *The maintenance of this old Government in office is tantamount to the complete overthrow of law and order, involving defeat on the battlefield, the end of the dynasty, and the greatest misfortune for Russia. We consider that the only means of salvation lies in a complete and final rupture with the past... and the summoning of a person enjoying the confidence of the nation.*

In other words, 'Don't come back'. This correspondent insisted that if the Tsar tried to maintain his position, the Socialists would take over: 'Yesterday the SDP issued a proclamation of a most seditious character, which was spread broadcast throughout the city.' The revolutionary SDP were summarily discounted by the British writer as 'mere doctrinaires' but he also correctly perceived the vulnerability of the populace to promises of peace, or a republic. Protopopov had surrendered his post; Moscow, said Our Correspondent, supported the 'anti-monarchist' Duma. 'According to this morning's reports all the troops at Tsarskoe Selo have gone over to the Duma. The whereabouts of the Empress and the Imperial Family is not known.'

Prince Lvov, who came from a long line of Russian princes and had a dramatically prolific beard to match, had been elected to lead the Government in place of Golytsin. Lloyd George sent him an effusive telegram:

The Revolution whereby the Russian people have placed their destinies on the sure foundation of freedom is the greatest service which they have yet made to the cause for which the Allied peoples have been fighting since 1914.

Hey, steady on. 'A little strong,' King George remarked. It wasn't the implied insignificance of Russia's twelve million dead that disturbed him, but the implication that revolution was a Good Thing.

The abdication had been a clumsy affair. On Sunday evening, fully recovered from his apparent illness at church, the Tsar knew that matters were getting out of hand in Petrograd, with bloodshed in the streets. Why had firm action not been taken? In time of war, this kind of thing was outrageous. He sent a sharp order to the Military Governor of Petrograd, then sat down to write to Alexandra. Protopopov, in his view, was not being decisive enough.

The next day, reports were even worse. General Alexeiev was urging him, he wrote, 'to appoint a very energetic man'. The energetic man would have to tell the ministers, who would have to order underlings to do something. All Nicolas himself could do was write to his wife about it. Suddenly a telegram arrived from Tsarskoe. 'Many units gone over to the enemy,' stood out from its terse contents. Alarmed at last, he ordered his train and set off at the crack of dawn on Tuesday morning, 13 March. All day it steamed north-west towards Petrograd and home.

At two on Wednesday morning, only 100 miles from its destination, the train stopped. Nicolas was awoken. Armed revolutionary soldiers were blocking the track. Rather than go back to Mogilev, Nicolas ordered a diversion west, to the military HQ of the northern armies at Pskov. The Imperial train pulled in to Pskov at 8 p.m. on Wednesday, 14 March. On the platform stood General Ruszky and his deputy General Danilov. Aboard the train Ruszky told the Tsar that the entire garrison of Petrograd and Tsarskoe Selo had gone over to 'the enemy', that is, the Duma. This included the Cossacks who patrolled his palace, as well as the Imperial Guard and the young nobles of the Corps des Pages. Nicolas was advised, gently, that he must make concessions.

He was outraged; this was treachery, but his power had melted away. He could no longer summon up the military on his side, and nor could the politicians his wife had put in place. *He could not give orders.* That was all he had ever done and he was defeated. He sent a telegram to Rodzianko. He was, he announced, ready to accept a constitutional monarchy. He would concede power to the Duma, presumably with Rodzianko in charge.

It was too late, Rodzianko replied; the current Duma was under tremendous pressure from the Soviets, the people's councils that had sprung up under Social Revolutionary leadership all over the city. The main Petrograd Soviet was vocal and strong. The Tsar must abdicate at once in favour of his son, and a Regency. This Nicolas did not want to hear. He went to bed.

Everyone, except himself, understood that if he did not abdicate he would face a violent death. As a last resort, the Duma obtained written reactions from everyone who mattered in the army and navy. Next day, Thursday, after breakfast, General Ruszky visited him again in his railway carriage. He produced telegrams endorsing Rodzianko's way forward. Every General and Admiral he had ever trusted, including Grand Duke Nikolai, was fervently in favour of his abdication; an Admiral implored that, without it, his fleet would mutiny. 'What do you want me to do?' the Tsar asked helplessly. It was simple. Abdicate.

He had to make the decision by himself. There was no telephone contact with, and no bullying from, Tsarskoe. He had no armed force to fight the Duma with, and even if he had, he did not want to disturb Russia further in wartime. At last he told Ruszky he would abdicate in favour of his son. He nominated Grand Duke Mikhail, his brother, to be Regent pending Alexei's majority. He and the Tsarina would very probably have to retire to Livadia, he thought. Alexei loved it there, and could stay with them until he was old enough to be crowned Emperor. At three in the afternoon, he signed a statement renouncing the throne.

Early that evening Fedorov, one of the Imperial doctors, discussed with him the likely progress of Alexei's haemophilia. In passing, he declared that this dream of retirement to Livadia was unrealistic. It was more likely, he pointed out, that both Tsar and Tsarina would be exiled abroad. In any case, Alexei's parents would no longer have the final say over his education or his care. Nicolas could not bear that. At nine that night two Duma members arrived. They had come to take formal acceptance of the abdication; the document must be signed in their presence. They saw Nicolas, alone in his small, dimly-lit study on the Imperial train. The two men were not by nature revolutionaries; most Duma members wanted a constitutional monarchy. They delivered a message about a complete and final rupture with the past and 'the summoning of a person enjoying the confidence of the nation.' The Tsar interrupted. He had changed his mind. 'I cannot part with my son,' he said. He would instead abdicate in favour of his brother, Grand Duke Mikhail.

He signed the revised papers and documents that made Grand Duke Nikolai Commander-in-Chief but he was replaced within a week by Alexeiev since the army would not accept a Romanov. Prince Lvov was made Prime Minister. At one o'clock on the Friday morning his train began the return journey to Mogilev, so that he could bid farewell to his commanders. He was as inflexible and uncomprehending as ever. 'All around me, I see treason, cowardice and deceit,' he wrote bitterly.

7

Alone, Despite Appearances

The previous Monday, the morning after the deaths of 200 people in Petrograd, Alexandra, preoccupied by her sick daughters, heard some rumour of unusually violent 'disorders' in the streets and invited her friend Lili Dehn for the day to find out more. There was nothing much to worry about, she was told. The strike was inconvenient, but Lili hadn't seen any trouble.

By the end of the day, the Tsarina knew that loyal regiments had deserted the Tsar. In the end, they were not loyal at all. Petrograd had succumbed to mob rule. There was drunkenness and anarchy. Lili Dehn stayed the night, preferring not to brave the uncertain city streets.

On Tuesday morning Benckendorf told the Tsarina that Rodzianko had urged her to leave and the Tsar was on his way back. Benckendorf himself had rung the station to order an Imperial train to be prepared for their imminent departure. They would have no need of it, she said; she was busy nursing Anna Vyrubova, the Tsarevich and three of the young Grand Duchesses through measles, so how could they leave? The Tsarevich had a temperature of 104. Benckendorf told her that, in any case, his request had been dismissed. None of the workers, he was told, would willingly get a train ready for them.

At 11.30 a.m. Benckendorf received another message. If the family did not take a train out at once, prepared or otherwise, they would be marooned. The lines were to be cut in two hours' time. He knew it was pointless to tell Alexandra this, and refrained. Unknown to him, in and around the Petrograd Soviet there were dark mutterings about the ex-Tsar's failure to return to Tsarskoe. Some thought he was organizing a German invasion. The question in Benckendorf's mind was, how was the Tsar to get unharmed past these outlaw bands of revolutionaries and back to Tsarskoe? A worse problem intervened. At nightfall a gang of drunken soldiers turned up to escort 'the German woman' and her son back to Petrograd. Benckendorf managed to summon up 1,500 armed troops to defend the Alexander Palace. 'They are so devoted to us,' Alexandra said fondly. He was not so sure. A field gun was rolled into the courtyard. Firing was heard from the grounds. The night passed without further incident but by morning there was no sign that the revolution was over. Alexandra could not contact her husband. This was Wednesday, and he was supposed to be back. On Thursday, he had still not returned, and the loyal troops, with their field gun, had melted away.

At the Alexander Palace, its russet walls only blurrily visible through successive blizzards, Alexandra did not suspect that abdication was even a remote possibility. There had been no telephone or telegraph contact for days. Water and electricity were cut off. Most of the servants had gone. The household, including the families of courtiers, now numbered about a hundred. They wore coats and scarves as they hurried up and down icy corridors in grey light. Snow-curves blocked the lower panes of the tall windows. Alexandra had difficulty breathing. She could not climb stairs without assistance and when she was not nursing her children, ostentatious in her Red Cross uniform, she was pushed across the parquet in a wheelchair.

On the Friday, she heard rumours from Petrograd that the Tsar had abdicated in favour of Grand Duke Mikhail. A Provisional Government held power. She didn't believe a word of it; why would her husband do such an outrageous thing all of a sudden, especially when he knew Alexei was so ill? But Grand Duke Paul came late that afternoon and confirmed it. They must go abroad as soon as possible, he told her.

She was seen after the children were asleep, 'sobbing bitterly'. At last she addressed her courtiers. 'She was very brave,' Benckendorf wrote, 'and said that the Emperor had preferred to abdicate the crown rather than to break the oath which he had made at his coronation to maintain and to transfer to his heir the autocracy such as he had inherited it from his father.' Benckendorf saw no logic in this, since Nicolas had in fact abdicated in favour of his brother, thereby violating his son's rights; but then there was no logic in any of her thoughts. He urged her that she must 'put her papers in order' since there might be 'a domiciliary visit'. She began to burn her diaries and correspondence. Petrograd newspapers came into the house, and Benckendorf and the ladies-in-waiting took pains to keep them away from her and her daughters.

Newspapers in Germany were quick to seize upon the Tsar's downfall. It would be even harder now for Russia to raise a War Loan. It had been weak before, but now! Who was going to run the country? Not that the Tsar would be missed. 'The disappearance of the person of the Tsar would signify nothing in view of the character of the world war as a people's war, and in view of the Tsar's whole personality,' opined the *Frankfurter Zeitung*, renowned for its pacifist liberal views.

That wasn't quite the story as Wilhelm read it. In this war he had suffered a certain unease at the habitual dismissal of his opinion by his own Generals, but there had been nothing like this. He had known, since Nicolas made concessions in 1905, that this would happen. Grand Duke Mikhail had renounced the throne already. The Petrograd Soviet was demanding a republic. There was no Romanov in charge at all. It just showed: once you allowed your monarchical principle to slip, you got what you deserved. His *Schadenfreude* was immense. Germany could make peace now, on its own terms.

The Americans came into the war at the start of April, so the British were cautiously optimistic. However, the British Ambassador, Sir George Buchanan, remained exasperated by the Petrograd Soviet; who did they think they were, these unwashed people? They should stand aside and let the Duma take charge. Oliver Locker-Lampson, the flamboyant young officer who wrote letters from Russia to King George, was more circumspect. He caught the excitement from the streets of Petrograd yet found time to speculate on the motive behind 'German money' in inciting the revolution.

The German Foreign Office and General Staff were both involved with Helphand. He, richer than ever, explained his plan to the German Minister in Copenhagen. Russia would shortly collapse into anarchy, he predicted; by the end of the summer German troops would be able to sweep in unopposed, break the empire into manageable chunks and impose efficient administration. To make certain of social and military collapse before invading, a summer of political upheaval would be necessary. Lenin and his band of similarly-minded Bolshevik demagogues must be transported to Russia forthwith, and given money to intensify the revolutionary propaganda campaign that Keskula had financed the year before. They could bring chaos out of order if anyone could. The alternative was to sue for a peace settlement now. This would leave Germany in much the same predicament it had started with: an enormous politically unified land mass on its eastern border.

Lenin's reaction to the revolution had been grumpy. He read the Swiss papers; the Provisional Government were simply instruments of the bourgeoisie. He telegraphed Bolsheviks everywhere: *no rapprochement*. At about that time he and his fellow-exile Zinoviev were informed that they would be given money to go back to Russia and that their friends, scattered about Europe, would follow. Lenin would have none of it. The Bolsheviks, he said, must arrive in Russia together. As is well known, over thirty Russian emigrés were finally transported ('like a plague bacillus' snorted Winston Churchill) by train in a sealed carriage from Switzerland across Germany, to arrive in Stockholm.

Lenin remained strained and truculent about taking German gold. Once he reached Russia, it poured in 'from an inheritance' of his sponsor in Zürich, Karl Moor. But this covered a tiny fraction of the money that Germany pumped into destabilizing Russia in that summer of 1917, which was between thirty and fifty million gold marks.

Lenin and other equally determined Bolsheviks reached Russia on 16 April. They set themselves up in a Petrograd palace vacated by Ksessinchskaia, the *Prima Ballerina Assoluta* of the Imperial Ballet, who had been Nicolas's lover before his marriage. Meriel Buchanan, passing along the street:

> noticed suddenly an enormous scarlet flag flaming vividly above the walls. Full of curiosity, I asked somebody the meaning of this and

was told that the house had been taken possession of by a new group of political exiles who had just returned from Switzerland, having been given passage across Germany in a specially guarded train, with the blinds drawn at the windows, and detectives and armed soldiers posted at the doors. There were said to be about thirty of them in all; they belonged to an extremist party and had been given the title of Bolsheviks.

Every day, Lenin addressed crowds from one of the balconies and explained how much better life could be under a Marxist system. Buchanan dismissed him as some kind of eccentric, but British Intelligence knew perfectly well where Bolshevik money was coming from and they were not quite so sanguine.

Before Nicolas returned to Tsarskoe, Alexandra was informed by an emissary from the Provisional Government that both she and her husband were under arrest. When the children had recovered, the entire family would be conveyed north to Murmansk. This was the new name for Port Romanov, an ice-free Arctic port founded only five months before. From its deep harbour a British cruiser would take them to England. This was the result of a flurry of cypher telegrams. Within days of the abdication, the Foreign Office was reminding Sir George Buchanan by cable that: 'Any violence done to the Emperor or his family would have a most deplorable effect and would deeply shock public opinion in this country.'

At about the same time the Provisional Government received a threatening message from the Kaiser sent via Stockholm. There was no nonsense about concern for public opinion from him; privately he might think Nicolas a fool, but a Tsar must not be murdered. If they harmed him he would hold them responsible with their lives.

Sir George was able to reassure London that the Provisional Government would not harm the Romanovs. The Tsar had agreed to leave the scene, but must be allowed to return to Tsarskoe to be with his children until they had recovered from the measles, when they could all travel together. Perhaps he was himself perplexed as to where they would go, because he added, in a cable the day after, that Miliukov, the Foreign Minister, seemed to take it for granted that the British were busy making arrangements for them to come to England.

Consternation. One imagines the blank looks in London. Who? Where? The King? Where would they live? What would they live on? How long would they stay? What would the papers say? Were we supposed to fetch them? And how on earth could one justify sending a fully manned and armed gunboat (for that would be necessary) through waters in which Russia's Baltic Fleet was reportedly weakened by mutiny? It would very likely come under attack, if not from Germany then from Russian forces hostile to the Tsar. The Foreign Office sent a telegram back. Perhaps Denmark (where the Dowager Empress came from) or neutral Switzerland might be more suitable?

Miliukov was alarmed. He made a formal request through Sir George Buchanan. Then he heard that workers had refused to allow free passage to the Imperial train, and that a night or two ago a band of drunks had gone to Tsarskoe and tried to take the ex-Tsaritsa away. He impressed upon Sir George that the Tsar's life was in danger from 'extremists' who were 'exciting opinion against His Majesty as much as they could.' But the Government could only let Nicolas leave with an undertaking that he must not return before the end of the war, and public opinion would not tolerate his being permitted to go either to Denmark or to Switzerland.

> I entirely agree [wrote Sir George to the FO] that it is most important that the Emperor should leave before the agitation has time to grow and I earnestly trust that... I may be authorised without delay to offer His Majesty asylum in England and at the same time assure the Russian Government that he will remain there during the war. The departure of the Emperor would certainly strengthen the Russian Government and help matters to settle down.

His cable arrived in London at 5.40 p.m. on Thursday 22 March, the day Nicolas arrived back at Tsarskoe. It crossed with two that had left London at 5 p.m., the outcome of a meeting between Lloyd George, his Deputy Andrew Bonar Law, Lord Hardinge (Permanent

Secretary, Foreign Office) and the King's Private Secretary, Lord Stamfordham. One, copies of which were circulated to the King and the War Cabinet, was headed:

PRIVATE AND SECRET.
After further consideration it has been decided that it would be better for the Emperor to come to England during the war rather than to a country contiguous to Germany. Apprehension is felt lest, through the influence of the Empress, the residence of the Emperor if in Denmark or Switzerland might become a focus of intrigue, and that in the hands of disaffected Russian generals the Emperor might become the possible head of a counter-revolution. This would be to play into the hands of Germany, and is a risk that must be avoided at all costs.

There followed a couple of paragraphs about the need to make sure, first, that the Russians understood this was an offer made at their own prompting, and second, that the Romanovs would not drain the resources of King or taxpayer. At exactly the same time, another telegram left, but this one Sir George could show to Mr Miliukov:

In order to meet the request made by the Russian Government, the King and His Majesty's Government readily offer asylum to the Emperor and Empress in England which it is hoped they will take advantage of during the war.

You should at the same time impress upon the Russian Government the necessity for making suitable provision for their maintenance in this country.

Miliukov reassured him that they would receive an allowance, but it was important not to let this be known in Petrograd, or the Soviets wouldn't allow them to escape. The next day, another telegram was forwarded to Buchanan in Petrograd. General Hanbury Williams, at Mogilev, had had an unofficial conversation with General Alexeiev and cabled London with his view of the stance that the FO, in other words Buchanan, should take:

You should immediately and urgently press Russian government to give absolute safe conduct to whole Imperial family to Port Romanoff and England as soon as possible... You should point out discredit which will attach to new Government in eyes of the world if Emperor or his family are injured, and you should add that we rely on Russian Government ensuring the personal safety of His Majesty and the Imperial Family.

It was true that if the Romanovs were lynched while in their care, it wouldn't look good; but the Russians knew that. The point was to get them away. The invitation to England had been accepted, but when would action commence? It seems that the FO was negotiating their safe conduct, by sea, with Wilhelm, via the Danish royal family. In later years the Kaiser did reveal as much, in conversation. What put an end to it was King George himself.

Nicolas was back at last. In his absence from Alexandra, he had spent some time with his mother, the Dowager Empress Maria Feodorovna, at Mogilev. She had arrived in her own train after the abdication and he spent three fraught days in one of its carriages with her, hearing yet again how deeply the family deplored his wife and her poisonous influence. These had been private discussions, very probably the most intimate, emotional and tragic they had ever had. There had been tears on both sides.

Now he was stopped at the Palace gate and addressed as Colonel. The Imperial lives, so placid on the surface, had been turned upside down. Pornographic cartoons and lurid stories of life at court, especially of the Tsarina's relationship with the late traitor Rasputin, were openly circulating in Petrograd. Rasputin's body was roughly exhumed from its chapel in the Tsarskoe park, doused with petrol and burned. In Petrograd, the silent army of Okhrana agents who had looked after them for so long were being thrown into the Fortress of St Peter and St Paul, the big city jail. All over Russia, Romanov estates were to be shared out among those who had lived and worked on them for generations. The Duma would soon begin redistributing farms, a prospect that made peasants forget residual monarchist sympathies at once. Soldiers were already deserting the front in order to get home and stake a claim. Calls to stop the war came from the powerful Petrograd Soviet, but as the Duma showed its mettle, and military planning and organization resurfaced, the soldiers began to regain morale. 'Wilhelm of Hohenzollern' had yet to be defeated and they were going to do it.

By the end of March it was clear to everyone that the Republic declared by the Soviet was here to stay. The Provisional Government had a precarious grip on power, but were kind enough to the ex-Tsar and Tsarina. An emissary reassured them that their relations had been in touch, by telegram, to wish them well. The Alexander Palace was provided with guards for the family's safety. The children were getting better. Alexei had quite recovered. Yet there was, as yet, no date for the projected journey to Murmansk. Nicolas was writing 'if we go to England' in his diary. Not 'when'.

In London, there seemed to be some hesitation. It wasn't just the Government, worrying about public opinion if Nicolas and Alexandra came to Engand. Lloyd George would gladly get the Tsar out of Russia because he feared that, otherwise, Nicolas would become a figurehead for monarchists aiming to start a civil war there. But no preparations had been made to get him out. The ship that would pick the family up had not yet been assigned to the task. The invitation so 'readily' made was hedged about with queries obviously inspired by the King, such as,

Can you possibly ascertain what are the private resources of the Emperor? It is very desirable that His Majesty and his family should have sufficient means to live in a manner befitting their rank as members of an Imperial family.

Their living expenses could not, for political reasons, be paid for from the Civil List, and the ultimate responsibility, if their Russian allowance were not paid, could be a disastrous drain on the Privy Purse. King George never liked spending money, and maybe he and Queen Mary were dismayed for other reasons. These Imperial cuckoos would have to be invited everywhere and provided with a grace-and-favour house of some size. They had four marriageable daughters and might well form a kind of alternative court, with emigré monarchists and Orthodox priests at its heart. Their social and religious attitudes were antique and would inevitably prove offensive; all this would reflect upon King George and Queen Mary. And the King could not expect to welcome a Russian despot without at least some public protest, which meant spending more on royal protection. In short, they would be a literally *intolerable* burden.

On 30 March, just one week after the firm British offer of asylum, came a bolt from the blue. Lord Stamfordham wrote to Balfour, Foreign Secretary:

> The King has been thinking much about the Government's proposal that the Emperor Nicholas and his family should come to England.
>
> As you are doubtless aware, the King has a strong personal friendship for the Emperor, and therefore would be glad to do anything to help him in this crisis. But His Majesty cannot help doubting, not only on account of the dangers of voyage, but on general grounds of expediency, whether it is advisable that the Imperial Family should take up residence in this country.
>
> The King would be glad if you could consult the Prime Minister, as His Majesty understands no definite decision has yet been come to on the subject by the Russian Government.

That arrived on the Friday. There were astonished consultations over the weekend. As always with these things, there was backstory here, for in recent months Lloyd George had refused to concede to the King's wishes over two other matters (the removal of his favourites from military office). So the response, sent on Monday 2 April, was cautious but firm. Pointing out that the original invitation had not been 'the Government's proposal' at all but a response to Miliukov decided by a triumvirate of Prime Minister, Lord Hardinge and Stamfordham (representing the King), it went on:

> His Majesty's Ministers quite realise the difficulties to which you refer in your letter, but they do not think, unless the position changes, that it is now possible to withdraw the invitation which has been sent, and they therefore trust that the King will consent to adhere to

the original invitation, which was sent on the advice of his Majesty's Ministers.

Grudgingly the King instructed Lord Stamfordham to reply that, in that case, 'His Majesty must regard the matter as settled, unless the Russian Government should come to any fresh decision on the subject.' But it kept him awake at night.

On Friday morning Stamfordham wrote a fretful letter: 'Every day the King is becoming more concerned about the question of the Emperor and the Empress coming to this country... ' His Majesty (who couldn't, in sustained argument, have distinguished between an anarchist and a Marxist or a Fabian socialist) suddenly claimed deep insight into the public mood. Evidently the Russian-imperial-family issue was being discussed 'not only in clubs, but by working men'. Labour MPs didn't like it. The King had always thought having the Empress (especially the Empress) here 'would raise all sorts of difficulties... and I feel sure that you appreciate how awkward it will be for our Royal Family who are closely connected both with the Emperor and the Empress'. Not only that, but 'people are either assuming that [the invitation] has been initiated by the King, or deprecating the very unfair position in which His Majesty will be placed if the arrangement is carried out'. And would they please get Buchanan to tell the Russian Government to send their royal family elsewhere.

Balfour – who did have a few other things on his plate – had barely drawn breath when another missive arrived. The King's temper had now risen to a crescendo of anxiety; the problem had assumed enormous, threatening proportions in his mind, like the lowering giant Rasputin in a cartoon. His querulous voice could be heard over Stamfordham's shoulder:

The King wishes me to write again on the subject of my letter of this morning. He must beg you to represent to the Prime Minister that from all he hears and reads in the press, the residence in this country of an Ex-Emperor and Empress would be strongly resented by the public, and would undoubtedly compromise the position of the King and Queen, from whom it is already generally supposed the invitation has emanated...

Buchanan ought to be instructed to tell Milyukov that the opposition to the Emperor and Empress coming here is so strong that we must be allowed to withdraw from the consent previously given to the Russian Government's proposal.

Lloyd George decided to give in gracefully. He did so without a qualm. Although it was true that anger was being stirred up on the left of British politics it was equally evident that nobody in Russia gave a fig for their ex-tyrant. It was time he made some kind of concession to the Palace.

Balfour forwarded the King's letter to the Cabinet secretary. 'We may have to suggest Spain or the south of France as a more suitable residence than England for the Tsar.' And 'try to keep an eye on anything that may be put into the War Cabinet minutes likely to hurt the King's feelings'.

A week later the offer of asylum was formally withdrawn, but nobody was to mention this to the Russians just yet. The War Cabinet minutes gave no hint that the withdrawal had been inspired by the King. Sir George Buchanan was told to prevaricate and suggest France might be a better destination; Lord Hardinge wrote to the British Ambassador in Paris asking whether the French would take them. 'It is a matter of grave embarrassment here.' That was true enough, but the Ambassador didn't think it would go down well; in his view 'the Empress is not only a Boche by birth but in sentiment'. Within a week *The Times* was reporting from Petrograd: 'Examining the events, it seems certain that the Empress and Protopopov helped to provoke disturbances in Petrograd... in order to get a peace favourable to Germany.'

Kerensky had confiscated certain papers from the ex-Tsarina, and the Allies drew their own conclusions.

8

Waiting

Kerensky, the young Minister of Justice, visited the Alexander Palace early in April to introduce himself. He was a man of strong will and principle who served simultaneously in the Provisional Government, and the Petrograd Soviet, of which he was Vice-Chairman. He had already talked the Duma into abolishing capital punishment. Nicolas, when he heard that, was horrified; it would be the end of discipline in the army, he said. Clueless as ever, he did not see that this was one decision for which he should be fervently grateful.

Kerensky politely made their reduced status clear. Frank, passionate, questioning, the socially acceptable face of the Social Revolutionaries, he was like nobody they had ever met before. Alexandra in particular, in her long Edwardian dress, and high, piled-up Edwardian hair, simply did not understand the twentieth-century world that had produced such a person. His men searched the palace from top to bottom. Kerensky insisted that the Imperial couple be kept apart for a few weeks. He was respectful enough, but when he left, he took with him a great deal of paperwork.

The family, together, waited for someone to arrange their move to England. Nicolas was passive by nature: 'meek', his wife would call him admiringly. Now that, for the first time, all their lives were entirely beyond his control, he rather liked it. The family kept one another's spirits up; none protested, all were simply patient. Olga, the one who read most, was academically clever and at twenty-one the oldest. She was also the most likely to argue with her mother. Tatiana was the most self-possessed, the one with the gift of leadership who could be imperious yet hated obsequiousness. They were 'the big ones', and shared a room. 'The little ones' shared too: Maria, at eighteen, was chubby, flirtatious, shallow and easy-going.

She went out of her way to make friends with the guards. Anastasia was sixteen, a good mimic, with a vicious streak and a taste for practical jokes. As the youngest, she was used to making a slighter impression than the others.

All the girls, when feverish from measles, had had their heads shaved as was customary then. As they had done all their lives, they learned French, English and German, they played the piano and sewed and read, and the older ones sat with their mother and her friends while the younger ones played. Alexei had lessons from all of them, as well as his tutor. He was twelve now and had a film projector and some flickering silent movies, so he put on shows for them; it was fun. They all indulged their little brother, the fragile bright child who could, in consequence, be delightful or a nuisance as the mood took him.

Alexandra's papers, hurriedly read by Kerensky's researchers, did not reveal the vast conspiracy with the Kaiser that everyone had expected. However, evidence has since come to light that she burnt an amount of correspondence before Kerensky's visit. More than once, Kerensky interviewed Nicolas and Alexandra separately. They were kept apart from one another during April and allowed to re-unite around the end of May. Kerensky did not want the ex-Tsar hanged; all he wanted was 'that for once in his life he should feel ashamed of the horrors that had been perpetrated in his name. That was the only revenge worthy of the Great Revolution.' Hopeless to expect Citizen Romanov to understand this, though. He showed no shame whatsoever. He could not grasp how monstrous had been the abuse suffered by ordinary Russians, or what his present predicament was. To that extent, his abdication was a failure. He was a 'slow-moving, diffident simpleton' pitiful in his 'utter loneliness and desolation'. He cared nothing for anyone, except his children. All the same Kerensky did not believe him a traitor.

Of the ex-Tsarina he could believe anything. He disliked her at once and her papers placed her firmly in the frame with Protopopov, a known German sympathizer; it was the release of this information that led to the hostility in *The Times*. In exile later, Kerensky wrote:

It is certain that Alexandra Feodorovna was directing the affairs of state during the last months of the autocracy, that she was the real ruler of the country. One had only to examine the visitors' book at the Alexandrovsky Palace, and see who were the people who called on the Empress, to understand the part she played in public affairs... she was the *de facto* head of the government that was leading the country straight into a separate peace. Whether any member of the Rasputin-Vyrubova circle was actually a German agent is not certain, but undoubtedly a whole German organisation was sheltered behind them and they were, at any rate, quite ready to receive money and gifts of all kinds.

Vyrubova was packed off to prison, where she stayed for only five months, and Lili Dehn was sent back to Petrograd to live by her own devices. She was surely relieved to escape. Alexandra 'depressed everyone around her by her languor, her misery and her irreconcilable animosity,' Kerensky wrote. There are hints of this in her daughters' letters. And everyone told him how much more cheerful Nicolas had been during his enforced separation from her at the Stavka.

The Tsar was often happy that summer, or at least as happy as one can be when suspended in a state of uncertainty. He was, as we say, on gardening leave, spending time with his family. Chopping firewood and playing with his children were what he liked best. He had inherited the job of Tsar; Alexandra had stood forcefully behind him for twenty-two years; but now he seemed light-hearted, like a man who had laid down a great burden. Also, he was convinced that the war would go well. He believed, wrote his private secretary Count Benckendorf later, that the army had since the beginning of the war never been 'so numerous nor so well provided with everything'. The Americans had just come in.

As to their personal future, it would perhaps be spent at Livadia, the white Italianate palace with its roses and mimosa above a blue sea, or otherwise England, where he would shoot with Georgie and make a new life. He would make the best of this temporary lull to enjoy the summer gardens and walks at Tsarskoe. He was restricted (at gunpoint, lest he forget) to an area quite close to the house; but in no time the girls and Alexei were planting a vegetable garden and accompanying him on his walks. Some of the guards were discourteous and, distressingly, they had shot a number of the park's tame deer. But one walked nevertheless. It was a kind of liberation. He smoked heavily; he always had. The whole family hoped soon to have a date of departure, to be able to plan rather than dream of the future.

In Petrograd Sir George Buchanan had received a shocking telegram from London: 'His Majesty's government does not insist on its former offer of hospitality to the Imperial Family.' He told Miliukov in confidence and Miliukov did not pass it on. Privately, Buchanan told his wife and daughter: 'They are afraid.' At that time he thought the danger of vote-losing anti-Tsar demonstrations had put Lloyd George off. He waited for further news. Early in May, when the Petrograd Soviet gained a voice in the Duma, the Russian parliament became a noisy coalition with nothing to lose. 'We have got to face the fact that socialism is now dominant,' Buchanan wrote to London. This did not bode well for the Imperial Family. It was high summer before attention turned again to their exile. The judicial enquiry into their conduct during the war had not found anything to indicate their personal involvement in a German plot. Better that they should clear out altogether. Where was this cruiser that was supposed to be picking them up? When would it come? Kerensky was in for a surprise.

I do not remember exactly whether it was late June or early July when the British Ambassador called, greatly distressed... He brought with him a letter from a high official of the Foreign Office, who was also intimately connected with the court. With tears in his eyes, scarcely able to control his emotions, Sir George informed the Russian Minister of Foreign Affairs of the British Government's final refusal to give refuge to the former Emperor of Russia...

Buchanan was certain the Tsar and Tsarina might be murdered if they stayed. King George knew too; in June he wrote to a former aide that if Nicolas were ever incarcerated inside the Fortress of St Peter and St Paul, he would be unlikely to get out alive.

From June 1917 to July 1918 there is no reference to the Imperial Family in the Royal Archive at Windsor, and his biographer Kenneth Rose speculates that there may have been some royal knowledge of, or sponsorship of, a secret-service-led escape plan. George had known the head of MI1c (today known as MI6), Captain Mansfield Cumming, for years, and maintained the friendship. They had played billiards together as young officers at Greenwich Naval College and had regular audiences during the war. The King seems to have loved Cumming's cloak-and-dagger tales of war-time espionage and on several occasions asked him to bring agents like Paul Dukes to Buckingham Palace to relate their tales of derring-do in person. George's diary mentions a discussion in which Cumming told him 'interesting things'. That had been late in 1916. Later tracks would have to be covered with care. All Russian governments were allies until March 1918 and officially neutral afterwards, but the Bolsheviks at least were likely to seize British assets in Russia if they had a mind to.

When his imprisonment began in 1917 Nicolas received 25,000 roubles a month from a Petrograd banking tycoon with lively British Intelligence connections called Jaroszyinsky. Jaroszyinsky was friendly with a young SIS agent called Leech. At thirty, Leech had knocked about a bit: he was a financier, he was an engineer, and he had worked in the oil industry. He had a room in the British Embassy in Petrograd and a Russian wife, and his company paid out of SIS funds for Allied propaganda to get in the papers. His most important job, later in 1917, would be to work with Jaroszyinsky to get control of the Petrograd banks and thereby pull the strings of Russia's oil industry, timber trade, railway builders and grain supplies. If the Tsar could somehow be rescued through the agents of the SIS, all well and good; but Cumming, at the time, had more pressing concerns.

So did the Provisional Government. An audit of Imperial funds had proved disappointing to the Petrograd Soviet and the Duma, and had there ever been a hope that Romanov wealth might prop up the war effort it was quickly dashed. By June it was clear that they appeared not to have nearly as much cash as one might expect. The Imperial assets were forests and prairie, parks and lakes, villages and palaces, serfs and animals and (although this seems to have gone unnoticed) their priceless portable treasure, held in gemstones. They all, children included, received incomes from fat bank deposits and farms, fisheries, forests and mines; however their incomes were largely disbursed in staff salaries, allowances to members of the Romanov family, and in improving and running numerous palaces and parks. A new guard commander at Tsarskoe insisted that the prisoners pay for their own food. They complied, although shortly afterwards Nicolas wrote to his bankers to enquire about his own finances. His letter was returned undelivered by the censor.

Lenin did not make much headway with the crowds around his balcony. There was heckling and disbelief when he called for peace, and derision when he wrote about disbanding the police. In May, Trotsky came back from New York after a long exile. With his return came better organization and better public relations. The Bolsheviks were listened to. They suddenly seemed more determined, more sophisticated and more competent, and their way forward had a new guiding principle behind it: Peace, Land and All Power to the Soviet! This was an inspiring idea when your life experience so far consisted of being trampled over by fusty priests and arrogant millionaires. As to brute force, the Red Guard was assembled from enthusiastic soldiers, sailors and working men.

Kerensky had been made Minister of War, had visited the southern armies and shaken hands and given pep-talks. The High Command ridiculed his efforts; he was too liberal by half; what armies needed was iron discipline, but he preferred to use reason. They sneered and called him the Persuader in Chief. When, after a short-lived victory, those same Russian troops were repulsed by Austria, and scattered in ignominy, they blamed Kerensky's soft way of doing things. In Petrograd after the defeat there were strikes, and German money was used to undermine morale among the Baltic Fleet.

The Stop the War movement, with its implicit backing for a Bolshevik coup, was gaining strength. The Bolsheviks came close to power, but the Provisional Government was getting money from the Allies – and on this occasion, all-important intelligence. The Allies supplied information and propaganda that confirmed German money was behind Bolshevik success. Proof appeared in newspapers and damaged Lenin enormously. The Bolshevik headquarters were attacked, and the offices of Pravda and the Soviet at the Fortress of St Peter and St Paul. He fled to Finland. Trotsky was held in custody. Kerensky was weakened, but the Provisional Government was saved.

Without a doubt it had almost been overthrown in favour of the Bolsheviks, socialism and peace. Kerensky in the second week of July had said to Nicolas: 'They are after me and they will be after you.' Now, in August, he was Prime Minister and it was time to move the former Imperial Family to a place of safety. The Petrograd Soviet wanted them out of the way this winter, but not in the sunny Crimea. Kerensky and two or three trusted conspirators made plans for their departure. They were a target for assassins, so he kept their trip strictly confidential.

He told Nicolas and Alexandra that they were leaving. For Livadia, they hoped? It was not until a few days before their departure that they knew they would be going north, as well as east. 'Take plenty of warm clothes,' Kerensky warned them. They would cross the Urals – it was for their own safety. That meant no escape by sea, because up there the Arctic was frozen from September to June. They were disappointed but stoic. 'The certitude that they would not be sent abroad, which they feared more than anything, pleased them,' wrote Kerensky. He impressed on them the need for secrecy. They told absolutely everyone they met as they walked in the grounds that they were leaving for Siberia.

During their reign, when the family travelled together, two Imperial trains had set off, one of them empty, a ruse designed to confuse and deter assassins. This time there was just one, a well-appointed international *wagon-lit* train with four separate carriages for the forty-two people who would accompany them: tutors, doctor, cooks, courtiers, valets and ladies' maids, chambermaids, footmen (ten), a wine steward, a nurse and a barber. The family, the courtiers and their servants packed a mountain of luggage. They took things like silverware and wine and the royal chef's *batterie de cuisine*, as well as personal effects, icons of course, family photographs and clothing. Surrounded by cabin trunks and hatboxes and tea-chests in the hall of the Alexander Palace, they waited most of the night for a train to appear. The ex-Tsarina sat on a trunk and wept. Alexei ran about excitedly with his spaniel. Like all the Tsar's children, he had been over-protected and was young for his age.

They were guarded by a force of 330 men and six officers, selected at the last minute, paid extra and exhorted to behave themselves. Grumbling, the soldiers had demanded a tip before they fetched the luggage down and dumped it higgledy-piggledy in the hall. They took another three hours to load the train.

Finally, at dawn that mid-August morning, the Imperial party rolled out of the railway station in carriages labelled 'Japanese Red Cross Mission'. The blinds stayed down for reasons of security. How long, asked Count Benckendorf, who was to remain behind, should they expect to have to stay? Kerensky told him that when the Government reconvened in November, they would be formally freed.

Russia's military problems were dire. At midsummer, with American money behind it, the army had defeated the Austrians. Now, once Russian soldiers were deserting or rebelling, Britain and France despaired. What use was an ally whose men could not be persuaded to fight and whose capacity to deliver was hopeless? Guns, shells, tanks, planes had been shipped to Archangel and Vladivostok by the ton, where most remained, and winter was coming. When the men did have guns, they turned tail and ran from the enemy regardless. As a condition of further aid, discipline must be restored. A British General interviewed General Kornilov, who had replaced Alexeiev as C-in-C. He reported that under Kornilov all would be well: draconian discipline would be enforced. The British pushed Kerensky to support Kornilov's aims. The Petrograd Soviet harangued him about peace. Politically, Kerensky was stuck.

Cables flew between the capitals of Europe; the residents of Petrograd queued and complained; weeds grew unchecked in the park at Tsarskoe. The Imperial train rumbled on.

9

Tobolsk

Doctor Botkin, one of the two royal doctors in residence, was on the train with them. The tutors were Pierre Gilliard and a Mlle Schneider. Mr Charles Sydney Gibbes, the English tutor, was not there. He had been away in Petrograd in the week of the February Revolution and abdication, and had not been allowed past the guards at Tsarskoe since. Alexei's big carer, Derevenko, had left months ago without a backward glance. Nagorny, who had been his assistant, was looking after the boy and would stay with him. Baroness Sophie Buxhoeveden, a lady-in-waiting, had to remain behind to have an operation, and Count Benckendorf must stay to look after his sick wife. Countess Hendrikov travelled as lady-in-waiting, Prince Dolgoruky (Count Benckendorf's stepson) would come with them as aide-de-camp, and General Tatishchev replaced Benckendorf as private secretary.

Tobolsk was their destination and Kerensky, who did not want harm to befall them on his watch, had chosen it with care. Livadia, in the Crimea, and Murmansk on the barely finished railway line north, would have been impossible to reach without the risk of attack. Tobolsk was about five days' journey through isolated communities and deserted forests and was not on the railway network at all. They would have to de-train at Tyumen and take a river trip to get there. A winter in Tobolsk, isolated from the world by the frozen river and snowbound landscape, would set them on the way to escape via Japan in the spring. Tobolsk was a conservative community, prosperous because of its location as an entrepôt for fish and furs from the Arctic; people would be respectful; and by all accounts there was a decent house empty, the Governor's residence.

The train stopped for half an hour a day, when Nicolas and the children would stretch their legs and walk their pet dogs in some remote spot. On the fourth day they reached Tyumen, a busy river station from which they embarked on a paddle steamer for the two-hundred-mile journey north-east along the Tura and Tobol rivers. They glided past Pokrovskoye, the big village Rasputin was from. For the first time Alexandra saw his house. A timber-built place, double-fronted, with faces staring from the windows; the rest of the town merely chickens and shawl-clad peasants, and low cottages along lanes of impacted mud. Did Alexandra wonder perhaps for the first time how one lived in such a place? Did Nicolas give a thought to the thousands his signature had committed to Siberian exile? Curiosity and doubt had not got them where they were today.

They arrived at four in the afternoon in Tobolsk. Colonel Kobylinsky, the sympathetic guard commander put in place by Kerensky before they left Tsarskoe, disembarked to inspect the house, a big rambling place with two rows of balconies on the upper floors that looked good only from the outside. He found it derelict, cobwebbed and grubby with a few sticks of furniture and filthy lavatories. He came back and explained that the house was not fit for habitation that night; it needed electrical and plumbing work as well as decorating, so they must stay on the steamer. They had to spend seven more days on the paddleboat before they could sleep in the house. For a week, they had ample opportunity to stare, from the deck, at Tobolsk. An old fortress and some churches dominated the town. Otherwise it was a backwater, with 20,000 inhabitants and no paved roads. Transport was by river in summer and by horsedrawn sleigh in winter.

In the end they took two houses, since the Governor's alone was not big enough for their entourage. For the first week or two they were allowed brief walks in the lanes around about. The household were not restricted in their comings and goings, and Mr Gibbes came from Petrograd to join them. The populace were kind and courteous to the visitors, and relations warmed between captors and guards.

At no time, at Tsarskoe, had there been any hint that the Tsar was other than passively accepting of their arrest and imprisonment. So far as we know, from abdication until the winter of 1917/18 he made no attempt to defend himself, argue for his family's freedom

1. Nicolas and Alexandra with
daughter Olga, 1896.

2. Nicolas and Alexandra, 1898.

3. Grand Duchesses Olga, Tatiana and Maria at Peterhof, 1900.

4. Alexandra signed this portrait of herself and Anastasia in 1901.

5. Grand Duchess Olga at Tsarskoe Selo, 1904.

Above left: 6. Grand Duchess Maria at Tsarskoe Selo, 1904.

Above right: 7. Nicolas with his newly born son Alexei at Peterhof, 1904.

Left: 8. Alexandra with Alexei at Tsarskoe Selo, 1906.

Opposite: 9. Alexei on the Imperial yacht *Standart*, 1906.

Above: 11. A saluting Alexei, 1907.

Opposite: 10. Alexei on the deck on the *Standart*, 1907.

13. The Imperial family at their Dacha, 1904.

14. Grand Duchesses Olga and Tatiana in regimental uniform, 1913.

Opposite: 12. The Imperial family at the Winter Palace, 1904.

15. Grand Duchess Maria in regimental uniform, 1913.

16. Nicolas and Alexei in regimental uniform, 1913.

Above: 17. The Imperial family in naval uniform, 1906.

Below: 18. Grand Duchess Tatiana on the yacht *Standart*, 1906.

Above: 20. Grand Duchess
Maria on the *Standart*, 1906.

Right: 21. A signed portrait
of Grand Duchess Olga at
Peterhof, 1913.

Opposite: 19. Alexei in
naval uniform and toy rifle,
1908.

Above: 23. A signed portrait of the Grand Duchess Maria at Peterhof, 1913.

Opposite: 22. A portrait of Grand Duchess Tatiana at Peterhof, 1913.

25. A reclining Anastasia.

Right: 26. A watercolour by Grand Duchess Anastasia, 1915.

Opposite: 24. Grand Duchess Anastasia, 1912.

29. Alexei with his bodyguard Andrei Derevenko and nurse Vishniakova, 1910.

Above: 30. Alexei and bodyguard Andrei Derevenko, 1910.

Previous page: 27. The four Grand Duchesses at the Winter Palace.
Previous page: 28. Alexei on holiday in the Crimea, 1910.

Above: 31. Nicolas
and Alexei on the
banks of the Dneiper
River, June 1916.

Right: 32. Alexandra
and Alexei, 1913.

Above: 34. Alexei, Nicolas
and Alexandra at General
Headquarters, Mogilev, 1915.

Right: 35. Portrait of Alexei,
1917.

Opposite: 33. Nicolas and Alexei
on the *Standart*.

Above: 36. Alexei with companions the Markov brothers, Mogilev, 1916.

Below left: 37. Alexei by the fountain, Eupatoria, 1915.

Below right: 38. Olga and Tatiana at Tsarskoe Selo, 1917.

Right: 39. Alexei at Tsarskoe Selo, 1917.

Below 40. Nicolas and Alexei at Tobolsk, 1918.

41. A signed portrait of Nicolas and Alexandra, 1917.

Above left: 42. A signed portrait of Olga and Tatiana serving as nurses during the war, 1916.

Above right: 43. British Agent Major Stephen Alley.

Opposite: 44. A cartoon of Alexandra, Nicolas and Rasputin.

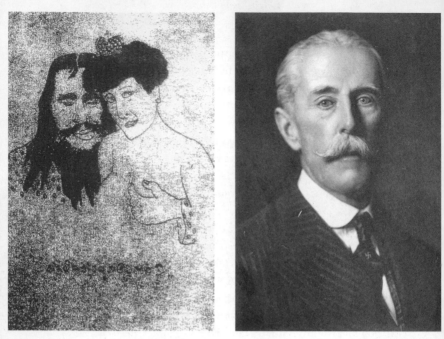

Above left: 45. A cartoon of Alexandra and Rasputin.

Above right: 46. British Ambassador Sir George Buchanan.

47. The Ural Regional Soviet who condemned the Imperial family to death along with other Romanov relatives they held captive.

48. Grigory Rasputin, the mystic holy man.

Opposite: 49. The corpse of Grand Duke Ioann, executed the day after the Imperial family on the orders of the Ural Regional Soviet.

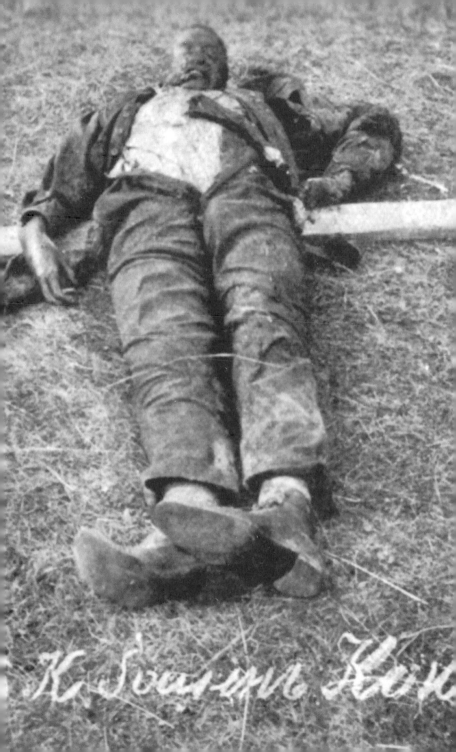

51. The Ipatiev House, Ekaterinburg.

Right: 52. Chekist Yakov Yurovsky, leader of the execution squad and murderer of Nicolas II.

Opposite: 50. The corpse of Alexandra's elder sister, Grand Duchess Elizabeth, executed by the Ural Regional Soviet the day after her sister.

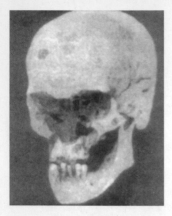

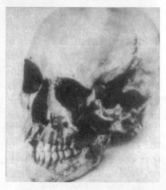

Left: 53. The skull of Nicolas II, identified after his exhumation.

Middle: 54. The skull of Grand Duchess Anastasia, identified after her exhumation.

Below: 55. Koptyaki Forest, location of the Romanov graves.

or bribe their way out. Perhaps he knew about Charles I, the English king whose plotting and conniving so exasperated his captors as to hasten his abrupt and horrifying death. As to the girls, they were treated as children and were naturally obedient. A young woman of twenty-two, as Olga was, would have more independence of spirit today; but they had always been infantilized.

At Tobolsk, as at Tsarskoe, the family settled down to make their own amusements, as though this were one long country house weekend. They played charades. The girls sewed. The tutors taught. They read their books. Sometimes Alexei and the Tsar spent time in the guardroom, playing board games or cards. The summer was short at Tobolsk, and the evenings rapidly getting longer.

After a month came two civilian Commissars, Pankratov and Nikolsky. As Social Revolutionaries, they had spent years in exile in Siberia and their roles were not an act. Nikolsky was an angry, vengeful and petty individual never missing an opportunity to be vindictive. Pankratov was somewhat milder and indeed kinder by temperament. The family remained calm; as individuals, none gave cause for offence.

While they settled in at Tobolsk, Kerensky, as premier, was buffeted between political extremes. At the end of August he convened a meeting of all parties. He found himself squeezed between the militarists who wanted a crackdown on the soldiery, and the Soviets and the Bolsheviks who wanted peace; both sides were intransigent. While they argued, Riga fell to the Germans.

The Bolsheviks had not recovered from the accusations about German money. Helphand, in Switzerland, had written an angry rebuttal of the propaganda branding him a German agent which was defiant rather than convincing. There is some indication that the stream of money funding the Bolsheviks dried up in August and September, perhaps because confidentiality could not be assured.

General Kornilov did not attend Kerensky's conference; he had been struggling for weeks to enforce discipline despite demands for peace from the soldiers' soviets and had pretty well decided to make an assault on the Petrograd government and take it over. The only two forces he could rely on were some Cossacks and Commander

Oliver Locker-Lampson, occasional correspondent to King George, who led a squadron of armoured vehicles and was not answerable to the Russians in any case. Threatened by Kornilov's putsch, Kerensky offered the Bolsheviks an olive branch. He needed all hands to resist Kornilov; Trotsky would be released, they could re-form the Red Guard and he, Kerensky, would make sure they were well armed. They accepted.

Within days of Trotsky's re-appearance the Petrograd Soviet was in Bolshevik hands and when Kornilov's cavalry joined forces with the Red Guards, the attempted putsch ended. It had been promoted by a mixture of political clumsiness, vanity, financial meddling, British interference and some real Cossacks, with real hand-grenades, who never did take Petrograd. The outcome was ignominy for Kornilov and the British and a short-lived triumph for Kerensky. With the smoke not yet cleared, Kerensky seized control. Safely in power, safe to stand down his defences, he asked the Bolsheviks for his guns back. They said no.

At this point the War Cabinet in London couldn't keep up. Communications were delayed by days. As soon as British Military Intelligence knew that Kornilov was disgraced they backed hurriedly away because support for him looked like support for the return of autocracy. At the same time they recognised that the long-promised improvement in Russian army discipline was not going to happen. Buchanan reported that since Kornilov was gone, Kerensky's Provisional Government must dance to the Bolshevik tune. As he saw it, between Government and Bolsheviks, the Bolsheviks were better financed, better able to propagandize and a leaner, meaner machine all round. They intended to win. Robert Bruce Lockhart, and (at this stage) General F.C. Poole, were more or less of the same mind: the way forward was co-operation and insidious influence through trade. General Knox was all for confrontation.

Meanwhile, the workers were striking, and the railways were in such a mess that no grain could get through. There might be food riots by October. The country was going bankrupt. Industries and rich individuals in Petrograd and Moscow were getting deeper and deeper into debt with English banks. The Germans were advancing through Russia's western borders. Berlin saw Bolshevik success in Petrograd as the satisfactory outcome of 'extensive undermining activities'. This Bolshevik rabble would press for peace, and the Germans would have Kerensky's Government just where they wanted it. In the third week of October, Lenin returned from Finland. He held a meeting of the Bolshevik Central Committee and moved a motion that 'insurrection is inevitable and the time fully ripe'. It was passed.

Kerensky was holed up in the Winter Palace, surrounded by armed men. Trotsky was already arming and training troops ready for an uprising. Buchanan knew about it; it was expected on 7 November. Everyone knew. People were taking their money out of the banks, getting ready to flee. Messages came to Kerensky from Britain, France and Italy. Order must be restored or the Allies would no longer provide assistance.

On 6 November, a Bolshevik crew positioned a cruiser in the Neva opposite the Winter Palace. Bolshevik Red Guards occupied telephone exchanges, post offices, banks, public buildings and railway stations. On the 7th, Kerensky drove away in an American Embassy car, flying the stars and stripes, having stated his intention to fetch support from soldiers stationed south of Petrograd. A few shells were fired from the cruiser and the Fortress, and by early afternoon, the Provisional Government had surrendered the Winter Palace.

There had been some kind of upheaval in the government in Petrograd and Kerensky was out. Nicolas knew that much. Presumably he did not know that Kerensky's men, searching Tsarskoe, had found a map of the entire front, in detail, among the papers of the Empress. General Alexeiev and Nicolas II should have been the only ones who saw this but it had probably been shown to Rasputin. Were he ever to come to trial, the Tsar would have to answer for such unforgivable breaches of security.

Now he was in Siberia, and with winter came long hours of darkness and fewer communications from the big cities. He and the children had explored the area around the house in the first week. As before they read, read aloud, taught Alexei – they all shared in doing that – or played the piano that had been bought for them. They acted out plays in English or French. Nicolas chopped wood. He loved doing that. Meals appeared on time, around the clock, as always. Nobody lost the will to live, or angrily demanded what was the point of it all. All but the perpetually miserable Alexandra carried on smiling and talking and making the best of their circumstances. If, as is possible, any one of them did have a black moment, they kept up appearances for the sake of the others.

The ex-Tsarina grew grey and lined, as well as wheelchair-bound. She was forty-five and looked sixty. She wrote in December:

> I feel old, oh, so old, but I am still the mother of this country, and I suffer its pains as my own child's pains and I love it in spite of its sins... although Russia's black ingratitude to the Emperor breaks my heart.

She took pleasure in small things, the few she could see from her window; the frost on the trees, the setting sun gleaming on the onion domes of the churches.

Their walks about the lanes had been curtailed. Exercise was now restricted to a small muddy yard behind a stockade and attendances at the church opposite. It was too cold to go out, minus 55°C, and minus 44°C in the draughty old house. Anastasia put on weight. At sixteen, she was treated as a child; the others put up their hair like young ladies, but she wore hers loose as she had when she was twelve.

To sew or knit, one's hands aching with cold, became impossible. Like peasants they huddled around the fire. As to the news, Nicolas pieced it together from the local papers he saw and what he was told, and by now it was clear that Lenin and Trotsky – two people widely regarded, when he left Tsarskoe, as German agents – were running the country and had opened peace negotiations with the Germans, who had driven the Bolshevik government back to Moscow.

The implications for his own safety were not promising, and in the months of January and February 1918, while every day Alexei and his youngest sisters had fun on the big snow-pile in the yard, matters worsened. The guards, more confident now that a Bolshevik government had officially reduced their prisoners to comrade status, became more insolent as money to pay them failed to turn up from Moscow. Colonel Kobylinsky, the loyal guard commander, was the household's quartermaster, and he had to borrow money, not only to pay his men but to keep the Imperial Family. Benckendorf sent a large sum from Petrograd which never reached them. Whether or not Jaroszyinsky's funds got through at this time is unclear.

Most of the guard were changed for younger men, who particularly enjoyed humiliating the girls with lewd graffiti. On 1 March, the family were restricted to soldiers' rations, by order from Moscow. The sum allocated for their keep would come from the interest on their private funds. A quick calculation made it clear that ten servants must go at once. The townspeople were kind; they sent gifts of food. But these were privations of a severity new to the Romanovs.

On 17 March, Gilliard wrote (with criminal carelessness, in the circumstances):

> Their Majesties still cherish hope that among their loyal friends some may be found to attempt their release. Never was the situation more favourable for escape, for there is as yet no representative of the Bolshevik Government at Tobolsk. With the complicity of Colonel Kobylinsky, already on our side, it would be easy to trick the insolent but careless vigilance of our guards. All that is required is the organised and resolute efforts of a few bold spirits outside.

The Russian 'bold spirits' concerned were monarchist groups and Romanov family members. Some of them had a lot of money, which would buy transport and an armed guard to defend them, but it would not buy ideas, and none could see an easy way to get a man, four able-bodied young women, one invalid and a handicapped child to safety undiscovered – because Nicolas insisted, as he had always insisted, that they remain together. The words 'human shield' spring to mind. They probably sprang to his too, if he ever saw his situation for what it was, but regardless of self-interest there was logic in his position. Were they to split up after an escape, they would certainly get away more easily – as long as they all escaped at the same time and didn't get caught afterwards. If even one of them was left behind, or recaptured in flight, that one would be held hostage. This would leave the successful escapees with a tragic choice between surrender and leaving the unlucky one to his or her fate.

He therefore insisted that rescuers must take them all together. To get them out of Tobolsk once the thaw had set in and the snow melted would be the only realistic option. Everyone agreed about that, but among the Russian groups nobody agreed about anything else. Those whose high rank allowed them to prevail were a spoiled, opinionated bunch unfamiliar with the principles of collaborative action and nothing was done, except for the sending of minions to spy out the land and smuggle mysterious notes, via the servants, into the house in Tobolsk.

Then Alexandra's saviour appeared, as she had known he would. In another guise, obviously – after all, Rasputin had been poisoned, stabbed, shot, drowned, frozen stiff, eaten by worms and burned to a cinder, so he was 'dead' – but from the messages she received, she knew he had blessed her escape from *the other side*. A note had been smuggled to her. 'Grigory's family and his friends are active.'

Last autumn, not long after they were taken to Tobolsk, Anna Vyrubova had been released from the Fortress. She quickly took her place at the centre of a spiritualist circle in Petrograd. This group were in the habit of receiving messages from Rasputin, among others who had 'passed over'; and as might be expected, Rasputin's daughter Maria came along out of interest. These visits made Maria increasingly exasperated with the shade of her father. When she got home, she wrote crossly in her diary: 'Daddy spoke to us again. *Boris*... Why do they all say the same thing: *Love Boris – you must love Boris* – I don't like him at all.' Despite private peevishness of this kind, she proved unable to resist. She had married Boris, the suitor of promise, the previous October.

He was Boris Solovyev, the son of the Treasurer to the Holy Synod. Her father would certainly have approved, for Boris had travelled to India and had studied in the school of Theosophy founded by Madame Blavatsky herself. Maybe he told Maria how he had supported the Duma, not the monarchy, last March, or maybe he didn't. Anyway, they both made their way to Pokrovskoye and had a kind of honeymoon in the Rasputin family home before travelling on to Tyumen. They didn't go from there to Tobolsk. There was no need. Tyumen was the railway junction, where every stranger to Tobolsk must necessarily stop and pass a few hours or a night. Boris's mission was to rescue the Imperial Family. Boris was gathering support for their escape. She was proud to be married to Boris.

In Tyumen it was easy to see who got on and off the train and the riverboats, to employ a network of local spies in the market and at the railway station and the quayside and know who was a stranger in town. Boris met them all, these nervous, secretive men and women, bringing money or letters but not quite sure how to proceed from here. Sometimes he met them on their way back, crestfallen at having been stopped at the gates of the Governor's house. When they had confided their story, he would say he felt he could trust them, and might whisper that a group with which he personally was associated had struck up a business relationship with a certain servant who 'lived out' from the Tobolsk house, and could come and go freely and smuggle notes or money in. He was already corresponding with Alexandra himself, and had 300 faithful officers ready to rescue the family when the time was right and the funds in place. She knew all about it. It was true, she did; excitedly she had decided that the 300 should be known as the Brotherhood of St John of Tobolsk. Already, one imagines, she was mentally designing the medal she would pin to their chests when the good times came back.

It quickly became known amongst monarchist plotters that getting anything past the guards was impossible, if you were a conspicuous stranger to Tobolsk. The only person with ways and means was Boris Solovyev in Tyumen. In January, February and March 1918 he received large amounts of cash, assuring the plotters in Petrograd and Moscow that men had been hired to help in the projected escape but requiring more money, rather than more man-power, to make success certain. Before too long, suspicions were roused, and a group of four monarchist officers arrived to ask searching questions. Unfortunately the Bolsheviks had just taken control in Tyumen and the officers had no sooner left Boris's presence than they were summarily arrested and shot, except for one, who escaped to tell the tale. Solovyev's lucrative business carried on as before. It seemed that he and the Bolsheviks were quite closely associated.

From these early months of 1918, there is evidence of British interests conspiring to effect a rescue. There may by now have been sentimental remorse on the King's part, but the real stimulus surely came from political intelligence – namely British suspicions of a German plot to kidnap the Tsar and use him as a figurehead promoting pro-German, anti-Bolshevik feeling. The German Ambassador in Moscow was Count Mirbach, and he was a formidable enemy. The British had overwhelming economic and strategic reasons to prevent the Germans from gaining a toe-hold in Russia.

The King's old friend from his days at Naval College, Mansfield Cumming of the Secret Service, was in communication with two key individuals with business interests in Russia. They were Jonas Lied, founder of the Siberian Steamship and Manufacturing Company, and Henry Armitstead, Archangel agent between 1916 and 1918 of the Hudson's Bay Company.

Lied was far more than a businessman out to plunder the fur and timber and minerals of Siberia's icy wastes. An honorary Russian citizen, he was a notable art collector and explorer whose efforts to open up the north-west passage have been compared to those of Amundsen. He had been Norwegian consul in Siberia until the revolution last November, had a unique art collection, and it was thanks to his efforts that an Arctic sea route had been opened, via the Kara Sea and two Siberian rivers, the Yenisei and the Ob. In 1913 the great explorer Nansen had joined Lied's second expedition from Tromsø to Siberia. This year, 1918, his company would be confiscated by the Bolshevik government.

Armitstead was a man of forty-four who had been born in Riga and was employed by the Hudson's Bay Company in an increasingly senior capacity between 1916 and 1927. He travelled extensively and in February 1918 was in London. Lied's diary, now in the custody of the Norwegian Maritime Museum, shows that on 26 February, Lied received a wire from Armitstead 'asking if he gets us visa, would I come to London to discuss expedition from England to Siberia. I wired consent.'

Lied arrived in Britain on 2 March – significantly, the very day before the Bolsheviks signed a peace treaty with Germany. Next morning he had a meeting in London with Cumming's deputy as head of MI1c, Colonel Frederick Browning. This was when he also 'met Armitstead and discussed expedition'. Two days later, he was introduced to Arthur Balfour, the Foreign Secretary, and the day after that, to Foreign Office Junior Minister Lord Robert Cecil. On 8 March he met the Director of Naval Intelligence, Sir Reginald Hall, who worked closely with MI1c. Hall's involvement would be essential to any plan to leave Russia by sea. In his diary entry of 20 March Lied referred directly to the purpose of these impressive introductions and meetings in London: 'Saw Sir Francis Barker and Grand Duke Michael at Vickers House about saving Nicholas II from Tobolsk by fast motor boat through Kara Sea.'

Sir Francis Barker was chairman of Vickers Ltd, which supplied warships, submarines, guns and torpedoes to the Admiralty and the Ministry of War. The escape almost certainly meant leaving Tobolsk up the Irtysh River via the Ob to the Kara Sea. From there they would travel, possibly by submarine, to Murmansk, where they would be accommodated before boarding a British vessel. The Ob/Irtysh river is the fifth longest in the world at 557 kilometres and only Lied would have known how much of it would be navigable and exactly when. 'As soon as possible' was the idea, if they intended to rescue the Tsar before the Germans did. Whatever the rescuers proposed to do, they would be well supplied with Vickers kit to do it with.

Snow lay on the ground in March but the hill of it in the yard, on which the youngest ones had had such fun, had been removed long ago as a security risk (they might signal from the top of it). Alexei still played on his makeshift toboggan, one of the wooden kind on rails. He liked to slide downstairs on it. One day, he fell and was injured. He haemorrhaged; he began to bleed into the groin; he was stuck, helpless, in this freezing house, with both legs paralysed.

Dr Botkin and the rest of the court were living across the way. Botkin was permitted to treat external patients from the town in a consulting room he had set up, but Alexei seems not to have received adequate pain relief; he lost weight fast and found it hard not to scream aloud in agony. Quite why this was is unclear, because one would be surprised if opiates were unavailable. One clue, and it is also a clue to Rasputin's success, is that Dr Botkin may well have been following accepted medical procedure for haemophilia at the time, which meant doses of aspirin. Aspirin is supposed to inhibit pain but it also thins the blood, making matters worse. Rasputin always insisted that medicines be withheld so that he could give his 'treatment' and this in itself could have led to a cure sooner than might be expected. If Dr Botkin was giving the little boy aspirin, he was slowly killing him with good intentions.

The boy was in constant pain but their rescue was imminent, Alexandra was certain. She believed, and prayed. Better weather would come. Changes were happening all around them. Soon, there would be a sign.

10

Confusion

The winter just past had been one of utter confusion. Berlin was annoyed and mystified by the Bolsheviks' continuing grip on power. It was a problem unforeseen in the plan of Herr Doktor Helphand, cooling his heels in Switzerland, and somehow it must be resolved to German advantage. Peace negotiations began in November, but dragged on despite the carrot of aid for the Russians if they settled, and the stick of invasion if they didn't. Procrastination was the Bolshevik strategy: 'neither peace nor war'; in other words, holding the Germans back with one hand while distributing propaganda behind German lines with the other. Lenin and Trotsky were deliberately undermining industrial relations in Germany, and with Russians being promised a land grab and workers' soviets to manage the factories, they had some success.

Trotsky continued to hope for a German revolution against the Kaiser and the creation of a workers' state which would come over to the Allied side. Early in 1918 Central Committee members who agreed with him were talking to Stephen Alley from British Intelligence. Alley was right behind their delaying tactics, since anything that kept the Germans out of France helped the British. That winter many German divisions were kept in limbo on the Eastern front.

More immediate war aims, as expressed in telegrams from London to Moscow, were confused. In November 1917 they were frustrated for weeks by a breakdown in radio communications out of Russia. The Allies pooled their impressions at a Paris conference at the end of November. Some still expected to see a regular Duma restored but Sir George Buchanan was adamant that that would not happen. Lenin and Trotsky had popular support, but they could run the country only if they achieved a peace settlement, saw the Germans turned back from their borders, and got the money to rebuild society in every way.

In these first months there was only a hazy understanding that they were dealing with a country run along structural, as well as ideological, lines different from their own. The Central Committee was not in a position to back up its orders with force, and every command was subject to local consent by the Workers' Soviet which, in a given area, might be more or less well disposed. Some, like the one in Murmansk, were dominated by Social Revolutionaries.

The Allied banks in Petrograd and Moscow were keeping a tight grip on the grain trade, to make sure it stayed out of German hands, but Romania, with its oil, was problematic. Should they assist Romania against the Germans, by asking Cossack troops to help Romania fight? If they did, would the Bolsheviks interpret their approach to the Cossacks as a hostile act? Should America give the Bolsheviks some money to keep them in the war? Nobody was quite sure what view the Bolsheviks might take about anything. Was Trotsky pro-German, anti-German or simply a genuine internationalist dedicated to victory for the workers? Opinions differed.

In January, when Buchanan left Petrograd and Robert Bruce Lockhart left Moscow for London (soon to return to Petrograd as unofficial Ambassador), it was all about money. Two British government-sponsored financial institutions remained behind. Their investment aims were more or less the same: to prevent Germany gaining a trade advantage in Russia, and plundering Russia's resources. To achieve this they must gain control of key banks and hence industry. Jaroszynisky (Leech's contact) was busy negotiating British money to buy up grain through the Russian Bank for Foreign Trade. The British military in the north (Murmansk and Archangel) had set up what must have looked like a damage limitation exercise, the Trade Barter Company. It had been promoted by General F.C. Poole. Whether Poole and Leech knew that each was working to the same ends is uncertain, but Poole also intended more: a torrent of British money would be insinuated via Russian banks, which would leave the Russians in hock for years, thereby achieving much the same economic-imperialist aims that the firm of Jardine Matheson had done in China in the nineteenth century, after defeating the Boxer Rising. Buchanan and Bruce Lockhart would have argued that the Bolsheviks were not a bit like the Boxers. The Bolsheviks were undefeated, and the only show in town and the only ones with a plan.

Months before, at the end of 1917 Poole had sent a stream of urgent demands to London. If they didn't do something now, get some astute businessmen out to talk to the Bolsheviks, get the timber and railway concessions, focus the initiative on Archangel and Murmansk, then 'in five years' time we shall mildly wonder how it is that the Germans have managed to collar the whole of Russia'. Within weeks he had got money to run an initiative in Archangel and was wondering how to get unused Allied matériel back, when relations between the British and Russian governments cooled to freezing, thanks to the intervention of Poole's then opponent in Russian matters – General Knox. Far away in London, the British had decided to send money to the Cossacks, the only force near enough to the Donetz coalfields to defend them. General Knox had pointed out that whoever got Donetz coal could get Russia moving again. The British must invest and gain control. But it was too late; the financiers squabbled, the Cossacks mutinied, the Bolsheviks took the Donetz basin and the British seemed to be trying to undermine the Bolshevik government.

In London there was desperation, and dubious information, including the forged 'Sisson' documents which showed Trotsky personally in the pay of Germany. Close to panic, the War Cabinet thought the Germans might overrun Russia all the way to Vladivostok. There was talk about a joint Japanese-American-British force to arrive from the East, and talk about getting control of the Siberian railways and joining up with the Cossacks in a line from north-east to south-east, but it was all ill-informed hot air. The Poles and Romanians, the Armenians and Ukrainians – and the French – all of whom had an interest in the outcome, collapsed or claimed triumph or demanded assistance from minute to minute. Every demand required an instant response and the War Cabinet was floundering. One useful, and largely accurate, report on the progress of Bolshevism all over the former Empire included: '*Siberia*: a series of small republics with a strong tinge of Bolshevism and anarchism. No probability of a central Govt being formed in the near future.'

Bruce Lockhart, in Petrograd, had talked to Trotsky, who in his view was anti-German and would be only too pleased to get Allied help. General Knox, bitterly opposed to Lockhart, insisted that the Japanese must be brought in. General Poole, temporarily in London, urged collaboration with the Bolsheviks and an end to backing for anti-Bolshevik forces (like the Cossacks, for instance). War Office and Foreign Office could not agree. Stephen Alley, a genuine, bilingual Russian/English railway expert already in Petrograd, was still talking, trying to keep the Russians on side. On the Central Committee Stalin was the most prominent supporter of an immediate peace with Germany. Alley wrote later:

> One telegram I got was that I had to liquidate Stalin. Seeing that I was negotiating with them at the time, it did not seem to be quite a good idea as it would have meant liquidating myself and him at the same time.

This was the situation when, on 3 March, the Bolsheviks and Germans having argued, delayed, conceded and argued again for three and a half months, peace was declared. The final Treaty of Brest-Litovsk meant Russia was no longer at war with Germany. Germany gained Poland, Finland, Estonia, Latvia, Lithuania and the Ukraine, the Crimea and most of the Caucasus: two strategically important coasts, oilfields, timber and grain and sixty million people. Germany could turn its attention to France.

The British feared that the next move would be a German-Russian alliance. Trotsky understood those concerns and saw that they would not need much excuse to start a mini-invasion. On the principle that the Allies were better inside the tent than out, he supported the British initiative in landing a small force, under General F.C. Poole, at Murmansk. Allegedly they were there to repel an anti-Bolshevik, pro-German band of Finns, and for that reason the Murmansk Soviet were content to have them there. But as Trotsky knew, Murmansk, the port open all year round, was key to British peace of mind. If there were to be a Germany/Russia alliance, German submarines might be transported overland on the wide-gauge Russian railway system, a new military branch of which had been completed only last year, and launched into the Kola Sea at Murmansk to harass British patrols. The British were also there to guard and distribute British matériel. Port warehouses at Murmansk, Archangel and Vladivostok were full of Allied military equipment.

With Russian territory drastically reduced, the Central Committee were left with a vast country to bring under control and the threat that civil war might break out in any of several weak spots. If it did their defences were few. Most of Russia's remaining troops had dispersed back to the land, and they were needed there. The Red Guards were ill-trained. There were some mercenaries: Lett soldiers, who did not want to go home now that Latvia was German; some Chinese; other groups of varying ethnicity and military skill. Numerically, it was not much. For local control, the Bolsheviks were reliant in the first months on local Soviets dominated by sympathizers, and a Tsarist-style network of secret police. The Okhrana was replaced by the Cheka.

From Moscow, the view was dismal. In the field, prepared to fight the Bolsheviks, were the ex-Kornilov forces led by General Denikin in the west, some right-leaning Social Revolutionaries, and a number of dubious forces in the north and east. The Social Revolutionaries were diffuse, but not in a good way, from the Bolshevik point of view; at worst, if they joined forces with the Allies they might try to seal off everywhere east of the Urals. More serious actual or potential opponents were those Allied elements (like Knox) and cadet elements of the Provisional government (like Admiral Kolchak, currently abroad) who saw Bolshevism as little better than a smokescreen for Germany. They included the Japanese, who landed unannounced at Vladivostok in the first week of April. The London newspapers were already propagandizing for a resistance force against Bolshevism, and the War Office advertising for recruits. If any or all of the Allies chose to fund the Whites, and the Social Revolutionaries joined them, defeat would be a real possibility. There were too many points of vulnerability.

It was late April in Tobolsk. They had lost a couple of weeks in February; the old Russian calendar had been changed to the European one. Now, with melting snow turning the roads to mud in wintry sun, Alexandra wrote to Anna Vyrubova about rumours that they were to be moved elsewhere. There seemed to be a lot of new soldiers about, and she did not like the look of them. Their commander was a Bolshevik Commissar newly arrived from Moscow. His name was Yakovlev.

Nicolas was horrified by the peace treaty, especially the loss of so much territory and resources. 'I then for the first time heard the Tsar regret his abdication,' wrote Gilliard. Also, ironically, he fumed about Kaiser Wilhelm having – by deigning to negotiate with the Bolsheviks – betrayed the monarchical principle. There had been rumours of a German demand for their release. 'I would rather die in Russia than be saved by the Germans,' Alexandra wrote. But the Bolsheviks were aware that they had a bargaining tool and in April, at the start of the brief period during which Tobolsk's roads and rivers were clear, there was a flurry of activity.

Nobody in the Governor's house knew it, but the Urals Regional Soviet at Ekaterinburg had demanded Moscow's permission to take custody of the Romanovs. Ekaterinburg, about 300 kilometres west of Tyumen on the Trans-Siberian Railway, was in the foothills of the Urals. It was not at all like sleepy, conservative Tobolsk. It was on a mining town with a working population that had been fiercely militant for years. Their Ekaterinburg Soviet had a great deal of influence in the Urals Soviet based in the same town.

Omsk, nearly 600 kilometres south-east of Tyumen, was a little different; a more sophisticated place, the state capital, the repository of Tsarist gold reserves, a centre of Cossack power. Later, when the civil war was raging, it would be briefly held by Admiral Kolchak and his White Army and declared capital of Russia. Right now it had a working Bolshevik Soviet. The Omsk Soviet sent a Bolshevik detachment to Tobolsk, coincidentally while Moscow was making its decision about allowing the Urals Soviet to guard the Romanovs.

Their task was unrelated – simply to set up a working Soviet in Tobolsk. (At the Governor's house, seeing the men from Omsk ride past, the Tsarina had thought they were rescuers, and waved; Nicolas hoped they were the advance guard of the '300 officers' promised by Solovyev from Tyumen.)

On their heels arrived a small deputation from the Urals Soviet to reinforce their claim to take the Romanovs back to Ekaterinburg. The Omsk Soviet argued with them. There was an impasse; nobody dared make a move without permission from Moscow.

When Commissar Yakovlev came from Moscow with a force of 150 men that settled it. He had backing in high places, and a telegraph operator who kept him in constant contact with the Kremlin, in fact with no less a person than the Chairman of the Central Executive Committee of the All-Russian Congress of Soviets, Jakov Mikhailovich Sverdlov. If opposed, Yakovlev was licensed to kill, and had the papers to prove it. Nobody in Tobolsk was going to argue with Commissar Yakovlev.

He was a man in his thirties of mysteriously cultured background. He said 'Bonjour, M'sieur' to Gilliard and called the Tsar 'Your Majesty'. He took tea with both of them when he first arrived, and proved courteous. On the second day, he asked to see Alexei, seemed worried and got an army doctor in to have a look at him. 'The boy is seriously ill.' He then telegraphed Sverdlov and got his agreement not to remove the family, but the Tsar alone. He then noticed that the representatives of the Urals Soviet had abruptly left for Ekaterinburg. That worried him; he did not underestimate their murderous intent; his job was to bring the Tsar to Moscow, not to allow him to be martyred. On the third day, he told the former Tsar and Tsarina that Nicolas must leave, but would not say where he would be taken. Nicolas refused to go. Yakovlev explained that if His Majesty did not consent, someone much less reasonable would arrive to ask him. He instructed him to be ready by four in the morning.

The ex-Tsar consulted Colonel Kobylinsky. Since they were preparing for a four, maybe five-day journey, Kobylinsky thought the destination might be Moscow. Nicolas, who was convinced that the Bolsheviks were working for Germany, concluded that this meant 'they' wanted him to countersign the Treaty of Brest-Litovsk, which he was determined not to do. In that case, his wife decided, she must go with him – to keep him up to the mark. And she would need one of the girls to help her get about. They all decided it must be Maria. Tatiana was competent to look after the others: Olga was unwell and Alexei too ill to be moved. Prince Dolgoruky, Doctor Botkin and three servants would go with them. Dr Derevenko remained with the children, as did the rest of the entourage. Commissar Yakovlev agreed that those who stayed behind could follow them later. General Tatischev, in Benckendorf's old position as manager of the household, was in agonies of trepidation and telegraphed a 'please advise' message to Benckendorf and his monarchist supporters, who were, of course, useless.

They travelled for five days towards Tyumen in a caravan of creaking carts, lying on straw, wading through river water, jolting over rutted roads, like anyone else. From Tyumen they would take a train to Moscow.

11

The House of Special Purpose

Alexandra was quite sure that this was probably a rescue attempt. These rough soldiers guarding them might well be the 300 in disguise. But when they descended, aching in every limb, from the carts at Tyumen, they got into a train without incident, while Yakovlev left for the telegraph office.

There ensued a mysterious change of plan. Instead of going west via Ekaterinburg in the direction of Moscow, Yakovlev got back on the train with his men and directed it south-east along the line to the great junction at Omsk. As it set off, Yakovlev entered the royal compartment. He explained that by taking this longer, southerly route, they could double back on the railway system and by-pass Ekaterinburg altogether. His intention was to avoid a confrontation with the Urals Soviet, who would take the Tsar off the train if they could.

If, as fate would have it, the signalman at Tyumen, alone at his post, had decided to mind his own business, Yakovlev's plan might have worked. Instead, the manoeuvre was noticed by someone who understood its significance. As they steamed eastward in the moonlight with the lights out, Tyumen telegraphed Ekaterinburg: the Romanov party was bound for Omsk. The Urals Soviet immediately suspected a rescue attempt, since beyond Omsk the line headed straight for Vladivostok. A message flew to the comrades at Omsk, who sent troops to intercept the train before it arrived.

The train stopped, in the night, in the middle of nowhere; men came aboard. Yakovlev, citing reasons of security for his choice of route, demanded to speak to the Kremlin. He was taken to a telegraph post at Omsk, leaving the Romanov party under guard in the train. When he got through to Moscow, Sverdlov replied that in the circumstances Yakovlev must give in; there was no choice but to go back to Ekaterinburg.

This they did. But it had been an odd interlude, and historians were later intrigued because later in the civil war Yakovlev joined the Whites. There was no connection between Yakovlev's choice of route and any Lied/Armitstead plan. It was Sverdlov who chose to double-cross them by making sure the Tsar would get detained in Ekaterinburg instead. Sir Charles Eliot, at Omsk, certainly seems to have known or thought that Count Mirbach, the German Ambassador, was double-crossed by Sverdlov over this affair.

Ten days before the journey to Ekaterinburg, Mr Rumbold, British Consul in Berne – whose informants reported on numerous Russian emigré confabulators, and had ears in the walls of the Russian Embassy – had reported to London:

> The German Minister said [to the Russian Chargé d'Affaires] that about four weeks ago the German government had made tentative proposals to re-establish the monarchy in Russia. They had not continued these because they were unable to get promises of adequate support. No member of the Romanov family would come over to the German camp, even for the sake of restoring the Russian monarchy... The Tsar's attitude much disturbs the German Emperor, who spends sleepless nights in mourning over the Romanovs' fate.

When Nicolas and Alexandra arrived in Ekaterinburg, Prince Dolgoruky was immediately taken away to jail. Otherwise, they met with nothing worse than a barracking from the mob at the railway station. Among the crowd was a man called Ermakov, who would be intimately involved in their fate. Years later, acting on orders from Moscow, he recalled for a Western journalist this, his first vision of the Imperial couple. Alexandra looked like 'a sharp-tongued German housewife' and was 'haughty' and generally a hard-faced piece of work. Nicolas was 'pale, undersized and weak-looking'. Remembering what he himself had gone through in Tsarist prisons, 'I could have strangled the little shit right there on the platform.' His wrists still bore scars of the manacles he had worn for a year in jail.

The Ipatiev house chosen to accommodate them had been vacated by its owner, a merchant, only the night before. Its door was opened to them by a man called Goloschekin, a personal friend of Sverdlov. If Sverdlov had for a single moment suspected Yakovlev of duplicity in taking the family east, he need do so no more, for Goloschekin would see to it that orders from Moscow were carried out.

The Ipatiev house, henceforth known as the House of Special Purpose, was a big, rambling, two-storey place. Because it stood against a hillside its rear elevation was partly built into the earth. In the hours before their arrival, workmen had erected a high wooden fence around its garden and covered the insides of five of the upper windows with white paint. These were the five rooms to which the Romanov group would be confined, and from which they would not be able to see out. The lower floor would be occupied by their guards, who assumed that in due course Nicolas would be taken to Moscow for a trial. Trotsky himself was planning to prosecute.

Alexandra wrote at once to her daughters in Tobolsk: 'Dispose of all medicines as agreed.' They began sewing diamonds and sapphires and rubies into their clothes. Three weeks later, they and their brother were allowed to join their parents. They brought Tatiana's little dog and Alexei's spaniel, and more servants, including Nagorny who carried the Tsarevich, and the tutors and Baroness Buxhoeveden, the Tsarina's lady-in-waiting.

Of the entourage who arrived with the children, Countess Hendrikov, Mlle Schneider and General Tatischev were for some reason singled out, imprisoned and shot. Gilliard, Gibbes, Dr Derevenko, Baroness Buxhoeveden and a number of servants were allowed to go free. They had nowhere to go so they slept in the railway carriage in which they arrived, and took to visiting Mr Preston, the British Consul. They discussed plans for the Tsar's escape and apparently decided that it was impossible. The town was crawling with Red Guards and the house itself was guarded round the clock inside and outside.

The Ekaterinburg Soviet had their spies, too. They saw plenty of promises being made, and monarchists hanging about. Those people were as conspicuous there as they had been in Tyumen. A note was 'intercepted'; it is couched in florid language, and was a plant by the local Bolsheviks to gauge Nicolas's response. It asked Nicolas to explain something of the set-up indoors. Eagerly he replied. He had counted thirteen guards inside the house:

> ... armed with rifles, revolvers and grenades. No room but ours has keys... The orderly officer makes the round of the house twice an hour at night and we hear his arms clattering under our windows. One machine gun stands on the balcony and one above it, for an emergency. Opposite our windows on the other side of the street is the [outside] guard in a little house. It consists of fifty men...

After ten days, that is, around the beginning of June, Gilliard and the others from the train were sent back to Tyumen. Left in the house were a valet, the cook and cook's boy, Dr Botkin and a lady's maid.

Ekaterinburg was worse than Tobolsk for them all. They were constantly watched, and strictly confined to their quarters except for a few hours in the garden in the afternoons. According to Ermakov, the ex-Tsarina began the day she came by writing out menus on gold-crested cards. He sniggered; their food was mostly black bread and soup. The Imperial Cook and his assistant did not have a lot to do. The cook's boy was called Leonid and with no scullery to scrub, no potatoes to peel, he played with Alexei. The Tsar 'smoked cigarettes all day' and kept very quiet. The Tsaritsa complained about the noise the soldiers made outside. Ermakov told her they weren't the prisoners, she was.

The guards undoubtedly fraternized with the Grand Duchesses; one was caught in a compromising situation with Grand Duchess Maria at the end of June. On the other hand they probably were drunken, rude and thieving, because in May, Nagorny, defending Alexei's property, had a set-to with one of them and ended up in the town jail. Four days later he was taken out and shot. The ex-Tsar carried his son after that. What he knew of Nagorny's fate, and what he told Alexei, cannot be known. They were not good at telling the truth to their children, so probably Alexei guessed, if he did not hear it from his friend the cook's boy, Leonid. Guessing would have been worse.

The British public were lamentably ill-informed by Our Correspondent from *The Times* in Moscow. On 30 April (the day Nicolas and Alexandra arrived in Ekaterinburg) he reported 'rumours' of a monarchist coup in Petrograd, with Alexei proclaimed Tsar and Grand Duke Michael, Regent. From time to time in the days afterwards, the Bolshevik government was reportedly expected to collapse 'in a few months'. The confused messages could indicate some form of disclosure, in that Grand Duke Michael appears to have been in London only months earlier, plotting something with Lied and Armitstead, and now there had been the sudden, suspicious removal from Tobolsk to a more secure prison.

On 10 May, the Soviet authorities confirmed to the *Times* correspondent that Nicolas, Alexandra and one daughter had been transferred to Ekaterinburg because of a 'conspiracy among the monarchists to assist him to escape'. He was now in Ekaterinburg with 'one or two attendants and no visitors'. Sverdlov was quoted as follows: 'Nicolas Romanov will have to reconcile himself to the fact that he is a prisoner of the Soviet and the question of his ultimate fate will soon be brought up for decision.' A search had been made among his belongings, and 80,000 roubles found and confiscated.

The documents now indicate a Plan B, with Armitstead at any rate still involved. On 21 May, Mansfield Cumming wrote to the Hudson's Bay Company at 1 Lime Street, London EC3, to place on record his intention to pay their agent for a little job he was about to do for MI1c – not, evidently, his first:

Dear Sir
As Mr H A Armitstead, the representative of your company for Russia, has, with your kind permission, temporarily placed his services at my disposal for a journey through Russia, I wish to put on record that I will refund to you all Mr Armitstead's expenses on the journey from the time of leaving London until his return to this town. I am agreeable, owing to the nature of his journey and in accordance with Mr Armitstead's usual agreement for travelling expenses with your

company, that his accounts shall be presented in a similar manner to those you have previously received from him.

May I take this opportunity of thanking you for your courtesy in this matter, which I much appreciate.

Yours very truly

Mansfield Cumming

Captain RN

The expenses of Henry Armitstead's 'journey through Russia' would eventually be reimbursed to him in December 1918. Right now, in May, the general outline was already agreed. His co-conspirator this time would be Stephen Alley, the intelligence officer who had been too cute to try and bump off Stalin during the peace negotiations. Alley was already in Murmansk and planning ahead. There were seven 'valuables' to deliver. Whether they were to be carried separately or together to Murmansk is unclear. Alley asked for a hand-picked force of four men, all of whom could pass as Russians. On 24 May he sent a cable to MI1c headquarters at Whitehall Court:

I should be glad if you can arrange to send the following officers if after interviewing them you approve:

A. 2nd Lt HILL, G. 13th London Rgt

B. Lt HITCHING; his address should be known to Maj SCALE in Sweden

C. Lt MICHELSON if he has left HELSINGFORS

D. Lt Commander MACLAREN if you do not wish him to come to England would be of great assistance to me. I should therefore be glad to have him put under my orders. Colonel Thornhill approves my request for officers.

E. These officers should clearly understand nature of employment which may require them to pass as civilians. All these officers are presently known to Col. Thornhill and myself.

Alley himself, who as we know had been born in a Yusupov palace, had been brought up and educated until the age of fifteen in Moscow at the prestigious Fiedler School. His mother, also, had been born in

Russia, where his family had a country estate as well as a grand town house. In his own words, he 'ran wild' as a boy – around 1890 – on the estate. His family were locomotive builders and marine engineers in Glasgow, the friends of his childhood the young aristocrats of Russia. At fifteen he was sent to London. Notwithstanding a bone-idle academic record he worked for the family, and for himself, in London and in Glasgow; then in Russia, on the first heavy-oil pipeline to the Black Sea, before the war. In London as a young man he had become an officer in a volunteer regiment and joined the St Stephen's Club, opposite the Houses of Parliament on Bridge Street, at the heartland of Whitehall and its Ministries. By the outbreak of war, his Russian having proved useful already to the War Office, he was co-opted at once into Military Intelligence and sent to Petrograd. He was close to the key players in the death of Rasputin. The picture that emerges is of a networker and man of action, a ruthless and clever soldier with a laconic sense of humour – but very much a loose cannon. He knew exactly who he wanted on the crack team for the task ahead: Hill, Hitching, Mitchelson and MacLaren.

2nd Lieutenant George Edward Hill should not be confused with his better-known cousin, Lieutenant George Alexander Hill of the Manchester Regiment and RAF, who also worked for MI1c. The Hill family had been traders in Russia since the middle of the eighteenth century, preserving their British nationality by sending wives back to Britain to give birth. Having grown up in Russia, they were all fluent Russian speakers whose knowledge of the people and customs of the country was second to none.

Lieutenant John Joseph Hitching of 16th Battalion, London Regiment, was from a Portsmouth family but had been born and brought up in Finland, which had been part of the Russian Empire until December 1917. Having spent most of his life in Russia he could easily pass as a native.

Lieutenant Ernest Michelson was also a fluent Russian speaker who had been working under cover as a journalist for the *Daily Chronicle* in Finland between late 1917 and May 1918. Now, like Alley, in his forties, he had lived in Russia since the 1890s working for the Neva Cable Company. He had married there in 1897; his two children were both born in St Petersburg, and oddly enough, he and his family had been living at Tsarskoe Selo in 1900.

Lieutenant Commander Malcolm MacLaren had a similar background to the others; he had married a Russian and according to his file was fluent in Russian and indistinguishable from a Russian.

It seems Alley got the team he wanted. They would presumably have trickled into Murmansk, after an interview and briefing in London, as fast as possible – by mid-June, anyway. He made an undated note about the trip back from Ekaterinburg to Murmansk with the 'valuables':

> I have made it clear to Armitstead, in no uncertain terms, that his role is strictly liaison and that he must leave all arrangements for the journey to Murmansk to us. We are responsible for securing and delivering the valuables, he is responsible for their safe passage out of Russia.

Armitstead seems to have understood the terms, because the Hudson Bay Company undertook to fit out a building held by the 'Murmansk Scientific Industrial Society'. It was to be supplied with 'luxury' (rather than standard-issue) beds, blankets and cutlery for seven persons. An ex-Tsar, his wife and five children could be quite cosy there, while they awaited their ship to another destination.

As to Lied, if he was involved in this second plan to rescue them from Ekaterinburg, or if he was simply on standby to assist if required, we do not know. His expertise would have been irreplaceable in getting from Tobolsk upriver to the Arctic in April, but seems unnecessary for an overland, or even land and river, journey from Ekaterinburg to Murmansk at midsummer, when nights were short and roads no longer snowbound. Archangel, while still on the European side of the Urals, was a lot closer to Ekaterinburg than Murmansk was, and at this time General F.C. Poole was planning to advance upon it and move south with a larger force that he commanded at Murmansk. (His views had changed; he was all for undermining the Bolsheviks now.) The drawback to Archangel was that after an escape all routes into it by river, road and rail would have been crawling with Cheka spies.

The overland trip to Murmansk was a long one and Alley's plan must surely have involved motor cars or lorries. Oliver Locker-Lampson and his armoured vehicles spring to mind, but they had been sent back to England, Locker-Lampson having disgraced himself over the Kornilov affair.

It is tempting to wonder how, once they were west of the Urals, Alley intended to proceed, but his immediate task was the rescue itself. All we know for sure is that somehow he obtained or drew a sketch map of the Ipatiev House and the crossroads beside them. On the sketch are reconnaissance notes setting out the need for: 'Road details: width, how constructed, what materials available on the spot for repair... any particular steep gradients such as would affect movement of carts.' These read like instructions to another person – a sort of 'this is the general layout and these are the details we need; go and get them'. Whoever sketched the rough map did not mark the Bolshevik gun emplacements or guardhouse. They either couldn't get a good view over the stockade, or had drawn it from memory, because when the Romanovs were installed, the Ipatiev house was bristling with defensive weapons. In late June, rescuers could not afford to miss machine gun nests on the balcony and ground floor, or the numerous armed guards overseeing the approaches, or the machine gun trained on the building from the church on the opposite corner.

The reconnaissance notes suggest a hope that they might head for the hills by some little-used route. Alley himself visited Ekaterinburg in June to reconnoitre and finalize decisions about the disposition of his men and those 'carts'. He would have found that the Ipatiev house was high up, in a prominent position; its yard must be crossed, and it was observed on all sides day and night; the guards were well equipped and machine gun nests covered all possible points of entry and exit.

Stephen Alley kept his secrets to the grave, so far as he could. In 2007 relative Michael Alley was interviewed for the television documentary *Three Kings at War*. He said:

There was a suspicion at the time that he'd been involved in a plot to try and rescue the Tsar and his family after the Revolution... there was also a rumour that grandfather had heard going around that he'd been sent to reconnoitre a passage to see whether they could get him (Nicolas) out of Siberia. The Tsar had been moved to east of Moscow to Siberia and of course it was quite a long way out of reach from Murmansk where the British were holding the port in readiness. And we understood that this was actually aborted because it wasn't possible to achieve it.

In short, the House of Special Purpose looked impregnable; the mission, suicidal.

In June, the Bolshevik government had a multitude of reasons to feel threatened. A significant British and American force landed at Murmansk. In the Ukraine, the white army was fortified by more Cossacks. Worst of all, Siberia – and the railway east – were insecure. Last year Kerensky had done a deal with about 40,000 Czech ex-prisoners of the Austro-Hungarian army, arming them to fight for their Czech homeland. Trotsky, when he took power in November, had agreed that they could go east by the Trans-Siberian railway, in order to travel back by sea and get behind the German lines; but in the course of his peace negotiations, the Germans had objected to this. They demanded he have the trains stopped and the Czechs disarmed.

Trotsky conceded, but the Czechs were having none of it. After a stand-off they got together with some anti-Bolshevik Russian officers and set off back west. Not only were they preparing the ground for an invasion from Vladivostok, but within weeks they might overwhelm opposition at Omsk. According to Francis McCullagh, who later interviewed Mr Thomas, the British vice-Consul at Ekaterinburg, at this stage the Bolsheviks were sending trainloads of gold and platinum back west (presumably from the Tsar's stores at Omsk). Trotsky and Lenin were hunkering down, concentrating the assets in one place further west. If the Czechs could take Omsk, they could pursue the Trans-Siberian railway to Moscow, and on their way, they would come to Ekaterinburg. They might well make an attempt to capture the Tsar as a figurehead for anti-Bolshevik armies everywhere.

On 27 June, the Tsar is said to have received a message about impending rescue by 'an officer'. The family spent the night fully dressed. Nicolas, one may assume, sat up smoking constantly. We now know from newly accessed Russian records that this message was a ruse by the Cheka to test lines of communication and state of mind; the family wisely stayed put.

12

Oblivion

A week or so after Nicolas's long, disappointing night of wakefulness, there began a new buzz of activity in the House of Special Purpose. A man called Yurovsky came at the head of a detachment of Cheka guards. Orders and receipts for additional parts and ammunition for the guns in the house show that, on 6 July, Colt pistols were swapped for new Maxims. Goloschekin left for Moscow to confer with Sverdlov. Hostile anti-Bolshevik forces were advancing into Russian territory from the north and east. The British in Murmansk were starting to suffer disturbances in the ranks, Bolshevism having proved quite attractive to men already tired of war, so the War Office's spring recruitment drive produced a new batch of 5,000 troops for Russia and made sure they were indoctrinated before leaving England. With these latecomers, 5,000 Americans and 1,000 Frenchmen added to his existing force, General Poole had expanded the area under Allied power well beyond the port. The Murmansk Soviet declared that they were happy to be defended by General Poole and signed an agreement to this effect on 6 July. The Bolsheviks promptly cut all telegraph wires and blew up railway bridges on the approach to Murmansk.

Japanese and American troops were soon to land at Vladivostok. General Knox was already there. Closer to Ekaterinburg, the 40,000 Czechs were still advancing along the Trans-Siberian line and the Social Revolutionaries had already declared a 'government' at Omsk. There was every reason for a Bolshevik to feel nervous. *They must not get the Tsar.*

Yurovsky was a local man with a house and shop in the town, and a wife and children. He had run a photography studio in Ekaterinburg before the war, became a field hospital orderly and on discharge was a founder member of the Ural Regional Soviet and the local Cheka. If Goloschekin came back with an affirmative reply, he, Yurovsky, would be undertaking the Special Purpose for which the house had been chosen.

On Friday 12 July Goloschekin returned from the Kremlin. Thumbs up. Whether it was Sverdlov who had decided that all should be killed, not only the entire family but also some of their staff, is uncertain. Yurovsky and Goloschekin were on the ground and must decide where, how and when to do it. Secrecy was imperative, since the Czechs were now closing in on Ekaterinburg. They would be cheated of a figurehead all right, but if they ever found proof that a massacre had taken place, they would have martyrs. Public sympathy might swing in their direction.

Among the guards was Ermakov, another local. All eyewitness accounts of what happened on and around the night of 16/17 July differ in the order of events and the personnel involved; some, such as Yurovsky, describe a long-drawn-out scene of horrendous violence and cruelty. Ermakov's story equally has the *echt* ring of makeshift arrangements and pressure of time. While he was allegedly drunk that night and framed his recollections with himself in the central role, he was no doubt an eyewitness.

The idea from the start was to shoot them all quickly, before the Czechs arrived, and to dispose of the bodies secretly. Today was Friday. Tuesday night was the date they set. That would give them four days from Sverdlov's go-ahead in which to prepare, and at least a few days afterwards to effect disposal and clear out of town. Yurovsky's men were mostly non-Russian mercenaries who would have no qualms about the act itself. Secret disposal of the bodies was more problematic. Where and how could they get rid of so many corpses?

Ermakov answered to Yurovsky, who instructed him and a sailor called Vaganov to find a remote spot where a bonfire would be unseen and cremated remains would leave no trace. They went to a place they knew eighteen kilometres away, where miners had dug shafts, found no coal, and moved on. They returned to Ekaterinburg, found Yurovsky, and all three went back to the mines on horseback.

Yurovsky pronounced it the perfect place. The following day – Monday – Ermakov obtained a truck, a crew, and large quantities of petrol, sulphuric acid and firewood, took them to the place and set a soldier to guard the supplies overnight.

On the Tuesday night, the truck and its crew were stationed at 'Cathedral Square before the Prison House'. Blankets were brought and loaded aboard. On a signal, they were to drive to the basement entrance of the Ipatiev House, stop there and leave the engine running. If they could get it to backfire, so much the better; the idea was to cover the gunshots with engine noise.

Yurovsky decided that he, Ermakov and Vaganov should do the shooting:

> Yurovsky had a Nagant revolver. Vaganov and I had Mausers. We each carried twenty rounds of ammunition. Yurovsky also gave revolvers to three members of the Executive Committee and rifles to seven of our house guards.

These, it seemed, were for use only in an emergency.

There was no point in removing the family for execution. Indoors, under guard, they could not escape. On the Tuesday afternoon Yurovsky, Ermakov and Vaganov met at the House of Special Purpose and decided that the semi-basement room built into the hillside would be the best location for the act. Noise would be muffled – Ermakov nailed the window up to make it more so – and it was the right size: about five and a half metres long by three and a half wide. It gave onto a corridor via a double door and was close to the basement entrance where the truck would be parked. The double door was wide enough for three executioners to block the entrance and shoot without getting mixed up with the targets or hit by stray bullets.

Darkness fell late. Vaganov and Ermakov drove the truck to Cathedral Square and left it with the crew. 'Come when we send for you.' They returned on foot to meet Yurovsky, who was with his three Commissars and seven hand-picked guards at the main entrance to the Ipatiev House.

They checked their weapons. They had decided to spare the cook's boy Leonid, since they had observed that he treated Alexei like any other boy, without undue deference. He had been sent away already. The others closest to the family – Botkin, Demidova the lady's maid, the cook and the valet – were all 'lackeys' who should die with them. There was a Bolshevik maid in the house as well. She would be brought down to the basement room with the rest, to allay suspicion, then told to leave.

At midnight Yurovsky knocked on the Tsar's door. (It seems he would have had to walk straight through the Grand Duchesses' room to get there, which apparently soldiers from the guardhouse had done often, at night, in recent weeks.) The Tsar, his wife and son were asleep together in the one room. Yurovsky went in and announced that there was fighting in the town. They would have to spend the night elsewhere. A car was coming for them. He wanted the whole family and their servants to get dressed quickly and come down to the guardroom by the basement entrance.

It took them over an hour to get ready. Their doors were closed but they could be heard talking and moving about inside. They emerged without hats and coats, because it was a warm night. Demidova was carrying a cushion, as were one or two of the others. Ermakov thought, he said, that Yurovsky must have suggested they bring cushions against the bone-shuddering motor journey ahead.

Ermakov watched them coming downstairs. The ex-Tsar seemed quite pleased. He must have thought rescue by the Whites was not, now, so far away. He was carrying his son. Ermakov, who, it is chilling to recount, had a seven-year-old boy of his own, volunteered to help, but the offer was declined.

They were installed in the basement, with chairs brought for the Tsarina and her son, and left alone, guarded by two Letts. A message was sent to the truck. After a while the three executioners went downstairs and gathered at the entrance to the room. They were followed by the seven Hungarians of the Cheka with fixed bayonets.

The Tsarina sat on a chair, and the boy was lying against the Tsar on two chairs with Botkin behind. Near the Tsarina, against the back wall, were the three eldest girls. The truck's approach was heard. Yurovsky signalled the Bolshevik maid to leave the room. She walked out past them. Ermakov said something about putting her in the car first. Yurovsky was to shoot the Tsar and the boy. Ermakov was to get the Tsarina, Botkin, the cook and the valet. Vagarov was to deal with the maid and the four daughters.

The truck had parked outside the basement now, and made a heck of a racket. The back door was open; it was deafening. The Tsar stood up. The boy put his cap on. The valet took the cushion from the Tsar's chair. Yurovsky began to read, shouting over the noise: 'In view of the fact that your relatives continue their offensive against Soviet Russia, the Presidium of the Ural Regional Soviet has decided to sentence you to death.'

The Tsarina *jumped up*. For the first and last time. The Tsar half turned to say something, didn't seem to understand. Yurovsky shot him dead; Ermakov got the Tsarina, then Botkin. Yurovsky had shot the boy, who was on the floor groaning. Ermakov got the cook, then the valet. Vagarov shot all the girls. They all kept reloading – their guns held six bullets each. Aim was hazy in the smoke and poor light. As the smoke cleared they saw Anna Demidova, the maid, was shielding herself with cushions and had not been shot and the boy was still alive. According to another eyewitness participant, Alexei Kabanov, it was Ermakov who bayoneted Maria, Anastasia and Demidova as well as the already dead bodies of Nicolas, Alexandra and Dr Botkin. Throughout Alexei remained seated and petrified – Yurovsky shot him twice through the head.

Yurovsky told the guards to take any jewels and other bits and pieces from the bodies and put them in one place. They then piled the blanketed bodies into the truck and drove away. They left behind them twelve men to clear up the 'red lake' full of bags and pillows and odds and ends.

The road was bad, the drive slow, and it was after two in the morning when they left. Nights were short at this time of year; by the time they reached the disused mineshafts, it was dawn. Ermakov claimed that he spent all of that day, Wednesday 17 July, collecting their jewels, icons, diaries and letters to be sent to Moscow, that by the time he had finished, everyone was too tired to cremate the bodies, and that he left Vaganov on guard with a squad of soldiers at the mineshaft and did not go back himself until late in the evening.

Meanwhile Yurovsky had reported at once to Goloschekin and Goloschekin had telegraphed Sverdlov. Sverdlov must have known by three in the morning. In Moscow that day, the Council of People's Commissars received a telegram from the Urals Bolsheviks: 'the entire family suffered the same fate as its head.' 'All of them?' said Trotsky, astonished, to Sverdlov. 'All of them! Why not?' Sverdlov allegedly replied. That very day, Wednesday, Bruce Lockhart heard a rumour in Moscow that Nicolas had been shot at Ekaterinburg, though it was not until Lenin made an announcement on Thursday 18 July that he noted: 'News that the Emperor has been shot is true – on the night of 16th. Evidently in connection with the advance of the Czechs who are now nearing Ekaterinburg.'

An official leaflet was being circulated. It announced that Nicolas Romanov had been shot and his wife and son were in a place of safety. The news took a while to reach Geneva. On that day, Thursday 18 July, Mr Edwards at the Consulate there reported a plot by some Russian emigrés:

> Berlin is considering kidnapping the ex-Tsar and his family and bringing them to Germany, and has asked the Swiss section of the League for the Restoration of the Russian Empire whether they agree to the plan that Berlin has hatched to kidnap the ex-Tsar and bring him to Germany whether he will or not.

Too late, too late. That Wednesday night, Ermakov said he returned and stripped the bodies at around ten. In the dim summer night, he found a lot more jewels, sewn into clothes, which were sent to Moscow. Afterwards he and his men made a great pile of clothes, dashed them with petrol and set fire to them. In the light of the fire they then reloaded the naked corpses and remaining supplies of petrol, acid and firewood into the truck and took them to another mine. There (he was lying now) they built a pyre, on which they burned all eleven corpses, filled the empty petrol drums with ash and scattered them. 'We had to keep the fire burning a long time to burn up the skulls,' he said. When they left the site of the bonfire they scattered the ashes to the winds over a wide area.

Richard Halliburton, the American journalist who heard Ermakov's story in the early thirties, was so convinced by this account of the multiple execution and cremations that 'Anastasia', who had been wow-ing New York when he left, was forever condemned in his mind as a fake. Indeed it is only the last part of this account, the cremation, that history has proved to be wildly distorted.

Captain Francis McCullagh, a British intelligence officer born in Omagh, County Tyrone in 1874, was a seasoned journalist who had covered the Russo-Japanese war for the *New York Herald* and subsequently worked for a number of Japanese, Russian and French newspapers. In December 1914 he joined the British Army and was commissioned as a lieutenant in Military Intelligence. On the strength of his fluency in five languages, he was sent initially to the Dardanelles and a year later to Serbia and Macedonia.

In July 1918 McCullagh was promoted to Captain and sent to Russia as part of General Knox's Military Mission to Siberia. McCullagh was able to visit the Ipatiev house after the Whites had re-taken it. He asked local people what had happened to the bodies. The stories he heard from various people are of great interest and are preserved among his papers. When the Bolsheviks re-took the area, he was able to pose as an insurance worker, and as we shall see in due course, in this guise got to meet and interview Yurovsky himself. As an expert linguist, he was, of course, able talk to the locals in Russian. His interviews confirm that *all* died on the night of 16/17 July:

The disturbance was caused by the appearance of five carts and one motor-lorry, the former filled with Red soldiers and some kind of baggage wrapped in white blankets, the latter containing also soldiers, five civilians, and two barrels. Instead of continuing straight on to the village, this strange procession turned off the road and on to the grass, for there was no side-track, and entered the beautiful sunlit recesses of the forest. The heavy lorry stuck fast, however, in a swamp near the road; and, after several ineffectual attempts to dislodge it, the civilian passengers got out and led the carts further into the wood, until they reached a birch-tree... Close by this tree was a disused shaft, known locally as the 'Isetsky Mine', about fifteen feet deep, with water and mud at the bottom. Near the tree the five civilians consulted together: their names were Urovsky, Goloschekin, Lovatnykh, Nicholas Partin, and Alexander Kostusov. Meanwhile, in obedience to Yurovsky's orders, the soldiers moved outwards into the forest in a circle, with ever-widening intervals between each man, until they halted at a distance of about 500 yards from the marked tree. Their object was to prevent any intrusion, but none took place, though the villagers soon became aware of their presence... The peasants remained awake all that night in a state of great trepidation... They did not go outside their houses, but they could see from their doors the reflection in the heavens of a great fire which the Bolsheviks had kindled in Koptyaki Wood.

He goes on to describe how soon afterwards, the remains of clothing and jewellery were found in the ashes, and nothing significant down the disused shafts of the Isetsky mine. He then attempts to summarize a 'systematic investigation of the site on the orders of Admiral Kolchak' (then running the 'government' at Omsk); this was Sokolov's enquiry of early 1919. He also includes an account 'from the Bolshevik side' which has it that the bodies were taken first to the Isetsky factory (in the town, beside the main road from the Ipatiev house) where they were transferred into carts before being taken north for cremation:

... Yurovsky was in such a state of nerves that he could not decide where to bury the bodies. He stopped once on the way and even had the bodies removed from the carts, only to the decision, immediately afterwards, that the place was too exposed. After he reached the Isetsky Mine in Koptyaki Wood, he wanted to go further into the forest, but as time was being lost and the soldiers were becoming impatient, Goloschekin finally insisted on the cremation being carried out at the Isetsky Mine. A pile of wood was then collected and the bodies were placed on it, that of the Tsar being on the top... [after the cremation] Yurovsky, Goloschekin, and the rest of the soldiers remained behind owing to Yurovsky's determination to stay in the forest all next day in order to see by daylight whether any traces of the bodies still existed.

Another of McCullagh's interviewees reported overhearing talk between some of those who had taken part in the execution of the Imperial family and been involved in their burial:

From the subsequent conversation Prokofy gathered that they had been buried in two places. First they were buried in one place beyond Ekaterinburg, and then taken up and buried in another place, where it was not stated. As a matter of fact, however, they were not buried the first time, but only taken out of the carts, and on the second occasion they were cremated.

McCullagh was eventually captured by the Bolsheviks on 6 January 1920 at Krasnoyarsk, near Lake Baikal, and was held as a prisoner of war until his release on 15 May the same year. Two years later he returned to Russia for the *New York Herald* but left the next year at the request of the Soviet Government, who already had a very thick file on him and his journalistic activities.

13

Doubt & Uncertainty

When Ekaterinburg woke up on Wednesday 17 July the Ipatiev House was deserted and unguarded. People whispered, but no one dared say anything. Mr Thomas passed the house often, and had noticed the exaggerated activity in the last few weeks and the jumpiness of the guards in the afternoon of the day before. Suspicions were officially confirmed by Lenin's announcement on the 18th: the Tsar was dead. On Friday 19th, the *Urals Worker*, the local paper, headlined the Tsar's execution 'in accordance with our new democratic principles', whatever that meant; later on, Goloschekin addressed a meeting and confirmed that the Tsar was dead and his wife and children in 'a place of safety'. In Moscow that day, Bruce Lockhart noted in his diary:

> As all bourgeois papers are suppressed, comments on the Emperor's murder are naturally one-sided. The Bolshevik press however reviles him as a tyrant and a butcher. States that he made a whorehouse of the throne, &c, and assays that the government will shortly publish the diaries, &c, which it has in its hand. Rest of people seem to take things indifferently. Their apathy is extraordinary.

Soon, though, there would begin a ninety-year battle between science and superstition which is not over yet.

The Whites took Ekaterinburg a week after the murders. According to a report received by the British Consul in Archangel, 'a few hundred' Cossacks arrived on Thursday 25 July, and within a day, they were joined by 800 Czechs. Whites would control Ekaterinburg and all points east on the Trans-Siberian railway for the next fourteen months. On that first day, some officers entered the Ipatiev House. They found (and rescued) Alexei's spaniel, Joy, half starved in the yard, and saw signs of uproar in the basement room. There were bullet-holes and bayonet slashes on the walls, and lumps of plaster missing, and the place had obviously been scrubbed clean. If an execution had taken place, either somebody had put up a superhuman fight, or more than one person had died.

According to Ermakov, the Whites found and shot the Bolshevik maid, and went looking for the executioners. Ermakov was in hiding, but they got his seven-year-old son, who was sick with measles, and threw the boy from a train. (He survived.)

In London that Thursday 25 July, King George and Queen Mary attended a service at the Russian Church in Welbeck Street, organized by Grand Duke George in memory of the Tsar. The King wrote up his diary as usual: 'We can get no details. It was a foul murder. I was devoted to Nicky, who was the kindest of men and a thorough gentleman: he loved his country and his people.' Nobody knew what had happened to the rest of them. There was silence.

The British escape plan had never happened. Alley had seen the Ipatiev House, complete with its machine gun nests and round-the-clock guard detail, and rightly decided a rescue attempt would be suicidal; he and his officers had melted away. Mr Lindley, at the Archangel consulate, was visited by a Polish officer at the end of August. The Pole had been in Ekaterinburg with the Whites until 3 August. He reported that the Bolsheviks had taken away to Moscow 36,000 pounds of gold and 7,200 pounds of platinum, and were now working hard to repel the Czech advance. Mr Lindley added that 'it was believed that the Empress and her children are at Verkhotur north of Ekaterinburg in which region Bolsheviks are still supreme'.

That was as much as anyone knew; rumour, no more than that. Nobody actively looked for them; there were no traces at all. And then, in September, the *Urals Worker* – which had sharply changed sides – solemnly announced that the Tsar's corpse had been exhumed by the White Army and was to be buried in Omsk 'in a zinc coffin encased in lavish wooden paneling of Siberian pine'.

It was a fleeting lie, whirled away like a leaf on the storm of events, and no more was heard of it. The Kaiser went into exile, and the armistice took place on 11 November. Twelve days later a British naval Commander, Charles Turle, went with Russian Lieutenant-Commander Korostovzov to visit the Tsar's mother in the Crimea. They arrived in HMS *Tribune* 'with HMS *Shark* for company'. Their mission was to inform the Dowager Empress Maria Feodorovna that King George V was concerned for her, and to invite her to leave with them for Constantinople, where a British battleship would be placed 'at her disposal'.

> Her Majesty who was in good health informed the officers that she did not wish to leave the Crimea and appeared to have little anxiety as regards her personal safety, which however was not entirely shared by her entourage. From enquiries she has caused to be made she seems to be of opinion that the Emperor may be still alive and on that account wishes to remain in Russia.

She was surrounded by relations, in-laws and assorted nobles including Prince Dolgoruky, who had been released and somehow made his way there. She sent a note back for the King: 'Just seen Commander Turle. So touched and thankful for your kind proposal. Love to all. Aunt Minny.' A separate note along the same lines went to the Dowager Queen Alexandra, widow of Edward VII: 'Hurrah. Delighted at last to wire... Love to you all. Sister Dagmar.'

In January 1919, the King got news which was not comforting. Sir Charles Eliot, British High Commissioner at Omsk, had sent a detailed report on Ekaterinburg early in October, with a telegram, but since it had to go via Tokyo, the report did not arrive until the New Year. Eliot's opinion was that the Tsar had certainly died and the rest may have been taken away in disguise. Any confusion 'may in great part be due to the unbusinesslike character' of the investigations held when the Czechs came to the town; to put Eliot's view less diplomatically, a procession of inadequates had been in charge. He had been shown over the place himself, by the man then in authority, who believed 'the chances were four to three' that there had been a murder. The question was, whose, besides the Tsar's? The rooms in which the Imperial Family had been confined were deserted and dirty. 'There is some evidence that sounds of uproar and shooting were heard in the house that night and that no traffic was allowed in the streets near it.'

The room where 'the murder' allegedly had taken place was opened for him. It had a wooden floor and wooden walls coated with plaster. He counted:

> the marks of seventeen bullets, or, to be more accurate, marks showing where pieces of the wall and floor had been cut out in order to remove the bullet holes, the officials charged with the investigation having thought fit to take them away for examination elsewhere. They stated that Browning revolver bullets were found in all the holes and that some of them were stained with blood. Otherwise no traces of blood were visible...
>
> There is no real evidence as to who or how many the victims were but it is supposed that they were five, namely the Tsar, Dr Botkin, the Empress's maid and the two lackeys. No corpses were discovered or any trace of their having been disposed of by burning or otherwise.

He added that the rest of the family had supposedly left in a sealed train; but that so much mystery surrounded them that conspiracy theories were springing up all over the place. And it was true that if the Empress and children had vanished but were still alive, why not the Tsar? The noise that night, and damage to the basement room, could have been caused by a drunken brawl. Eliot then added, ominously: 'I fear that another train of thought is nearer the truth.'

He went on to refer to Gibbes' account of the Yakovlev railway journey; the diversion of the train to Omsk, then back to Ekaterinburg. He suspected a Bolshevik–German conspiracy to get them to Germany. He also suspected that in July, with the Czechs approaching, the custodians of the family had panicked at the thought of Bolshevik defeat and the Tsar's escape.

He was inclined to think the Tsar had been murdered but his wife and children had been taken away. (The King's heart must have sunk;

the implication was that the Germans might have them; but Eliot had written this in October, and the Armistice was now in place and there was still no news.) The story that they were burned to death elsewhere probably came, Eliot said, from the discovery of a great deal of burned clothing, and a diamond, some distance away, and some hair concealed in the house. 'It therefore seems probable that the Imperial Family were disguised before their removal.' However, 'Subsequent stories about the murder of various Grand Dukes and Grand Duchesses cannot but inspire apprehension.' That was true enough. Grand Duchess Elizabeth, Alexandra's sister, had been thrown down a well at Perm and killed on almost the same day, along with a Grand Duke and a couple of Princes.

As Sir Charles Eliot's report reached London that January, the Russian General Dietrichs, working for Admiral Kolchak's white government in Omsk, commissioned the Ekaterinburg prosecutor Sokolov to carry out an investigation. Sokolov went about his work methodically, unlike the first curious visitors to the Ipatiev house. Gibbes and Gilliard were consulted. It cannot be said that he approached the task with an open mind; so strong was the propaganda locally that when he visited the disused Isetsky mineshaft area, he expected to find cremated remains. He found evidence of burning all right. He oversaw the collection, collation and labelling of finds and fragments, including jewels habitually worn by the family; six corsets (those of the five women and the maid); spectacle cases; spectacles; Dr Botkin's false teeth; cut bones; a severed finger; a few scorched or acid-affected bones and bullets; the unburned body of a dog; the contents of the little boy's pockets.

But, as Sokolov himself admitted, no proof of the number killed. He did his best to follow the route that the truck had taken. The question nagged at him. A railwayman near one of the bridges along the road had said some old railway sleepers had been stolen from his yard that week in July, when all the Red Army soldiers were about. The soldiers' lorry had got stuck and they must have nicked the sleepers then, the man said, but when he got to the spot and tried to dig them up they wouldn't budge. Sokolov went to have a look, and sure enough the sleepers were still there. Impacted, presumably, by the weight of the truck struggling out of the mud. He took a picture but didn't pay much attention; the incident seemed irrelevant.

In the end, all he had to show for the search was burned clothing. That confounded him but he insisted, nonetheless, that the bodies had been burned, in the same place:

> ... situated in a dense forest. The work of destroying the bodies was carried on here during the space of three days. First they were dismembered, then destroyed by fire on piles of burning wood and benzine and then decomposed by the action of sulphuric acid.

It was a horrifying picture, but it seemed certain that all five children and both parents were dead. In 1919, he presented his findings to General Dietrichs who promptly confected a story about how, before the burning took place, their heads were decapitated, pickled and despatched to the Kremlin for use in some kind of Judaic ritual. It was widely believed by the White, anti-Bolshevik side.

In September of that year, the Bolsheviks re-took Ekaterinburg. Everyone locally knew, from hearsay, that all members of the Imperial family had died, so the Bolsheviks had no choice but to confirm it.

In 1920, the Romanov massacre of July was still not universally believed. On the one side, Halliburton and McCullagh and others of their kind presented the murders as evidence of Bolshevik evil. On the other, writers gleefully published 'Could they have survived?' articles of the kind that were circulating in that asylum in Berlin in 1922. The confabulators of mystery gave millions of people something exciting to hope for; glamour, magic, proof of God's benevolence and justice.

Halfway between the two points of view came Robert Wilton, former *Times* correspondent, whose two-volume account of the deaths, published in London in 1920, was full of 'Red Jew' accusations. In another respect, he was onto something. He had visited the alleged site of the cremations in July 1919 and made a young Bolshevik contact called Fesenko. Fesenko insisted that no bodies had been burned; they would have left traces of something other than clothing and none of significance had been found. Wilton put this to Sokolov, who agreed. He said: 'The fact is, he touches a sore point. Where are the cinders? That is the question. We have found too few. They must be hidden somewhere.'

Yet as early as 1920, Yurovsky had secretly given his own account. He recounted exactly how many had died, who they were, and what had happened to the bodies, to an official Bolshevik historian called Pokrovsky. The clothes had been burned near the Isetsky mines. The bodies had been put down a mineshaft but had to be fished out, since they wouldn't sink deep enough. They were put back in the lorry and driven further north in a long and futile search for a deeper mine. (Yurovsky blamed drink-sodden Ermakov for most of this bungling.) He recounted a nightmare journey in which a truckload of corpses was trundled hopelessly about the countryside for days on end and Yurovsky, half crazed with sleeplessness, felt the wrath of the Urals Soviet at his neck. Finally the bodies were partly dissolved in sulphuric acid, and the burial was effected in utter desperation, impromptu, with all sorts of stray observers having cottoned on to something nefarious in the woods. They were buried near a railway bridge, in two spots close to the road – Alexei, and a woman mistaken for the Tsarina (perhaps a maid, he was not sure), having been partly burned, and interred somewhat apart from the other nine. The nine were hidden under railway sleepers in boggy ground.

The Yurovsky Note, as it came to be known, was placed under permanent embargo by the Soviet authorities. Notwithstanding this, among the Urals Communist cadres of the twenties, local understanding was that they were all buried off the Koptyaki Road, and well-placed visitors were offered excursions to the country to view something that may or may not have been the site. Yurovsky's account of the burial in two groups, in slightly different places, was confirmed by others who had been present. A man called Sukhorukov said:

We decided to burn two corpses on the fire and did so. For our sacrificial altar we got the last heir. The second body was the youngest daughter Anastasia. After the corpses were burned, we scattered the ashes, dug a pit in the centre, shovelled in all the unburnt remainders, made a fire again on the same spot and finished the work.

Pavel Bykov was a member of the Ekaterinburg Soviet who later became chairman of the Ural Regional Soviet. He had been among the execution squad, and published an essay in Ekaterinburg in 1921 in which he said that the victims had not been, as Sokolov thought, burned in the open mineshaft but buried near another disused mine site, several kilometres further north, called the Four Brothers; and the bodies had been concealed 'in a bog'.

Bykov's was the first publicly available document that admitted the Bolsheviks had killed the whole family. Not until 1934 did the Communist Party officially state that Lenin and his closest colleagues had organized the deaths. Ekaterinburg had been renamed Sverdlovsk in 1924, though, so it is safe to say that people may have wondered.

In Stalin's Russia it was best not to discuss these things. Not even to think them. 'Not another word about the Romanovs!' Stalin growled, when asked in the late twenties whether some of the executioners could publish a book. In America and Europe, and to those few mystic Russians who dared meet for clandestine church services, the possibility that one or two of the Imperial Family were still alive – had escaped the Forces of Evil – was much more seductive than the Bolshevik cremation story. In Germany, the Gothic Dietrichs version, with the heads sent to the Kremlin, was a gift to the Nazis. A version surfaced in 1928 in the *Hannoversche Anzeiger*, which printed an account allegedly by Iliodor the Monk (an old enemy of Rasputin's), who claimed to have seen Trotsky burning the Tsar's head at the Kremlin in 1918.

The Romanovs' role in history was over, yet their anachronistic Edwardian look, their unworldliness and fabulous wealth stuck to their memory like an accretion of barnacles. Many times before and after the next world war, mostly in Europe and America where speculation was safe, they were written about. Somehow theirs resembled the Sleeping Beauty myth; sooner or later, in some remote place, the four princesses and the sad little prince would be found, not aged, not changed.

Their murder was a key event of the cataclysmic Russian

Revolution, so when the war, and the civil war, were over and the dust had settled, exiles and witnesses wrote down their recollections. In England, the aborted escape invitation of 1917 had to be hushed up. The authorities were nervous of exposing the Government – more especially, the King – to public scorn. However scathing one's opinion of the Tsar, there was such a thing as family loyalty, and an almost atavistic dislike of pusillanimous betrayal. Nobody ever got a medal for leaving a wounded comrade to be bayoneted on the field of battle.

In the first draft of Sir George Buchanan's *My Mission to Russia*, for instance, the King appeared less than welcoming to the Romanovs, but once the Foreign Office had had a word, it was published with the story of the withdrawn invitation removed. Kerensky's book, published in France in 1927, boldly said that the British had been unwilling to receive the Russian Imperial family. This was seized upon and written up in the Continental edition of the *Manchester Guardian*, and Major-General Sir Arthur Knox promptly bought a copy of the book and read it on his way down to the Riviera Palace Hotel at Monte Carlo. Is this by any chance true? he wrote to Oliver Locker-Lampson in London – because he, General Knox, was telling everyone it wasn't. Locker-Lampson took advice and wrote back, explaining that in March of 1917 a hasty exodus of the Romanovs had been halted by opposition from Russian workers, not because the British had refused to receive them. Knox wrote back; he suspected there was a bit more to it; Kerensky was now talking about conversations that summer. General Knox had got the bit between his teeth. Airily Locker-Lampson wrote another disingenuous reply, which boiled down to: 'It's a mystery. Why don't we meet somewhere quiet and talk about it?'

Lloyd George also was made to sacrifice accuracy for the sake of the King's reputation. His war memoirs had, in the usual way, been submitted in draft to the Cabinet Secretary. According to the diary of A.J. Sylvester, Lloyd George's Private Secretary:

> 9th April 1934 – Tonight I received two letters from Hankey [the Cabinet Secretary]. He thought the chapter on the Tsar's future residence should be suppressed altogether. Hankey thought the King

would object to this and to the extract from Cabinet minutes on the subject. The Court is very jumpy and nervy and they might take the line that we must not publish anything.

Sylvester's diary wasn't published for forty years, and the censored chapter appears to be lost, apart from Lloyd George's draft notes. Meanwhile the Duke of Windsor had hit a resounding six for the home side:

> It has long been my impression that, just before the Bolsheviks seized the Tsar, my father had personally planned to rescue him with a British cruiser, but in some way the plan was blocked. In any case, it hurt my father that Britain had not raised a hand to save his cousin Nicky. 'Those politicians,' he used to say. 'If it had been one of their kind, they would have acted fast enough.'

It was all very well for the King to come up with these self-serving remarks, although some have suggested it was more to do with his fear of having to support them. When the Dowager Empress finally left the Crimea she occupied a palace in Copenhagen supplied by King Christian. There for the next decade or so, until her death, she refused to pay any bills or to sell any of the jewels she kept under the bed. Lights were left burning all night; the house was tropically hot; King Christian must pay.

Relations soured somewhat. In the 1930s, among those reminiscing, modifying their views or making admissions was Trotsky in exile. He made a diary entry on 10 April 1935; with hindsight he saw that the deaths of the children could not have worked 'in a legal sense'. Underlying this is the knowledge that it could not have been right in a moral sense either. Punishing the Tsar's family would, of course, have been impossible in the legal sense. The Tsar's family was a victim of the principle that forms the very axle of monarchy: dynastic inheritance.

That begs another question about guilty people, as well as innocent ones, as victims of some 'principle'. As a 'return match for the pogroms', though, eliminating the lot of them must have seemed justified at the time.

The man and woman in the street, in Chicago or Liverpool or Marseille, never considered any of this. For them, it was Anastasia who kept alive the idea that an escape may have taken place. The Russian government no longer went out of its way to crush such rumours. Chicherin, Commissar for Foreign Affairs, in an interview with the *Chicago Tribune*, mischievously said in 1922, 'The fate of the young daughters of the Tsar is at present unknown to me... I have read in the press that they are now in America.'

Sokolov, exiled in Paris, published the report of his investigation there in 1924. Conspiracy theorists loved the book; there it was in black and white: the ashes were missing, so had there ever really been any? Anastasia' and her publicity machine lived on, and on.

14

Buried Bones

The Ipatiev house was used as a Bolshevik club; later it became the Sverdlovsk Museum of the Revolution, and Yurovsky and a couple of others donated their weapons to it. Resurrection Square, between the house and the church, was the wonderfully named Square of the People's Vengeance until the 1940s.

In the 1970s, as nostalgia for life before the two world wars overwhelmed Europe and America, Russians became fascinated by their recent past as well. Knowing this, and seeing the sixtieth anniversary of the Tsar's death looming, in 1977 Boris Yeltsin, who had recently become First Secretary of the Sverdlovsk Oblast Party Committee, ordered that the Ipatiev house be demolished.

Too late. Since 1971, a Sverdlovsk geologist and local history buff called Avdonin had been fascinated by the fate of the Romanovs. He and his wife had found Bykov's account: the one that said the family were not burned but buried 'in a bog'. He was curious. It was still less than sixty years after the event and although few witnesses could be found, there was a lot of hearsay evidence. He went out of his way to find older inhabitants of Sverdlovsk/Ekaterinburg to note down exactly what they said about that night in July 1918.

In 1976, he met a former policeman, detective and screenwriter from Moscow called Ryubov. Ryubov encouraged him; they must not give up; together, they would find this 'bog'. Investigation took them through oral history to Yurovskaya, the widow of Yurovsky in Leningrad (as Petrograd had been renamed in 1924). She would say nothing, but recommended that Ryubov talk to her brother. It was this brother who told him that the 'Yurovsky Note' existed, somewhere in the archives of the Kremlin.

Ryubov, having been a policeman, pulled strings. He had been allowed to read the Sokolov account in the archives, so he learned the story of the railway bridge and the sleepers firmly embedded nearby, and now he was given sight of the Yurovsky note and discovered that only two bodies had been burned. The nine others had been doused with sulphuric acid, buried in a wet pit, and concealed with railway sleepers on top.

It was Avdonin who noticed that Yurovsky's squad, in the lorry, had stopped in one place for *five hours*. Why would they stop for so long, with bodies on board, unless they were doing something? This must be the site where the railway sleepers had been laid; but where was it? There was nothing but grass and trees to be seen now. Avdonin and a geologist friend walked the long quiet stretch of road near the railway bridge and finally decided on a place not far from the road where damp ground seemed to have sunk. Surreptitiously they drove a home-made borer in as far as they could – which was not very far. Extracted, the earth proved to contain an oily black substance which tested as highly acidic.

Disturbing a grave was illegal. They applied for a permit to dig for purposes of 'geological research', and waited until warm weather had dispersed the snows of winter completely. Avdonin, his wife, a geologist friend and his wife, Ryubov and another man drove out to the site on 31 May 1979. They dug and scraped at the damp, hollow place until they hit the remains of the wooden sleepers and a lot of this black, oily stuff. Beneath the sleepers, higgledy-piggledy in the ground, were bones. And skulls. But they couldn't open the area completely for fear of discovery.

They put three skulls in their cars, carefully restored the site so it would not be noticed, and drove away really, really scared. Now that they had found them, how could they proceed without serious trouble? Ryubov approached people he knew at forensic labs in Moscow. They wouldn't touch the job; skulls of unknown provenance – no paperwork – a criminal offence had been committed, obviously, and they didn't want anything to do with it. Five weeks later, the conspirators returned. They brought the skulls back, having had plaster casts made, and re-buried them with a time capsule that explained what they had done, what they had found, and when.

In 1984 'Anastasia' died. Ten years after the secret discovery by Avdonin and Ryubov, Russia's 1989 revolution brought *glasnost*, a new spirit of openness. The archives were opened. In Moscow, Ryubov wrote a screenplay based on the story and boasted about his finds, refusing to reveal the whereabouts of the remains unless they were given a 'Christian burial'. He was interviewed several times and never once mentioned Avdonin, the key collaborator whose curiosity had led to the discovery in the first place. Avdonin and his wife, who lived in Sverdlovsk, saw a trail of bonehunters turning up on the once-lonely road every weekend.

Avdonin was furious. In 1991 he approached the head of the Urals Soviet, and through this connection got the next President's backing – the President shortly to be inaugurated being, by popular demand, Boris Yeltsin. Avdonin was given police permits to exhume the remains and enlisted the help of an archaeologist, Ludmilla Koryakova. The exhumation now had official status; Isvestia reported that it would be undertaken, and the local Prosecutor also turned up at the site at the appointed time, accompanied by two police officers, two forensic experts, and two epidemiologists.

Directed by Avdonin, supervised by Ludmilla Koryakova, they uncovered the remains with the time capsule hidden in 1979. By degrees the whole grave was opened. It turned out to slope, and to be only four feet deep at its deepest point. The greater part of nine skeletons were found, crammed in layers, into an area six and a half feet by five; that is, the length and width of a double bed. There was slight damage on one side where a power cable had been laid.

Koryakova, the archaeologist, expected this to be run as a painstaking professional dig over weeks or months. Sketches would be made, the earth carefully brushed away, bone fragments photographed before being lifted, soil samples taken and so on. There was to be none of that. The Prosecutor overruled her. Impatiently, he pretty well said: 'There are nine of them, all we have to do is take the bones out, put them in bags, and reassemble them in the warm and dry.' She, as a mere expert in forensic archaeology, had no authority; he, crudely viewing this as a scene of crime, did. Some of the remains crumbled or broke as they were roughly removed. Twelve ammo boxes were filled, locked and sealed. Inside ten of them were the bones from the graves. including the three skulls from 1979; in the other two, odds and ends.

The remains were surrendered into the care of the police. In October 1991, a second search revealed more bone fragments and teeth. When the bones were reassembled into skeletons, there were four men and five women, identified as Nicolas II, his wife, three daughters, Dr Botkin, the chef, the valet, and the lady's maid. Political pressure meant the remains stayed in Sverdlovsk, which was now called Ekaterinburg again. The mystery was not over yet; the Tsarevich and one of the two youngest girls were missing. This made sense, since various accounts had declared that there were two gravesites, not far apart; but given a radius of several hundred metres in which to search for scorched bones and ash-heaps buried so long ago, who could find them? The resources did not seem to exist.

The results of the excavation were made public. The Patriarchate of the Russian Orthodox Church did not believe a word of it. They had the Sokolov cremation version firmly in their minds and would not lightly concede the Dietrichs/Iliodor version either. They clung to their conviction that decapitation took place before burning, and the skulls were ritually cremated, in Moscow, by Trotsky. If there were any skulls, it was because another family had been buried to put people off the scent.

It was therefore necessary to prove, for sure, who these people were. DNA testing was not very sophisticated in Russia in 1992, so American scientists got involved. Fifty scientists from Russia were called in, all expert in different fields of forensic pathology, to work with a team from Florida and another from the United States Government. They knew whose bodies these must almost certainly be but they could not be sure which girl, of Maria and Anastasia, was missing.

In 1993 at a laboratory in Aldermaston in Berkshire, bone samples from the nine sets in the grave were DNA-tested against DNA from Romanov relatives. Finding living relatives was far from straightforward. A Romanov nephew was alive in Russia, but the Russian Orthodox authorities objected to British or any foreign scientists having anything to do with him. One of the Tsar's brothers could theoretically have been exhumed, but the Church objected to that too. The only way the Russian government could possibly silence these people was to designate this a criminal investigation, for murder. They therefore put an astute policeman (coincidentally called Solovyev, like Rasputin's daughter's husband) in charge, and stood by as Aldermaston completed the investigation between 1993 and 1995.

Nuclear DNA is equally inherited from father and mother; mitochondrial DNA (mtDNA) comes unchanged from the mother. Those who share a common female ancestor, generations apart, have matching mtDNA. Aldermaston showed three offspring of two people in the grave, plus another four unrelated (i.e., the three servants and Botkin). Prince Philip, husband of Queen Elizabeth II of England, had descended directly from Princess Alice, his great-grandmother via Victoria of Hesse (Alexandra's sister and his grandmother). His mitochondrial DNA matched that of the Tsarina and the three young females.

It was also necessary to find a person of unbroken matrilineal descent to match DNA in the skeleton believed to be that of the Tsar. Countess Xenia Cheremetev-Sfiri came forward. Her grandmother had been Yirina Yusupov, whose own grandmother had been Louise of Hesse-Cassel – as had the Tsar's. There was a match, as there was with the mtDNA of the Duke of Fife, another great-great grandchild of Louise of Hesse-Cassel. The only caveat was a tiny, unusual discrepancy in the Tsar's mtDNA.

In 1995 Grand Duke George, the Tsar's brother, was finally exhumed and examined by a Russian scientist at the US Armed Forces laboratory in Maryland. The Aldermaston results were confirmed in every respect; a discrepancy in the Tsar's mtDNA was common to Grand Duke George as well; the likelihood overwhelmingly was – this is the Tsar.

As to 'Anastasia', mitochondrial DNA was retrieved from a tissue sample of hers in an American hospital, and tested against a sample from Prince Philip. No match was found. The same 'Anastasia' sample, tested against a great-nephew of Franziska Schankowska, the Polish factory worker, matched perfectly. The girl on the Berlin bridge had never been a Russian princess at all.

The scientific results were announced in a respected, peer-reviewed scientific journal. The Russian Orthodox Church, split between indigenous and diaspora branches, divided in opinion. Some still insisted upon decapitation and/or 'ritual murder'. There were scientists, media-savvy ones, willing to support the church of course. The decapitation theory was supported by a forensic odontist called Popov, who said that two teeth belonging to an adolescent male had been found in the grave – but no adolescent male. The heads had been swapped! Obviously. The Ekaterinburg authorities had allowed an American scientist called Maples to remove bone samples for testing at Berkeley. He insisted that some samples sent to the laboratory at Aldermaston had been contaminated, so some of the evidence was wrong.

Popov and Maples and other scientists refused to believe that all were dead. In any case the police case number included 666. What further proof did one need? All this was a cunning plot.

Meanwhile Vladimir Solovyev, the police commander, had been trying to identify the weapons that killed them all. There had been, it was said, thirty-two bullet holes in the basement room. Twenty-five bullets were retrieved from the grave, having evidently emerged from the bodies during decomposition, and it seemed that over fifty had been used. Solovyev's enquiry confirmed the makes and models of gun. Ermakov and others had presented their weapons to museums and they matched. All had been handguns. Ermakov was right; the rifles provided to the Cheka men were not used except as bayonets. The Tsar had been shot repeatedly in the chest; two of the girls had been shot through the temple and their faces smashed. Beyond that, it was hard to say.

In 1998 the only living relative died, leaving permission for tests to be carried out using his DNA after death. Yet again there was a positive identification and a full, comprehensive report. Solovyev was confident enough to confirm that the grave had contained a Romanov father, his wife and three young adult females of an age to be Olga, Tatiana and Maria, although they thought the third one was Anastasia.

That still left one girl (probably Maria) and the Tsarevich to find. One scientist used a cranial matching technique. He got hold of a weird picture, taken by Gilliard in 1917 when the four Grand Duchesses had their heads shaved because of measles. Their four bodies were concealed by a sheet, and their four bald heads and faces alone were visible. This he matched against the skull in question and decided it was Maria's; it followed that the missing girl must be Anastasia. But his result was derided as mere opinion.

Some people still were not satisfied. Some insisted that the bones of Grand Duke Michael, the Tsar's brother, had been substituted for the Tsar. But the Tsar, Skeleton no. 4, could be identified for all sorts of reasons; he had backache, rode a lot (it changes the bones), and had once broken a rib. He had proportionately short legs, dental decay and periodontal disease, presumably exacerbated by those endless cigarettes. In life, he must have had dreadful halitosis. Alexandra had exquisite platinum and porcelain crowns and gold fillings. The maid had gold teeth and all the Grand Duchesses had numerous amalgam fillings. Dr Botkin had no teeth in his upper jaw at all; hence the false ones that were found. The Soviet authorities, in a futile attempt to quell rumour once and for all, insisted on another report which would answer the church's questions in full, and Solovyev produced it in 1998.

The Patriarchate insisted that the Bolsheviks had destroyed all traces of the bodies and that was 'incontrovertible fact'. He did however agree that on the eightieth anniversary of the deaths, a reburial of the remains of a person or persons unknown could take place in the old Imperial chapel at the Cathedral of St Peter and St Paul. The Patriarch would simply hold a memorial service for all victims of the civil war 1918–1921. The case was closed. In the year 2000, the Tsar was canonized.

Franziska Schankowska was dead, but there had been no shortage of deluded claimants elsewhere. In the course of their long lives they had produced descendants in California or Eastern Europe who were now busily filling web-pages with their own theories. And there was no stopping them, because after all, where were the other two bodies?

15

Delusions Persist

The second grave must be found. Rather than dig up half the *oblast*, they would return to the documents for a clue. Between 1991 and 1998 historians and archivists trawled through the Russian State Archives as well as those of the Interior Ministry, the KGB, the Foreign Ministry, the Ministry of Culture and material held abroad; no clue.

There was also the question of blame. Had this been a crime, or a deliverance? Should the memory of the regicides be publicly disgraced in some way? There might be a precedent. For a long time it was thought that Sokolov, as prosecutor, had not carried out his investigation with the aim of commencing a criminal case. Then a Sotheby's auction brought to light Sokolov papers in the estate of Count Orlov, and they included an order for the institution of criminal proceedings.

But there was still no trace of the second grave. It was local knowledge that led them to the truth in the end. Andrei Grigoryev, of the Ekaterinburg institute devoted to preserving historical monuments, and his team discovered vital extra clues by examining the original shorthand records of a speech delivered in 1934 by Yurovsky. He had been talking to a loyal Bolshevik audience; the notes had been taken and typed up by two local secretaries, and later edited by Yurovsky in his own hand.

It seems to have been this text that helped two searchers narrow down the search to a precise spot. It was, as they had expected, not far from the railway bridge. Indeed it was only sixty metres from the first grave. On 29 July 2007, hunting with probes and metal detectors, they uncovered parts of a container of sulphuric acid, nails, metal strips from a wooden box, and bullets; and buried together, two partly destroyed skeletons. The case was reopened. On 30 April 2008, scientists confirmed that yes, these were the two they had been looking for. In July, with most of the investigation complete, police commander Solovyev and Nikolai Nevolin held a press conference. It was minutely detailed; it had to be. They would be endlessly challenged and they knew it.

The testing process had not been easy. After death by shooting, Yurovsky's men had tried to destroy these two bodies, not only with acid but by burning. DNA testing had been carried out by forensic scientists from the laboratory at Sverdlovsk, the best of its kind in Russia, supplemented by distinguished collaborators from top-rated labs elsewhere. Leading the DNA testing team were a Russian, Evgeny Ivanovich Rogaev, a specialist in mammoth genotype reconstruction; an American, Michael Coble, who was employed by the Pentagon to identify dead soldiers; and Walther Parson, an expert from Innsbruck, Austria.

Historical and archival research was the responsibility of Sergei Mironenko, Director of the Russian State Archive. The Archive had painstakingly hunted down the Sokolov documents, which had at one time been scattered all over the world, and now had the entire collection. They were also able to study the transcript of the revealing speech Yurovsky had delivered to Bolshevik veterans. Handwriting analysis confirmed that it had been edited by Yurovsky himself.

Ballistics tests were carried out by people from the Russian Ministry of the Interior, the equivalent of the British Home Office. Sokolov had found a lot of bullets and shell cases in the Ganin Pit – that is, not the Isetsky mine where the clothes were burned but a second, more northerly mine (sometimes called the Chetyrekhbratsky mine), which had been rejected as a burial site during the long schlep with the corpses. Ballistics experts compared the bullets and shells with those discovered in 1991. They matched perfectly and had been fired from the same barrels. Two guns, the Nagant and the Browning, deposited by the executioners with museums, were used for those tests, and proved the link between the Ganin Pit and the 1991 site.

Several independent expert teams did a full anthropological analysis of the remains; three independent DNA tests were carried out on the bones found in 1991 and those discovered in 2007; and the results were conclusive. So were ballistic examinations. All indicators were that the latest bones were those of Alexei and Maria.

Nikolai Nevolin, the forensic scientist from Sverdlovsk, explained to the world's press that all they'd had to go on were forty-four bone fragments, some of them tiny, and seven teeth. Some of those were of no use at all, because of the high temperatures to which they had been subjected, but others could be classified by age and sex. Forensic dentistry and anthropological assessment showed that one set of bones belonged to a 'Europoid' female aged 17–19, and another, of sex not determinable by this particular examination, to a 'Europoid' individual aged 12–14. Milk teeth, the ones that fall out when we are about six, are actually pushed downwards by adult dentition, but all the adult teeth can take six or eight more years to appear. This appears to have been the case with Alexei, as traces of milk teeth were found. There was also an anomaly on the tooth surface which had been found in teeth of all three girls in the first grave: a 'loop-shaped curve of the second groove of the dental crowns' chewing surfaces'. Further, the amalgam fillings had been mixed in *precisely* the same proportions of mercury, silver, cuprum and tin.

DNA testing had come on since 1991, when Y chromosome examination didn't exist. The Y chromosome is inherited from fathers over generations without any changes, and the Y chromosome of the boy aged 12–14 was the same as that of the male discovered in the first burial pit. The same Y chromosome was found in other direct male descendants of Tsar Alexander III. It was possible to state conclusively that this male was a son of the male in the first grave and the female was his sister. The remains from both graves belonged to the Russian Imperial family.

The journalists at the press conference had a lot of questions of which one was uppermost in every mind: how would the Church take this? The Russian Orthodox Church had made no comment so far, although as Solovyev said, 'If the results of our work are accepted, the next question to decide will be re-burial of the remains.'

This had caused problems enough the first time. Tests were still going on. There were bloodstains on a shirt in the Hermitage, for instance, which were those of Nicolas II. Solovyev did not say so, but really the scientists were just piling up evidence to convince those who would not believe any science whatsoever unless it supported their own prejudices. Then, they would be only too glad to accept its scientific validity. Not otherwise.

This went not just for the Church, but for many others. The Grand Duchess Maria Vladimirovna, for instance. Her father and grandfather claimed to be the rightful heirs. A spokesman for other Romanovs told Moscow Radio that people should 'be very careful' about the finds until 'more evidence' was presented.

The last word should probably go to the most recent claimant. In June 2002, an old lady who claimed to be Grand Duchess Anastasia, and therefore the legitimate heiress to a fortune conservatively valued at one trillion dollars, held a press conference in Moscow. She was, she agreed, 101. She had not been shot in 1918 at all, but had fled to Georgia, where she had married. She made these claims also on a video, which was shown on Russian television. People were not unimpressed; at least this claimant could speak Russian, which some of the other ones had apparently forgotten through 'stress'. She had left it until 1995 to make the claim, though.

Others sighed, for as it turned out, the claimant was already dead. She had been born in 1900 and died in 2000, and a hospital in Moscow had tested her claim and found that she was actually one Natalya Petrovna Bilikhodze. Quite who the lady at the press conference was is unclear; but although the fate of the Imperial Family is known, their legend refuses to lie down and die.

APPENDIX 1

The Yurovsky Note (State Archive of the Russian Federation, Moscow)

On the morning of the 15 July, Filipp arrived and said that things had to be finished off tomorrow. Sednyov the kitchen boy (a boy of 13) was to be taken away and sent to his former birth place or to somewhere in central Russia. It was also said that Nicolas was to be executed and that we should officially announce it, but when it came to the family, then perhaps it would be announced, but no one knew yet how, when, and in what manner. Thus, everything demanded the utmost care and as few people as possible – moreover, absolutely dependable ones.

On the 15th I immediately undertook preparations, for everything had to be done quickly. I decided to assemble the same number of men as there were people to be shot, gather them all together, and told them what was happening – that they all had to prepare themselves for this, that as soon as we got the final order everything was going to have to be ably handled. You see, it has to be said that shooting people isn't the easy matter that it might seem to some. After all, this wasn't going on at the front but in a peaceful situation. You see, these were not bloodthirsty people, the people performing the difficult duty of the revolution. That is why it wasn't mere chance that, at the last minute, the situation arose that two Latvians refused to participate – they didn't have it in them.

On the morning of the 16th, I sent away the kitchen boy Sednyov under the pretext of the meeting with his uncle who had come to Sverdlovsk. This caused anxiety among the arrested. Botkin and then one of the daughters asked where and why they had taken Sednyov and for how long. Alexei missed him, they said. Having received an explanation they left, seemingly calm. I prepared twelve Nagant revolvers and determined who would shoot whom. Comrade Filipp warned me that a truck would arrive at twelve o'clock at night. Those who arrived would give a password; they would be allowed in and would be given the corpses, which they would take away for burial. Around eleven o'clock at night on the 16th I gathered the men together, gave out the revolvers, and stated that we would soon have to start liquidating the arrested. I warned Pavel Medvedev about the thorough check of the sentries outside and in; about how he and the guard commander should be on watch themselves in the area around the house and at the house where the external guard was lodged, and about how they should keep in contact with me. Only at the last minute, when everything was ready for the shooting, were they to warn all the sentries as well as the rest of the detachment that if they heard shots coming from the house they shouldn't worry and shouldn't come out of their lodgings, and that if something was especially worrying they should let me know through the established channel.

The truck did not show up until half past one in the morning; the fact that we waited longer than expected, couldn't help but create anxiety, in addition to the anxiety of waiting in general, but the main thing was that the summer nights were so short. Only after the truck came – or after I learned by telephone that the truck was on its way – did I go to awake the arrested.

Botkin was asleep in the room closest to the entrance; he came out and asked what the matter was. I told him that everyone had to be woken up right away as the town was uneasy, that staying upstairs was dangerous for them, and that I would transfer them to another place. Preparations took a lot of time, around forty minutes. When the family was dressed, I led them to a room previously selected in the downstairs part of the house. We had thought this plan through with comrade Nikulin. Here I have to say that we didn't think in advance that the fact that the windows could not contain the noise; second, that the wall against which those who had to be shot were to be lined up was made of stone and, finally that the shooting would take on a chaotic character, but this was impossible to foresee. This last thing wasn't supposed to occur because each man was going to shoot one person, and so everything was to be orderly. The reasons for the chaos – that is, disorderly and confused shooting – became clear later. Although I warned them through Botkin that they didn't need to bring anything with them, they nevertheless gathered up various little things – pillows, little bags, and so forth – and I believe, a little dog.

Once they descended to the room (at the entrance to the room on the right is a very wide window, almost the size of the whole wall), I suggested they stand by the wall. Apparently, at that moment they still did not imagine anything of what was in store for them. Alexandra said: 'There aren't even chairs here.' Nicolas was carrying Alexei in his arms. And he continued to stand with him like that in the room. I ordered a pair of chairs to be brought. Alexandra sat on one of them to the right of the entrance almost in the corner and by the window. Next to her, toward the left side of the entrance, stood the daughters and Demidova. Here Alexei was set down beside them on a chair; after him came Dr Botkin, the cook and others, and Nicolas was left standing opposite Alexei. Simultaneously, I ordered the people to come down and ordered that everyone be ready and that each be at his place when the command was given.

Nicolas, having seated Alexei, stood so that he was blocking him. Alexei sat in the left hand corner of the room from the entrance, and I immediately, as I recall it, told Nicolas approximately the following: that his imperial relatives and closest associates both inside the country and abroad had tried to free him and that the Soviet of workers deputies had decreed that they be shot. He asked: 'What?' and turned to face Alexei. Right then, I shot him and killed him on the spot. He didn't manage to turn and face us to get an answer. Now, instead of order, chaotic shooting began. The room was very small, but still everyone could have entered the room and performed the shooting in an orderly way. But, apparently, many shot across the threshold, and the bullets began to ricochet, since the wall was made of stone. Moreover, the firing intensified when those being shot began to scream. It took a great effort on my part to stop the shooting. A bullet from one of those shooting behind me whizzed by my head and I can't remember whether it was the palm, hand or finger of someone else that was hit and pierced by a bullet.

When the shooting stopped, it turned out that the daughters, Alexandra, the Lady in waiting Demidova, I think, and also Alexei were alive. I thought that they had fallen out of fear or perhaps on purpose and that was why they were still alive. Then we began to finish them off (I had earlier suggested they be shot in the region of the heart so that there would be less blood). Alexei remained seated, petrified, and I finished him off. They shot the daughters but nothing happened, then Yermakov set the bayonet in motion and that didn't help, then they were finished off by being shot in the head. Only in the forest did I discover what hampered the shooting of the daughters and Alexandra.

Now that the shooting was over, the corpses had to be moved, and it was rather a long way. How could they be carried? Here someone thought of stretchers (they didn't think of it at the proper time). They took harness beams from sleighs and stretched sheets over them, I think. Having checked that everyone was dead, we began to carry them. Then we realized that blood stains would be everywhere. I immediately ordered that the stretchers be lined with available soldier's blankets and that the truck be covered with them. I assigned Mikhail Medvedev to remove the corpses. He is a member of the GPU. He and Pyotr Yermakov were supposed to take the corpses and drive away with them. When the first corpses were taken away, someone, I can't remember who, told me that one of the men had appropriated some valuables for himself. I then understood that there were valuables among the things the family had bought with them. I immediately stopped the carrying of the corpses, gathered the men together, and demanded that the stolen valuables be handed over. After a certain amount of denial, two men returned valuables they had stolen. Threatening anyone who looted with execution, I dismissed these two and, as I recall, assigned comrade Nikulin to supervise the carrying of the corpses, having warned them the valuables were present on the bodies of those shot. I gathered together all the items containing objects that they had seized, in addition to the objects themselves, and sent them to the commandant's office. Comrade Filipp, apparently sparing me (as my health wasn't the best), warned me that I shouldn't go to the funeral but I was very worried about how the corpses would be hidden. That was why I decided to go myself, and I did the right thing as it turned out; otherwise, all the corpses would certainly have fallen into the hands of the Whites. It is easy to see how they would have used this matter to their advantage.

Having ordered that everything be washed and cleaned up, we departed around three o'clock or a little later. I took a few people from the internal guard along with me. I did not know where they were planning to bury the corpses. As I said, Filipp had apparently assigned this matter to comrade Yermakov, who took us somewhere near the Upper Isetsk factory. I think it was Pavel Medvedev who told me that the same night, when he was running the detachment, he saw comrade Filipp walking by the house the whole time and looking more than a little worried about how things would go there. I hadn't been to these parts and wasn't familiar with them. About one or two miles from the Upper Isetsk factory, we were met by a whole convoy of people on horse back and in light horse drawn carts. I asked Yermakov who these people were, what they were here for, and he answered that these were the people he had prepared. I don't know to this day why there were so many. I heard only isolated shouts: 'We thought that you would deliver them to us alive, and now it turns out they're dead.' Then, I think it was two or three miles further on, the truck got stuck between two trees.

During this stop, some of Yermakov's people started to pull at the girls blouses where they discovered the valuables. The stealing was starting up again. Then I ordered that people be posted so that no one could come near the truck. The truck was stuck and couldn't budge. I asked Yermakov: 'And is the place chosen for them far?' He said: 'It's not far, beyond the railway embankment.' And, on top of being stuck between the trees, this was a marshy place. No matter where we went, it was swampy. I thought to myself, he brought so many people and horses; at least there should have been wagons instead of lightweight carts. But there was nothing to be done. We had to unload and lighten the truck; but even this didn't help. Then I ordered the bodies loaded on the horse drawn carts, since we couldn't wait any longer: dawn was coming.

Only when it was already beginning to be light did we reach the well known clearing. Peasants were sitting by the fire about twenty paces or so from the mine selected for the burial site, apparently spent the night there after hay making. Along the way, lone people could be seen at a distance, and it became utterly impossible to continue working within sight of people. I have to say that the situation was becoming difficult and everything could have been ruined. I still didn't know then that the mine wasn't worth a damn for our purposes.

And then there were those cursed valuables. I didn't know then that there were rather a lot of them. The people that Yermakov had gathered weren't at all right for this sort of job, and there were so many of them, too. I decided that the people had to be got rid of. I immediately found out that we were about one or two miles outside the village of Koptiaki. A large enough area had to be cordoned off, which I ordered done. I selected people and instructed them to surround a certain area. In addition, I sent people to the village to advise the villagers not to go anywhere, saying that Czechoslovaks were near by, that our units had been brought here, and that it was dangerous. Then I said to send anyone they saw back to the village and, if nothing else worked, to shoot those who were stubbornly disobedient. I sent the other group of people back to the village, because they were no longer necessary.

Having done this, I ordered the corpses unloaded and the clothing removed and buried. That is, I ordered the things destroyed without a trace, and saw to it that any incriminating evidence was removed, in case someone was to discover the corpses. I ordered bonfires to be built. Things that had been sewn into the daughters and Alexandra's clothing were discovered when the corpses began to be undressed; I can't remember exactly what was discovered on the latter or if it was simply the same sort of things as was sewn into the daughters' clothing. The daughters had bodices made up of solid diamonds and other precious stones that served not just as receptacles for valuables but also as protective armour. That was why neither bullets nor bayonets yielded results during the shooting and bayonets blows. No one is responsible for their death agonies but themselves, it has to be said. I posted sentries and guards at the spot, took the valuables and left.

There turned out to be about eighteen pounds of such valuables. By the way, their greed turned out to be so great that on Alexandra there was a simply huge piece of gold wire bent into the shape of a bracelet of around a pound in weight. All these valuables were immediately ripped out so that we wouldn't have to drag the bloody clothing with us. Those valuables that the Whites discovered when they were excavated were undoubtedly part of the things that had been individually sewn into the clothing and that remained in the ashes of the fire when the clothing was burned. The next day, comrades gave me a few diamonds that they had found there. How could they have overlooked the other valuables? They had enough time to look. The most likely thing is that they just didn't think of it. By the way, some valuables are being returned to us through Torgsin stores, for it is likely the peasants from Koptiaki village picked up some valuables after our departure. We gathered the valuables, burned the things, and threw the stark naked corpses into the mine.

And here another muddle ensued. The water barely covered the bodies; what to do? We thought of blowing up the mine with bombs to cave it in. But nothing came of this, of course. I saw that we were getting nowhere with the burial and that the bodies couldn't be left as is and that everything had to be started all over again. What to do? Where to put them? Around two o'clock in the afternoon I decided to go to town because it was clear that the corpses had to be extracted from the mine and transferred to a different place. Besides, even a blind man could find them with the place being so churned up by people.

I went to the Regional Soviet Executive Committee and I told the authorities how badly things had gone. Comrade Safarov, and I can't remember who else, listened and had nothing to say. Then I found Filipp and pointed out the necessity of transferring the corpses to another place. Filipp summoned Yermakov, severely reprimanded him, and sent him to dig up the corpses. I simultaneously instructed him to take bread and dinner, as the men had been there almost twenty-four hours without sleep and were hungry and worn out.

They were supposed to wait there until I arrived. It turned out not to be so easy to pull out the corpses, and we suffered rather a lot over it. We had set out late, and we fiddled with it all night.

I went to Sergei Yegorovich Chutskaev, then chairman of the Ekaterinburg city Soviet executive committee, to ask whether he perhaps knew of a place. He recommended some very deep abandoned mines on the Moscow highway. I got a car, took someone from the Regional Cheka with me, Polushin, I think, and someone else, and we left.

About a mile short of the designated spot, the car broke down, so we left the driver to fix it and set out on foot, looked the place over, and found that it would do. The only thing was making sure there weren't extra, watchful eyes. Some people lived not far from there, and we decided we would go and remove them and send them to town. At the end of the operation we would free them; that was what we decided on. When we got back to the car, the car itself needed towing. I decided to wait for chance passers by. Sometime later, some people were tearing along, driving a pair of horses. I stopped them, and it turned out that the boys knew me and were hurrying to get to their factory. They weren't very keen on it, but they gave the horses up.

While we rode, another plan came to mind; to burn the corpses. But no one knew how. It seems to me Polushin said he knew how, which was fine, since no one really knew how it would turn out. I still had the mines on Moscow highway in mind and consequently decided to obtain carts to use for transport. Besides, in case of bad luck, I thought of burying them in groups in different places along the thoroughfare. The road leading to Koptiaki, which is next to the clearing, is clay, so if they could be buried there without anyone seeing, not a living sole would ever guess. They could be buried and carts could be driven over the site. The result would be a rough pathway and nothing more. And so, three plans.

There was no form of transportation, no car. I went to the director of the military transport garage to find out if they had any cars. There turned out to be a car, but the director, whose surname I forget, later turned out to be a scoundrel and I think they shot him in

Perm. Comrade Pavel Petrovich Gorbunov was the garage director or deputy director, I don't remember exactly, and is currently the deputy chairman of the state bank. I told him that I needed a car quickly. He said: 'And I know what for.' And he gave me the director's car. I went to Voikov, supply director for the Urals, to obtain gasoline or kerosene, sulphuric acid for disfiguring the faces, and a shovel. I obtained all of these. As deputy commissar of justice of the Ural region, I saw to it that ten carts without drivers were taken from the prisons. Everything was loaded up, and they left. The truck was directed to the same place, and I myself stayed to wait for Polushin, a specialist in burning, who had disappeared. I waited for him at Voikov's. Even though I waited until eleven o'clock at night, I didn't find him. Later they told me that he was on his way to me but fell from his horse, hurt his leg, and couldn't make it. I could have used the car again but around twelve o'clock at night I mounted the horse with a comrade whose name I don't remember now and departed for the place where the corpses were. Misfortune befell me too. The horse stumbled, rose to its knees and somehow fell awkwardly on its side, crushing my leg. I spent an hour or so lying down before I could mount my horse again.

We arrived late during the night and went to work extracting the corpses. I decided to bury a few corpses on the road. We started digging a pit. It was almost ready by dawn when one comrade came up to me and said that, despite the ban on allowing anyone near, a person had shown up from somewhere, an acquaintance of Yermakov's, whom he permitted to remain at a distance. The person could see that people were digging around here since piles of clay were lying around. Although Yermakov assured us that this person couldn't see anything, other comrades started to illustrate, that is, to show, where the person had been standing and how he undoubtedly could not help seeing.

That was how this plan was ruined too. It was decided to fill in the pit. We piled everything onto the cart as evening fell. The truck was waiting in a spot where it was pretty nearly guaranteed that it would not get stuck (the driver was Liukhanov, the worker from the Zlokazov factory). We headed for the Siberian highway.

Having crossed the railway embankment, we loaded the corpses into the truck again and quietly got in. We had been struggling for two hours, so it was getting close to midnight, and I decided that we had to bury them somewhere around here because at this late hour it was certain that no one at all could see us. I had sent for railway ties to be brought to cover the place where the corpses would be piled, so there was only one person who might see a few of the men – the rail road night watchman. I had in mind that if anyone found the ties, they might guess that they were put down to let a truck pass through.

I forgot to say that during that evening or more precisely, during the night, we got stuck twice having unloaded everything, we got out, but then we got hopelessly stuck a second time. I have to say that we were all so devilishly exhausted that we didn't want to dig new graves, but, as always happens in these cases, two or three began doing it and then the others joined in. We immediately lit fires, and while the grave was being readied, we burned two corpses, Alexei and apparently, Demidova, instead of Alexandra, as we had intended. We dug a pit by the spot where they were buried, piled in the bones, evened it over, lit another big fire, and covered all traces with ashes. Before putting all the corpses in the pit, we poured sulphuric acid on them, then we filled in the pit, covered it with railway ties, drove the empty truck over them, tampered the ties down a little, and were done with it. At five or six o'clock in the morning, we gathered everyone together, explained the importance of what we had accomplished, warned everyone to forget what they had seen and never speak of it to anyone, and left for town. The boys from the Regional Cheka who had lost track of us – comrades Rodginsky, Gorin, and someone else – arrived when we had already finished with everything.

I left with a report for Moscow on the night of the 19th. It was then that I gave the valuables to Trifonov, member of the third army's revolutionary council. I think Beloborodov, Novoselov, and someone else buried them in a basement in the earth and floor of a workers house in Lysev.

The Sir Basil Thomson Papers (National Archive, Kew)

The Director of Intelligence
Scotland House, London SW1
3rd July 1925

<u>Confidential</u>
Dear Mr Palairet
I have got together such evidence as is available about the murder of the Imperial Family in Russia. Copies have been sent to Lord Stamfordham, the Home Secretary and the Public Record Office, where the documents can be available to historical students in the future. There is sure to be a crop of claimants, and there was a danger that the sources of evidence might die, leaving no record behind them.
Sincerely yours
Sir Basil Thomson
Director of Intelligence

11th June 1920
Colonel RODZIANKO called and gave the following account of the murdering of the Tsar and his family by the Bolsheviks at Ekaterinburg: The Emperor, as you know, was living in Tobolsk with all the family in a private house. The Bolsheviks wanted to make him sign the Peace Treaty with the Germans – the Brest-Litovsk Treaty. He refused. Then they said that they would take the Emperor and Empress away and leave the Tsarevich behind and that if the Emperor then refused to sign they would murder the Tsarevich. They thought by that that they would succeed in frightening the Emperor into signing, but they were mistaken. He said they might cut off his

right hand before he would sign. They suffered terribly in the journey from Tobolsk to Ekaterinburg. From Tobolsk to the railway station is a distance of 250 miles, and the journey was done by the Emperor, the Empress, and family in cart without any springs, running full speed and surrounded by Red Guards on horseback. You know the state of the roads there so you can imagine their suffering. When they came to the station they were put in a third class car. They were given half of the car and the Reds were all the time wailing about guarding them, so that they should not escape. When they arrived at the house in Ekaterinburg – Ippatieveky House – during the first few days they had only two beds, one for the Emperor and one for the Empress. The Tsarevich slept on the floor. The Grand Duchesses had no beds at all. Later on the Emperor called the Chief Commissar and insisted that the Grand Duchesses should be supplied with beds, and about a week later they brought them in. Practically all the time the Emperor was there they tried to persuade him to sign the Peace Treaty, but they did not succeed. Then they said: 'It is enough.' The Czechs came and the Russian White Guards were streaming on Ekaterinburg, and they had to look after themselves. It meant either making the Emperor break or killing him, and they decided on the latter course. That is the reason they were at Ekaterinburg. The murdering took place about the 16th or 17th night of July, about eight o'clock in the morning, when they were all in bed, they came to them and said that it was necessary that the whole family should go downstairs and the White Guards were waiting in the town and it was dangerous for them to stay where they were. The Emperor asked if it was necessary to take their things downstairs. I think it was Crevsky who said: 'No it is not necessary, but you can take your cushions if you like. It would be just as well.' So, as far as I remember the Grand Duchesses took their cushions and they carried the small Grand Chair (the Tsarevich) downstairs. The Grand Duchess Tatiana took a little Pekinese dog with her. (The body I saw later). The maid also came down, and they brought in Dr Botkin and the cook. Altogether I think there were eleven people, including the Imperial family, ordered downstairs. They all had to dress in a hurry and go downstairs. I cannot remember what dress the Empress had on, but it is all written down in the papers that General Bietriona had. When they had them downstairs they started the shouting. Crevsky, the Jew, who has a chemists shop in Ekaterinburg, read the Order of the Republic of the soldiers and workmen of Russia that the Emperor and all his family were condemned to death. The Emperor walked forward, as far as I remember in the papers, and tried to say something. What he meant to say was: 'If you want to shoot me you can do so, but you must not touch my family.' But they did not give him time actually to finish the sentence, they shot him through his throat. He fell dead on the spot, there were about ten soldiers in the room. They came in and blocked the passage. The size of the room where the murdering took place was, I should say, 18ft x 15ft. I have the plans of the place, which I will let you see. In any case, they were shot against the wall and the soldiers guarded the entrance. Then they shot the Tsarevich and the Empress. It is proved that the Empress did not move. She stood absolutely calmly. Then the Grand Duchesses were shot. One of the Grand Duchesses – Tatiana, I think – was only wounded. The poor girl fell down and naturally fainted, and when she recovered they bayoneted her. I found on the floor eighteen bayonet thrusts that had gone through her body. General Dietriche later on cut out a piece of the floor and all the walls were cut out, and the pictures, so we have them all. Probably there was a certain amount of fighting in the room because when I looked up at the walls I found bullet marks all over the place. Some bullets had apparently passed through the ceiling, wall, door and hit the wall in the other room. It looked as if somebody had tried to defend themselves, and later it was proved that the maid tried to fight the Bolsheviks with a pillow, which probably hit the rifles when they were shooting, so some of the bullets went all round the room. But, anyway, she was shot, as was also Dr Botkin and the rest. It was simply a massacre. Almost immediately after the murder – the same night – they sent for some lorries. They came and the bodies were put in sort of white blankets, carried through a small door and put in the lorries, which went off to the Isetsky factory. I have the plans of the place. The little dog that I mentioned, which the Grand Duchess took with her in the room, was killed, no doubt by a hit on the head with something. The body of that dog was also thrown in the lorry and it went off to the same place. I forgot to say that the little boy who helped the cook was let free. He was only about thirteen years old. They did not kill him, they let him out of the house before the murder.

As I was saying, they sent these bodies to the factory. There they took off the bodies from the lorries and put them on carts. They crossed the railway about three miles from that factory and took them straight to the forest. It is about 14 miles altogether from the town. I have the place indicated on my map. I went on horseback with other British officers to see the place later on. It was about a year after my first visit, and nothing had been touched. Of course, General Dietriche had started the work of finding out the details in the mine. We went by exactly the same road that had taken the bodies of the Emperor and his family. When we came to the place in the forest where they are supposed to have buried the bodies, we found it a most extraordinary place. It was full of disused mine shafts, and there is no doubt that they used these mines during the process of burning the bodies. In fact, it was proved later on that they threw all the stuff that they did not need in connection with the burning into the mines. We found the stuff later on. Well, when they brought the bodies here they started a big fire first of all and then they brought a certain strong stuff that burns everything, and the first thing they did was to burn the bodies with this stuff, then they threw the bodies in the fire. What they did during three days and nights there I cannot say but no doubt they were all the time burning the bodies. In the forest there was one finger, which is kept in spirit, false teeth that belonged to Dr Botkin and other small details, such as pieces of dress that the Empress probably had – petticoats, the irons of the corsets that did not burn, a big diamond belonging to the Empress, a certain amount of brooches and pearls. They were found in the ashes of the fire, of course the diamonds etc. did not burn. The Empress had sewn all her jewellery under her clothes. They stole a tremendous amount of things but these they did not find. We do not know whose finger it was, I think it must belong to the Empress. It is very difficult to tell because it is so very swollen.

They probably wanted to take off the ring, and so the fingers were so swollen and they could not get it off, they cut off the finger. It was lying in the ashes as were the false teeth. After the burning, they threw all the remains in a coal mine that was covered with water – a flooded mine – and no one knew anything about it till a year later. Of course they tried to destroy and hide everything. They threw all the ashes away so that we could see a large area covered with ashes when we got there. I forgot to say one thing, in the ashes we found pieces of bones, but it could not be definitely said at the time that these belonged to a human being. They may have belonged to a rabbit. They were very small and all burnt. It may have been that they were burned by that stuff. Maybe these people were very hungry and they may have shot them and ate them and threw the bones there, but it was established later that these bones really belonged to human beings. They also found, when they examined the earth there, a certain amount of human fat, which all goes to prove that the bodies were burnt there. When they had finished with all that burning they left the place, and said that if anyone went near there they would be shot, but the peasants were very curious, and they went there, and the Russian officers that were in Ekaterinburg also went to see the place, and they found these things – diamonds, brooches, etc. Later on in the forest was found the body of the sailor who looked after the Tsarevich. He had been shot through the head later on, and his body was found in another part of the forest. About a week or two after that – I do not exactly remember the date – the Prince Bolgoroski was shot, the General that remained with the Emperor, the court petitioner and the countess Gendrikoff, who was waiting on the Empress. They took her away and shot her. I saw one of the servants of the Emperor later on. He ran away when he heard the shots in the house. He was serving with the high Commissioner in Siberia, Sir Charles Elliott, as far as I remember. He says that the Imperial family had a rotten time the last two weeks. The Emperor was treated very badly in the house. They have proof of it. During the dinner these Bolsheviks would come into the room and eat from the Empress's plate, they put their fingers in and would say, there is too much there for you. They used to tell horrible stories during meal times. In fact, they insulted them all the time. The real persecution of the family began a fortnight before the murders and continued getting worse and worse, during the last week. It must be remembered that the guards were very often drunk. One thing is certain – whenever the Empress or her daughters had occasion to go to the lavatory they were followed by two or more red guards, who used to stand over them all the time, loading their rifles. General Dietrichs said that he was satisfied that there was no outrage, but I wish I could say the same. I saw in the room in which the murders took place obscene drawings with inscriptions, partly obliterated since, but clear enough to read. There were horrible pictures of Rasputin and the Empress and inscriptions boasting of outrage, and the shrieks that were heard at night tend to confirm this. Anything more horrible than the last week of the family cannot be imagined. The Emperor used to send for a priest. I met the priest and spoke with him. It was very difficult to speak to him as he was overcome every time he mentioned it. I know myself what he must have felt. He was absolutely horrified at what he had seen in the house. He had hysterics every time he spoke of it. He was a very good fellow. I eventually forced him to speak. He said that the Empress always looked very calm. As far as he could notice, they all prayed very hard. The Emperor changed tremendously. Each time he went to service he was thinner. He had a long beard and his face was, the priest said, changed to such an extent that he looked like a man who had just had a very bad illness. The Tsarevich could not stand. He was sitting all the time and looked very bad. The priest said that he looked like a child that could not possibly live long. The commissars told the priest that if ever he tried to talk to the Emperor or make any sign or movement, he would be shot along with the whole family. So the poor man conducted his services under the most trying circumstances, not knowing what would happen at any minute. And yet he went. The last prayers were said two days before the Emperor was murdered. Which was the last occasion on which the priest saw the family. Of course the Bolsheviks used to jeer at the services the whole time. They laughed at the Emperor and said, why do you want all this rubbish? God won't help you. They made fun of religion the whole time, but the Emperor took no notice. They also used to laugh at the priest after the services. When the priest had finished the last service, as he passed out the Grand Duchesses were standing near the door, they said thank you for the service. They were the last words he heard. Even for that he got into trouble. The commissar on duty said: 'Why did these people talk to you? They had no right.' The only thing they were allowed to have was a certain amount of milk from the monastery set far from the house. Through these nuns some of the officers had the chance of sending letters when the milk was brought, but there was never any answer. (Colonel Rodzianko knows the name of the monastery but for the sake of the nuns who are still alive and who would certainly be shot if this transpired, he does not wish to divulge it unless absolutely necessary). Of course they were allowed no baths, and they had no privacy at all. They suffered tremendously. It was very hot during July, and sometimes they would ask for water and were brought dirty water. They were not even allowed privacy in their bedrooms. The guards would come in at any moment. They would come in several times during the night. It was practically impossible for the family to sleep. The man who was actually in charge of them was this Jew, Yurovsky. He was a local chemist. That was how it was easy for him to get the stuff to burn the bodies. I am convinced that the custody of the Imperial Family was given to him by the Moscow government. He is alive still and is probably in Ekaterinburg now. Captain McCullagh, who was captured by the Bolsheviks but being a correspondent, not touched, went to see him quite lately and said that he was dying from heart disease.

Two days after the murder of the Imperial family they murdered the Grand Dukes, then after that they murdered the Grand Duke Michael in Perm, and a week after that they murdered the Countess Gendrikoff, also in Perm, and all the other people, and two weeks after that Prince Dolgourouki and Count Taticheff were murdered. So it stands to reason that the government in Moscow knew perfectly well what was happening. They murdered the Grand Dukes in Alapaievsk, not far from Ekaterinburg, and later on they murdered the Grand Dukes in Petrograd. It is a lie when they say they knew nothing about it. They lie now because we have found out all the details. They thought we would never find that forest and never find the other things, but the hard work done by General Dietrichs a year after the murder had happened had the result of discovering all this. General Dietrichs named another man – a Mr Sokoloff, a very clever man who took the matter in hand and found out many things. The first thing he did was to go to the mine and take out all the water and all the mud from the bottom. He passed that mud through a very fine sieve and found pearls, a certain amount, I think, of diamonds, etc. All kinds of small decorations belonging to the Emperor were found in front of me. The dog also found them. They did not trouble to burn that. They just threw it down and it was there just as they had left it. We could see the hole in its head. The people that were living near the house during the night the Emperor was murdered heard all kinds of shooting and screaming. There is no doubt about it that they are all dead. The people around also heard screaming in the night during the fortnight before the murder. The house was surrounded by machine guns – they were on the roof, on the balcony and all round the place. It was surrounded outside by a very high wooden wall which had been built up on purpose.

When they murdered the Grand Dukes they simply came to the house and took them fourteen miles away and just threw them in the mine. They were lying there alive for about two hours. That was proved by the post mortem afterwards. It was about sixty foot deep. They were the Grand Duchess Elizabeth, the Grand Duke Serge and all the rest – they just threw them in. I have the photographs of the bodies.

I don't know if anything belonging the Tsarevich was found in the forest. There may have been something found when I was not there. In any case, it would be in the papers. I remember finding something belonging to the Emperor – a little flag of his regiment that he always wore. Of course it's important to establish the death of the Tsarevich. Already there have been claimants. The only things that were found in the place where the bodies were burned were things belonging to the Emperor, the Empress and the Grand Duchesses – a piece of the dress of the Empress and pieces of underclothing. The little boy who was assistant to the cook knew nothing. He was in the house, but they let him go, and he ran away. He did not know what happened. I am convinced that the men who did the shooting were not drunk. There were many German officers leading all the time. Their whole system was German. One of the terms of the Peace Treaty was that all the German officers should leave there. Officially they disappeared, but unofficially they were working hard there, and are still working there.

We left for Ekaterinburg to start this enquiry on the 16th October. General Knox knew that it would be of personal interest to the King. I asked permission to find out what I could and he gave me two days because we had to move on as the Bolsheviks were rather active on the Front, and General Knox had to go back to Omsk to form the new Russian army. During these two days I spoke with Mr Sergieff. He was the man that had taken the matter in his hands and had been trying to find out what happened to the Emperor's family. So I went to his place – it was at the Palace of Justice – and I insisted he should open the door of Ippatisvsky House, where the murdering had taken place. They did not allow anybody else in the house, but I told them that I was particularly anxious to find out what had happened, and after persuasion they opened the door. When I came into the room it struck me at once that the walls were covered with holes from the bullets. It was a room on the ground floor, about 18ft x 15ft, one wall in particular was absolutely covered with these holes. Mr Sergieff, as I have said, had been investigating the murder but had not been very successful. He started about two or three weeks after the murder had happened. He only went by what he found in the room, although he said he had been all round the country to find out things. When I got there I was three months late. The room at the time of the murder happened was no doubt covered with blood – not the walls, but the floor. You could see that they had washed the floor with some sand taken out of the garden. I compared the sand in the room with the sand in the garden and found that it was the same. They must have washed the floor with it to take up all the blood. They did not want any evidence of the murder to be seen. Later on General Dietrichs ordered the floor to be pulled up. When they did so they found heaps of blood under the floor that had evidently soaked through. That in itself is evidence of the murder.

From the proofs that have been collected it is clear that the murder was done by order of the Central Government in Moscow – not by the local Government. They are telling lies when they say they executed a man for having killed the Tsar. Five of the men who did the shooting were caught and shot. They behaved idiotically with them. Directly they caught a Bolshevik that had been connected with the murder they shot him on the spot. These five men who were caught signed statements containing more or less the information I have give you. I have read these papers. Yurovsky was the man who fired the first shot, I know. Many things were found in the house that had been looted – things that belonged to the Emperor and all the family. There were the private images that belonged to the Emperor and Empress, the diamonds and the Ikons. They were very old ones that were given by his father and grandfather. They were surrounded by diamonds and rubies. The stones had disappeared, but the Ikons were found. All these things were found in a hole in the yard where they threw all the rubbish. In the chimney was found the hair of the Grand Duchesses, which the Empress had cut off just before they were murdered. They had beautiful hair. Also part of the beard of the Emperor was found in the chimney. It has all been kept. General Dietrichs has it. General Dietrichs has all the papers, the statements, and everything in connection with the murder. If you could get into communication with him you could perhaps get copies.

All the time I was there the Bolsheviks tried to pull my leg. In order to prove that the Emperor was not killed by them. On one occasion a man came in and said: 'I think I have found the body of the Emperor. The night of the 16th or 17th we saw many bodies of people that were shot on a certain station, and I recognized the face of the Emperor and his son and I have buried him and I know the place where he is buried. If you can go there you will find his body.' Naturally I dashed to the place. When I got there I found a place absolutely covered with crosses. I thought: 'Is it possible that all these have been murdered?' Anyhow I had three coffins out. I had taken the doctor of the Emperor with me – Dr Derevenko. I looked at one body and I thought that it really was the body of the Emperor. They were very decomposed, but had a certain amount of hair left. We could find out by the teeth and the wound on the Tsar's head. We discovered that it was not the body of the Emperor. Then we found a smaller body. I had to take out about six coffins before I found it. It was the body of a young boy who had been shot in the chest. It was very difficult at first to tell whether it was a girl or a boy, as it was so decomposed, but I thought his foot looked rather the foot of a distinguished person, and the toe was not that of a peasant. It was too small. I asked the doctor and he said: 'I can assure you it is not the little Grand Duke. I know the teeth of the Grand Duke well. It is not he.' I buried them again.

I have with me a dog that belonged to the little Grand Duke. Of course, he is in quarantine now. He was in the house of Ekaterinburg, but was so terrified at the noises on the night of the murder that he escaped when the door was open, and after that they left him alone.

The Murders of the Grand Dukes and Grand Duchess Elizabeth
Colonel Rodzianko stated as follows:

When the Tsar arrived at Ekaterinburg, the Grand Dukes John Constantinovich, Serge Constantinovich and Constantin were there, but in order to make room for the Imperial Family they were removed to Alapalsvsk a week later. They were lodged in a deserted school (photograph attached) without any furniture and had to sleep on the school forms. After a day or two of demonstrations, beds were furnished to them by the population of Alapalsvsk. The Grand Dukes gave their word of honour that they would not try to escape from Russia, the Bolsheviks having told them that if they attempted to do so the Emperor would be murdered at once. So although they had many opportunities of escaping, they remained in Alapalsvsk. The day after the massacre of the Imperial family the Bolsheviks came late to the house where they were and said to them: 'You are to be transferred to another place, so have your dinner now.' It was then only six o'clock and they usually had their dinner at half past seven. As they had a certain amounted of luggage with them they asked about it and were told that they must not take it with them as it would be sent on later, but that they could take a certain amount of things in their pockets if they wanted to.

After their meal they were taken outside, put into carts that were waiting and driven about fourteen miles from the place. Then the carts were stopped and they were made to walk altogether surrounded by the Bolsheviks. Meanwhile, the Bolsheviks circulated the rumour that the Grand Dukes had escaped. To make this appear true they started firing and throwing bombs into the house (it will be noticed on the photograph attached that the windows are all broken and the state of the house looks as if some fighting has taken place there). The population believed this, so for a month or two no one knew what had happened to the family. Even the carts were stopped at a place near where there were coal-mining shafts and the family were ordered to walk, they began to understand that something was going to happen to them, so as they all walked on together they sang religious hymns, while the Bolsheviks laughed at them. The Grand Duchess Elizabeth, who was a nun, and who had previously lived in a monastery, was dressed in nun's clothes. She was one of the first to be thrown in the mine. She asked only one thing – that they should wrap her head in something (it will be noticed on the photograph attached that her body was found with something wrapped round her head). The other Grand Dukes were thrown after her. The Grand Duke Serge wanted them to shoot him before throwing him down the mine, they did not want to do that, so he started fighting with them. As a matter of fact, in the end they did shoot him through the head before throwing him down the mine. When they had thrown them all into the mine they threw down hand grenades, big pieces of wood – props and stones, and then they left the place. When the bodies were found it was proved by the medical inspection that some of them had lived two hours at least, because the food they had eaten before leaving the house had been digested about six hours, and they were thrown into the mine about nine o'clock. There is another proof that they did not die at once, in the photograph of the Grand Duke John it will be noticed that he has his fingers crossed as though he were making the sign of the cross. His body was found with his hand on his forehead, he had probably tried to do his last prayers before dying. The depth of the mine was about 60 feet, and on the bottom was a certain amount of water. The bodies were in an awful state. They were covered with bruises and many of them had wounds on the head. Some of the arms and legs were broken, and it was obvious that they had suffered tremendously before dying. With the exception of the Grand Duke Serge, they were all – the Grand Dukes, the Grand Duchess Elizabeth, her lady in waiting and Count Faley – thrown into the mine alive. The servant of the Grand Duke Serge, though he fell to the bottom of the mine, was found in a tunnel about 15 feet from the shaft. Judging by the position of his muscles and hands, he must have crawled there.

They had apparently not been robbed of anything. The things they had on them when they left the house were found on their bodies. A certain amount of money, letters, cigarette cases and all kinds of small things were found. What happened to the rest of the things I do not know, but I myself saw the clothes and things they had on them, and they were absolutely intact. I remember a wooden cross that was found of the Grand Duchess Elizabeth, which she always wore. I also saw a letter written by the Grand Duke John to his wife, the daughter of the King of Serbia, begging her to save herself and the children and not to worry about him as if he were killed it would be the will of God. He asked her to take great care of the children. I think she is safe now in Serbia. I do not know whether she ever actually received the letter. It was found in the pocket of the Grand Duke's clothes. All the things that were found on the bodies are now in the possession of General Dietrichs, who is in Ghita, Siberia.

When the bodies were discovered, the Countess Tolstoy, who came through the Bolshevik line especially to the help the Grand Duchess Elizabeth, went to the place herself with the people who were engaged in taking up the bodies, and brought coffins with her.

Captain McCullagh's Report on the Ipatiev House (From His Private Papers)

A steep flight of steps descended into the cellar from the dining room. The cellar is now used as a Bolshevik club, and the entrance to it is from Post No. 4. Over this entrance is a large Bolshevik signboard giving the name of the club, but containing no reference to the murder, which the Reds seem anxious to forget. The only reference to it in Ekaterinburg is contained in the name of the square, which I have already given.

When the ex-Emperor was first brought to Ekaterinburg, Ippatievsky House was surrounded by the Bolsheviks with a high wooden fence to prevent the inmates from looking out and outsiders from looking in. All that the Tsar could see from his window was the cross on the lofty dome of the church opposite, and, beyond that, the sky – a symbolism that probably did not escape that superstitious mind, ever on the lookout for omens. But, to such as cared to look, there were plenty of omens. From the roof of the church, for example, several Bolshevik machine-guns were permanently pointed at the Tsar's place of internment. The little stone shrine in the street outside the bedroom of the Emperor was dedicated to his patron Saint, St. Nicholas. Lastly, the name of the house, Ippatievsky, was the same as the name of the monastery where the boyars had elected Michael, the first of the Romanovs, to rule over Muscovy.

On the south side of the house is a short street, Ascension Lane, leading down to the lake; and on the other side of the street from Ippatievsky, is another house, which was used as a barrack for the thirty-six soldiers who guarded the Tsar. In this house there also lived one civilian Bolshevik who, in accordance with the loose military system that prevailed among the Reds at this time, commanded those soldiers with the title of Sergeant of the Guard, though not himself in the Red Army. Which he joined, however, after the murders. His name was Paul Metvietev, and he had formerly been a workman in the Sysertsk factory. Metvietev, with whom I afterwards travelled from Ekaterinburg to Moscow, was the right-hand man of Yurovsky, a shopkeeper and civilian, who was 'commandant' of Ippatievsky House and, as such, responsible for the 'safety' of the Tsar, whom he ultimately murdered with his own hand. The evidence against him is overwhelming and conclusive. Not only did all the trustworthy testimony collected by Admiral Kolchak's Government indicate that it was Yurovsky personally who had fired the fatal shot, but all the Bolsheviks whom I consulted on the subject, while I was living last March in Red Ekaterinburg, unanimously pointed him out to me as the Tsar's murderer. I had, by the way, a strange and terrible interview with him, which I will describe later.

On the north side of Ippatievsky House a large wooden gate leads into an ample courtyard. The front door, which faced east, was known by the Bolsheviks as Post No. 1, and was always guarded by some of the Lett soldiers who lived in the house. Post No. 2, on the balcony, was also guarded by Letts, but how verses in Russian came to be written on the wall there I cannot explain except on the supposition that Russian soldiers went there also. Post Nos 3 and 4 were guarded only by Russian soldiers from the house opposite. Post No. 3 opened into the yard, and was the door through which the dead bodies were carried into the yard after the massacre. Post No. 4 was the name given to the side entrance from Ascension Lane.

The house looked fairly large from the outside, but really contained, on the first floor at least, only four or five living rooms reached by six stone steps at the end of vestibule. There was a balcony at the back of the house, but the Imperial party were not allowed to use it. Several soldiers were always there, and it is probably to them that we owe the lascivious verses and pornographic drawings, which still adorn the balcony.

A large room near the entrance was occupied by Yurovsky, who slept there every night, though he had elsewhere in the town a shop and a house of his own, where he lived with his mother, his wife, one son and one daughter. A small room at the south-east corner was assigned to the Tsar, the Tsarina, and the Tsarevich, who slept in three beds, which were as many as the room could hold. The one door in this room led into the bedroom occupied by the four Grand Duchesses and their maid Demedova. Dr. Botkin, the medical attendant of the Imperial party, and the other members of Nicolas the Second's sadly diminished suite, slept with the guards in another room, so that the Tsar and his family had only two small rooms to themselves, and the use, in the daytime, of the dining-room and of a drawing-room which was used on Sundays as a chapel. Guards, all of them Lettish, slept in the room next to the dining room, and no Russian slept in the house, Yurovsky being a Jew. The thirty-six soldiers who were quartered in the house on the other side of Ascension Lane were not forbidden to enter Ippatievsky Dom, and they frequently passed through the dining-room; while the Commissars and the Lettish soldiers were in the habit of entering the bedrooms of the Imperial family as often as they liked, day or night. This privilege they exercised very frequently during the week before the murder, so that the prisoners got very little sleep. The girls were sometimes heard to scream at night, but there is no evidence that any assault was ever committed on them, and the most likely explanation of their screams is that they woke up at night frightened at finding somebody in their bedroom. The back room, which was used as a dining-room by the prisoners, was always rather dark, as it opened on to a covered balcony.

Mr. Thomas, who was with the British Consul, Mr. Preston, in Ekaterinburg when the tragedy occurred, told me that as the Czechs drew nearer in July, the alarm of Bolsheviks grew greater, though they tried to reassure the people by printing proclamations to the effect that they would never leave the town, and by shooting men who remarked casually in the street and elsewhere that they probably would leave, since they were certainly sending away trainload after trainload of gold and platinum.

Meanwhile the very air around the sunken house became heavy with a sense of impending tragedy. According to all the neighbours this feeling reached its climax on the night of 16 July 1918, the night of the murder. Although all traffic on the streets was not stopped till midnight, the obvious nervousness of the sentries and the fact that machine-guns were being placed all around the villa as well as on the roof and on the balcony drove most people indoors, where they cowered till daybreak. All of them heard firing inside the house during the night, and some of them heard screams as well. Late in the evening, as Mr. Thomas passed Ippatievsky on the way to the Consulate, which is only three hundred yards further on, he was ordered by a sentry, who seemed to be labouring under some emotion, to walk on the other side of the street, and was nearly shot because he did not obey the order quickly enough. This excitement of the guard was in strong contrast to the absence of all military precautions at the same point next day and to the deserted appearance of the house, but the reason for this change was soon apparent.

The Reds had been in the habit, at this crisis in their history, of keeping up their courage by holding Communist Revival meetings, as I may call them, in the great municipal theatre; and on 19 July Goloshokin, the leading Commissar of the town, was the principal speaker. He did not conceal the gravity of the situation. 'The Czechs,' he said, 'those hirelings of French and British capitalists, are close at hand. The old Tsarist Generals are with them; the Cossacks also are coming; and they all think that they will get back their Tsar again. But they never shall.'

He pronounced these last words slowly and solemnly, and then paused for a moment while a deep hush fell on the audience. Mastering himself by a strong effort, the orator then shouted out at the top of his voice those terrible and historic words: 'We shot him last night.' This was the first public and official announcement of the fact Nicolas Romanov, the last Tsar of Russia, had ceased to exist, but its effect on his audience was so different from what Goloshokin had expected that he quickly added: 'And we have sent his wife and family to a place of safety.' Taking their cue from Goloshokin many of the Bolsheviks then circulated reports of the Tsar and all of his family having been sent to Perm, with the result that many simple people were deceived, and that, until quite recently, some of the relatives of the Tsar refused to believe that he was dead.

Captain McCullagh's Report on His Meeting With Yurovsky (From His Private Papers)

McCullagh's report begins when he arrives at Yurovsky's front door, which was opened by the cook:

When the cook returned, her face was still gloomier than before, as if she had been communing with some dark spirit, and she asked me sharply and with the air of one repeating a lesson learnt by heart, what precisely was the business I wanted to discuss with her master, what was my name, and who had sent me. Recollecting an official report on his life insurance activity for the previous six months that Yurovsky had published in that morning's paper, I replied that I was a journalist, and wanted to speak to Comrade Yurovsky on the subject of life insurance. I also mentioned the name of a powerful Bolshevik who had given me permission to say that he had sent me, though he had refused emphatically to accompany me, and I gave of course my own name and some particulars about myself. When she left again, still unmollified and once more glancing at me darkly over her shoulder, it suddenly struck me that the regicide might see something sarcastic in a request to be consulted about life insurance; but luckily was not so, for the cook soon returned with a smiling face and invited me to 'Step this way, please.'

It was with a certain amount of constriction of the heart that I accepted her invitation and walked into the passage, making no noise in my Canadian felt boots. The passage was long and dark, but led into a well-lighted room, and in that room at the end of the passage a man stood, slightly bent and in a suspicious and expectant attitude. From his photographs I at once saw that it was Yurovsky the Tsaricide. It was in exactly the same attitude that this terrible monster had waited outside the door of the Tsar's bedroom at one o'clock on the night of 16–17 July 1918.

I knew beforehand that he was a man of about forty years of age, but as I came nearer I saw that he was grayish, wrinkled, and looking much older. He wore an unkempt, grayish moustache and uncombed brown hair, and from the stubble on his cheeks and chin I saw that he had not shaved for some days. His face was sallow, square, and not distinctively Jewish. His eyes were greenish in hue and filled with a hard look of distrust. He wore a great black fur coat or shuba which reached to the ground, and underneath it were pyjamas, for apparently he had not dressed. On his feet he wore cloth slippers, and his whole appearance gave me the impression that he had been asleep when I knocked: for perhaps, like Cromwell, he does not sleep well o' nights. I tried to overcome a strong feeling of repugnance which suddenly swept over me as I reached out my hand and clasped the limp, clammy, and a rather unwilling hand which hung by his side, the hand which had murdered the Tsar.

I introduced myself and began to speak with rather hectic haste about his report, trying at the same time to convey the impression that I took a deep and expert interest in life insurance – a subject of which, by the way, I know absolutely nothing. About some obscure points in his report I was extremely anxious, I said, to get further information. For about two minutes he continued to stand and did not invite me to sit down. But gradually his distrust began to diminish, though it never quite disappeared throughout the course of our interview and flared up several times in an ominous manner. He talked to me about the Bolshevik whose name I had used as a talisman, said he knew him by sight, but complained somewhat wistfully that they had never spoken. Then he recollected that he had heard of me, and asked me to sit down.

He himself collapsed heavily into an armchair from which he had evidently risen when I was announced, and remained silent for a few seconds. Then he apologized for him costume; saying that he was ill, suffering from heart disease. I was going to ask him since when he had suffered from that complaint, but refrained in a sudden panic, just as the words were on the tip of my tongue, for I felt that it was probably since the night of 16 July. To judge from his face, he is not long for this world. He may be dead even now, and, if so, one of the last of the men who took a leading part in the murder of the Tsar and his family will have gone to render an account of his deeds. He told me that his former colleague Goloshokin, the Commissar who had signed the Tsar's death-warrant, had died of typhus in Samara on 7 March, and that, only a week ago, his own mother had died in the house where we were sitting. Sergiev, the war correspondent of the Pravda whom I have already mentioned, had shown me the photograph of this old lady, whose face looked like that of a prematurely aged young man, and had made my blood curdle by telling me how savagely proud this old Jewess had been of the fact that her son had now a secure place in the history of the world, and that the humble name Yurovsky will be till the end of time linked with the mighty name of Romanov. The Tsaricide spoke for a long time and with evident feeling about his mother, whose death seemed to have given him a great shock. He had left her behind in Ekaterinburg when he himself fled to Moscow, and the Whites when they came had arrested her; but, when they evacuated Ekaterinburg, they had forgotten to take her with them as she happened to by lying ill of typhus at the time in a local hospital. The disease to which she finally succumbed was also typhus, of which she had had a second attack.

Yurovsky then began to speak of the atrocities committed by the Whites throughout Ekaterinburg Government and in Perm. He was very vehement on this subject, and I know that there was truth in what he said. He told me incidentally that the first post he had held in Ekaterinburg when he returned to it was that of President of the Extraordinary Commission, and he said that in that capacity he had put to death sixty White suspects. 'What are sixty men?' he asked contemptuously, and this terrible question made me suddenly realise what I was beginning to forget, that I was in the lair of a human tiger, that I was face to face with a devil incarnate. I thought of a graveyard near Ekaterinburg where they are buried – most of them in their everyday clothes, some of them wrapped in blood-stained blankets, very few of them in coffins – hundreds of victims of the Bolsheviks, executed during the first half of 1918, and of the awful tales told by a family living in a lonely farmhouse close by. Every night after dark they used to hear the creak of cartwheels bearing a fresh burden of dead bodies, and this went on for hours; while many executions took place against the cemetery wall. On one occasion a man, thought to be dead, got up and staggered away in the early morning. He was a well-known inhabitant of the town and is still alive – but not in Ekaterinburg.

What monstrous children will grow up in the houses like these! I have seen Siberian infants playing among the naked, frozen corpses of Kolchak's soldiers, stripped by their comrades for the sake of their warm clothes. What a monstrous generation is growing up in Russia! How much has he to answer for who, without the most extreme necessity, kindles the fires of Revolution and Civil War!

I had not heard before that the regicide had been head of the Extraordinary Commission. He had, it appears, been too bloodthirsty in that capacity even for the Bolsheviks, and had been transferred, evidently by someone with a grim sense of humour, from the department of death insurance to the department of life insurance.

But though Yurovsky speaks lightly of large numbers done to death, he cannot bear to speak of the eleven deaths about which I was anxious to get details. He always referred to his Imperial victim as the 'Autocrat,' and a baleful light came into his eyes every time he used the word. But he has the same reluctance to speak of the murder in the cellar as a man suffering from partial insanity sometimes has to speak of his delusions. Approach the subject and he trembles with rage or horror or incipient insanity. As my own precarious position made it impossible for me to probe deeply into that festering mental wound, I got no information on the murder from him during the whole course of this strange interview. I got a great deal of information from him, however, about the life insurance system which the Bolsheviks have established, and which embraces Old Age Pensions, maternity benefits, workmen's compensation, and a number of allied subjects.

Among other things he talked about the maternity classes that had been started by him in the town, in order to teach intending mothers how to care for their children, and thus to reduce 'the high infant mortality'. When he used this phrase I started and looked at him. He looked at me and read my thoughts. Then he raised himself slowly to his feet and said that he would go into another room to get me some statistics which he had compiled. While he was gone I looked around me for the first time since I had entered the room, and saw that it was well and tastefully furnished. The house had belonged, in fact, to a wealthy Jewish newspaper proprietor whom I had known, and who, though he was a Social Revolutionist, had fled with Kolchak. It contained a large piano, open, and with some sheets of Russian music on the holder.

When he had shuffled back again he handed me some papers with his left hand and, as he did so, I noticed that he had lost the tips of three fingers. As if he again read my thoughts he at once held up his hand for my inspection, and explained rapidly that this mutilation was due to an accident which had happened to him while he was a subbotnik. Subbotniki, I should explain, are workmen who work on Saturday (Subbota) for the benefit of the Government: there is quite a large subbotnik movement in Russia. I said, 'Yes, yes,' without listening to a word that he was saying, and tried to look sympathetic, but my voice sounded hollow and unnatural and my face was strained. I looked up from his hand to his eyes, and he looked at me and saw that I knew all. The papers which he had given me seemed to vanish like things which one receives in a dream, and I probably left them behind... He told me that he was a Siberian, born in Tomsk, and that he had served his apprenticeship as a watchmaker. He is an intelligent man, has studied Bolshevik ' literature' a good deal, and evidently peruses the Bolshevik newspapers very carefully. He looks at foreign politics from the extreme Bolshevik point of view, and cannot understand how the workmen of England allow themselves to be duped and exploited by the bourgeoisie. He has only contempt for what he considers to be the extreme moderation and self restraint of men like Mr Ramsey Macdonald and Mr J.R. Clynes. To him this moderation is only servility, and there is no salvation save in violence and terror, bloodshed and revolution. In short, he is the quintessence of Bolshevism, an infernal machine charged with diabolical forces of destruction; and his frightful theories were only rendered all the more frightful by reason of the contrast between their violence and his own physical weakness.

Press Conference at the Tass-Ural News Agency – 16 July 2008

THE ROMANOVS MURDER:
INVESTIGATION & IDENTIFICATION

Vladimir Solovyev: Major identification tests of the remains discovered near Ekaterinburg on 29 July 2007 are over. It was extremely hard work. We didn't hope for success as the remains represented the tiniest fragments of bone tissue that had been burnt, bore traces of acid exposure and damage that appeared to have been made by bullets. Now we can say for sure that the recovered remains belong to the Crown Prince Alexei and Grand Duchess Maria.

The identification testing was conducted jointly with experienced experts from the Sverdlovsk Forensic Bureau. First of all, we needed to conduct DNA identification tests. Among those who performed the DNA testing was the outstanding Russian DNA expert Evgeny Ivanovich Rogaev, professor of several universities, a specialist in mammoth genotype reconstruction. Another scientist involved in this project was Michael Coble, Director of a Pentagon laboratory for identification of unidentified bodies. This laboratory identifies remains of dead military personnel. The third laboratory dealing with DNA identification studies is led by Walther Parson from Innsbruck, Austria. There are only ten licensed laboratories in the world that have high credibility rating. So we trust their conclusions. The DNA identification tests have also been conducted by experts from the Sverdlovsk Forensic Bureau, and this work still goes on. This is the best laboratory in Russia to perform DNA identification tests. Its equipment complies with international standards, while the laboratory's experts are on exchange programs in the US and Austria.

For the purpose of exploring documentary evidence, we commissioned historical and archival research, led by Sergei Mironenko, Director of Russian State Archive. By now, we have a complete collection of the Sokolov papers. We also studied the transcript of Yurovsky's speech before Bolshevik veterans. The handwriting analysis showed that the editing was done by Yurovsky himself.

A very interesting ballistic test was conducted by Russian Interior Ministry forensic experts. While investigating the murder of the Romanovs, Sokolov had found a great number of bullets and shells in the Chetyrekbratsky mine (better known as the Ganin Pit). The ballistic experts compared the bullets and shells with those discovered in 1991. The tests showed that the bullets from 1991 burial site not only perfectly matched each other but had been fired from the same barrels. The test was done with two sample guns; a Nagant and a Browning. It has proved a connection between the Ganin Pit and the gully where the remains were found.

One of the DNA identification tests is called paternity testing; its results are internationally recognized. Our experts have improved this testing by employing their own know-how methods. Its results will be argued, of course. At this stage, we shall draw on leading international experts, and the more errors they find, the better it will be for us. There are new identification methods that need to pass evaluation tests before being put into practice.

In conclusion, I want to say that several independent expert teams did a complete anthropological analysis of the remains. They were followed by three independent DNA tests of the remains found in 1991 and those discovered in 2007. The results of those tests were conclusive. In addition, ballistic and handwriting examinations were performed. Their results clearly indicate that the discovered remains belong to Nicolas II's children, Alexei and Maria. But the research hasn't finished yet.

Nikolai Nevolin: As for the tests done by Lev Zhivotovsky and Tatsuo Nagai, I can say that no respectable laboratory will ever test biological samples whose origin was not identified or established, because it can undermine its reputation. All samples of bone tissues sent to US Armed Forces DNA identification Laboratory and Innsbruck Forensic Institute were testified by accompanying documents and went through customs control with all formalities observed.

In 2007 we examined 44 bone fragments, some of which were very tiny. They can be classified into three groups. The first group includes bone fragments by which we could determine the sex, the second group includes the fragments by which we established the age, while the third group represented the bone fragments that were totally unfit for sex and age-based DNA analysis. Many bones had traces of high temperature exposure and heat. An anthropological study found the presence of two human remains in the grave, one belonging to a female aged 17–19, and another, whose sex was impossible to determine, of 12–14 years old. The age was determined through the discovery of tooth anlage. During permanent development, teeth erupt into the mouth with age. Before that they remain in the anlage. Dental examination of a teenager aged 12–14 found a rare structure of two teeth, one of which had an anomaly – a loop-shaped curve of the second groove of the dental crowns' chewing surfaces. The same loop-shaped curve of chewing surfaces of the crowns was found in all female remains discovered in the first grave.

Inside the teeth we found amalgam fillings containing 47% mercury, 38% silver, 0.6% cuprum and 0.06% tin. The same proportion of metals in silver amalgam fillings was found in the teeth of the human remains found in the first grave. Based on the teeth structure, we established that they were permanent teeth belonging to two humans of Europoid race.

Next we began a genetic examination. Male sex is determined by the presence in the genome of two different sex chromosomes, X and Y, while female sex is determined by X chromosomes. Sex is determined by the same zone that corresponds to amelogenin. As the remains were severely damaged, we employed spectral and fluorescent methods. They allowed us to identify micro elementary composition of all tiny bone fragments. As a result, all bone fragments were broken down into two groups by their micro elementary composition. Other groups were not identified, which led our experts to conclude that the graves contained the remains of two humans: a female aged 17–19 and a male aged 12–14.

We also re-examined the samples found in 1991. The DNA chain is very long and its regions can be compared. While in the 1990s an examination at only six loci was possible, contemporary methods allow testing at as many as seventeen loci. The tests identified both nuclear DNA and mitochondrial DNA. Let me explain what nucDNA testing is. DNA is inherited from parents in the 50:50 ratio. If we examine the first generation, nucDNA testing can easily determine child's kinship to his or her relatives. If this chain is traced over two generations, DNA would be passed down to children by 25%, not 50%. Here we say about the fourth or fifth generation. NucDNA was tested at seventeen loci. Each one has its own name and represents a specific sequence of alternate combination of tetra nucleotide repeats. Depending on how many of them are found in each locus their quantity is determined. In our case, the father has 7, 9 and 3, while the mother has 8 and 8. The DNA testing of the remains discovered in the first grave found that Olga has alleles 8, 9 and 3 (allele 8 was inherited from the mother, while alleles 9 and 3 were passed down from her father); Tatiana possesses allele 7 carried from her father and allele 8 inherited from the mother, Anastasia has allele 8 inherited from the mother and alleles 9 and 3 carried from the father. In the second grave containing female remains, alleles at the Tn locus were found to be 7 and 8, while in the male remains alleles were found to be 8, 9 and 3. Such matches were found at all loci examined. If there is just one mismatch at two loci, those people can't be relatives.

The DNA testing clearly indicates that the bone fragments discovered in the first and the second graves belong to relatives. The human remains of a male aged 50 belong to the father, while the remains of a female aged 40–48 were identified as the mother's. Apart from the two bodies, the graves also contained the remains of three daughters. In the second grave we discovered a daughter and a son. This conclusion was made based on DNA tests.

All human mitochondrias have their own DNAs, but they are inherited exclusively from the mother. There are no paternal mitochondrias. The examination of mitochondrias was conducted for two lines, one of which was Nicolas II's maternal lineage. We did a test and all the sequences matched but one. The results raised doubts that the remains didn't belong to the Tsar. So we made a decision to uncover the grave of George, Nicolas's brother. The testing of biological material revealed that heteroplasm found in the remains of Nicholas II matched those of George. It was inherited from the mother. All five children had the same mitochondrial DNAs as those found in the female from the first grave.

Next we compared the remains with the sample of Prince Philip's blood. Their mitochondrial DNAs were inherited from Princess Alice, daughter of Queen Victoria. They proved to be the same.

It may be concluded that the first and the second burial pits contain a family group of mother, father and their five children – four daughters and one son. The mitochondrial DNA pattern of the children and the mother in the female's maternal lineage is the same as Prince Philip's.

Q: It is true that forensic tests have been financed from the local budget?

Nikolai Nevolin: In order to conduct tests of degraded DNA we needed additional equipment for our laboratory. The government of the Sverdlovsk region allocated funds for the acquisition of this equipment. Our laboratory helps law-enforcers solve crimes that couldn't be solved using old forensic methods.

Q: How serious is the historical analysis?

Vladimir Solovyev: The idea to conduct a historical analysis was once put forward by Academician Alexeev. The historical research is carried out by a panel of highly qualified historians and archivists. In the period 1991 to 1998 they checked all state Russian archives, as well as the archives of the Interior Ministry, KGB, Foreign Ministry, Ministry of Culture and foreign archives. The research has not been finished yet.

We were lucky. Some time ago, Sotheby's auctioned the Sokolov papers that had been passed on by the investigator to Count Orlov. As a result of long negotiations, the records were acquired by Hans Adam II, Prince of Lichtenstein, who passed them on to the State Archive of the Russian Federation. Among the Sokolov papers we found three inventory books and a book titles *Other Records* opening with an order on institution of criminal proceedings (the first documents were drawn by Namyotkin) and finishing with documents Sokolov had drawn in France. The inventories list all criminal records. By now, Russia has eight volumes of the criminal case including the most secret papers that Sokolov had entrusted with Count Orlov.

I examined other criminal cases Sokolov had conducted. It is worth noting that he hadn't faced a crime with so many victims involved. Murders of this kind were quite rare in those times. So Sokolov, for natural reasons, had no experience in solving crimes that contemporary investigators have today. If I had met with Sokolov, it would have taken us less time to ascertain the truth.

In the 1990s, methods of Y-chromosome examinations didn't exist. The point is that Y chromosome is inherited paternally over generations without any changes. It has also been tested at seventeen loci. It turned out that Y chromosome of the teenager aged 12–14 from the grave is the same as the one identified in his father – the male discovered in the first burial pit. The same Y chromosome was found in Andrei Andreevich Romanov's DNA pattern. The DNA test findings have led the experts to conclude that all the remains from both graves belong to the Russian Imperial family.

Apart from this evidence, the Hermitage Museum has a shirt with stains of blood originating from the wound that was inflicted on the Emperor in 1891. The blood's DNA pattern is supposed to match the DNA of skeleton No. 4. This will be a unique opportunity to conduct direct identification. The test also identified skeleton No. 2 from the first grave belonging to Evgeny Sergeevich Botkin. His relatives live abroad, so we can conduct a comparative DNA test.

Q: Is the Russian Orthodox Church ready to recognize the remains as belonging to the last Emperor's family?

Vladimir Solovyev: I don't know. I haven't heard any statements from them.

Q: Would you say the examination findings you have reported can be considered official?

Vladimir Solovyev: By now, we have an official conclusion made by acknowledged experts. If the results of our work are accepted, the next question to decide will be re-burial of the remains.

Q: Have the DNA tests found haemophilia in Alexei's remains?

Nikolai Nevolin: Tests for haemophilia are currently under way. This is a very complicated analysis as his DNA is degraded.

Q: When are you going to conduct a DNA test of blood stains on the shirt?

Vladimir Solovyev: We are planning to conduct this test this month. However, we anticipate certain problems may arise while conducting the analysis. The shirt could have been touched and cleaned. So we cannot guarantee positive results. If the shirt hasn't been dirtied by other inclusions, the result may prove positive. But we are committed to conducting comprehensive analysis.

Nikolai Nevolin: Extracting biological components from old blood stains is not an easy job. Normally, before beginning the extraction procedure, forensic experts cut the tissue into tiny pieces. In our case, this procedure is not allowed. We shall extract biological components directly from the blood stains.

Sources

Background

FO 371/2995	15 March 1917	Grand Dukes call on Tsar to grant reforms. (FO file 811/55582)

Abdication

FO 371/2995	15 March 1917	Tsar's train stopped. Duma's conditions for his abdication. (FO file 811/55576)
FO 371/2995	15 March 1917	Tsar's train stopped again, by troops demanding his resignation. (FO file 811/55824)
FO 371/2995	15 March 1917	Report of Tsar's abdication, and appointment of Grand Duke Michael as regent. (FO file 811/56408)
FO 371/2995	16 March 1917	Report that abdication decided by Executive Committee but not yet carried into effect. (FO file 811/56488)
FO 371/2995	17 March 1917	Report on the renunciation of the Tsarevich's right of succession. (FO file 811/57143)
FO 371/2995	17 March 1917	Report of Tsar's abdication in favour of Grand Duke Michael. (FO file 811/57147)
FO 371/2995	18 March 1917	Text of abdication. (FO file 811/57871)
FO 371/2995	18 March 1917	Report that Grand Duke Michael unwilling to accept throne unless elected. (FO file 811/57873-4)
FO 371/2998	19 March 1917	Sir George Buchanan's opinion on the succession question. (FO file 3743/58189)

| FO 371/2995 | 5 April 1917 | Report by Mr Walpole on the revolution, and on the Tsar's abdication. (FO file 811/71223) |
| FO 371/2998 | 5 April 1917 | Tsar's manifesto of abdication. Grand Duke Michael's manifesto of renunciation of throne. (FO file 3743/71222) |

Treatment & Whereabouts of Tsar & Imperial Family
from the February Revolution 1917–16 July 1918

FO 371/2995	16 March 1917	Report that Empress and her children in Alexander Palace under guard. (FO file 811/56426)
FO 371/2995	16 March 1917	Report suggesting whereabouts of Tsar unknown. (FO file 811/56484)
FO 800/205	19 March 1917	Telegram to the Tsar from the King expressing distress at the turn of events, and professing continued friendship. (FO file 53)
FO 371/2998	21 March 1917	Report of conversation with Dowager Empress about the Tsar's plans, and telegram stating that Tsar given permission to go to Tsarskoe Selo and then to Romanoff. (FO file 3743/59540)
FO 371/2998	21 March 1917	Report of possible arrest of Tsar. (FO file 3743/60126)
FO 371/2998	21 March 1917	Report that Tsar deprived of his liberty and placed under escort. (FO file 3743/60234)
FO 371/2998	24 March 1917	Note that Tsar at Headquarters Staff. (FO file 3743/62484)
FO 371/2995	24 March 1917	Assurances received as regards safety of Tsar. (FO file 811/62233)
FO 371/2998	25 March 1917	Assurance from Russian Minister for Foreign Affairs regarding the Tsar's safety. (FO file 3743/62969)
FO 371/2998	4 April 1917	Report of removal of Tsar from Tsarskoe Selo to villa at Peterhof. (FO file 3743/69859)

FO 371/2998	5 April 1917	Above report incorrect – Tsar still at Tsarskoe Selo. (FO file 3743/70713)
FO 800/205	9 April 1917	Report of conversation with Kerensky concerning delay of Tsar's departure from Russia pending examination of seized documents. (FO file 82)
FO 371/2996	19 April 1917	Report by Mr Lindley includes opinion on position of Imperial Family. (FO file 811/80675)
FO 371/2996	26 April 1917	Report by Mr Lindley that Imperial Family still at Tsarskoe Selo under guard. (FO file 811/85500)
FO 800/383	29 April 1917	Protest by the Royalist Club at the lack of government action to help the Tsar and Tsarina. (FO files 31–35)
FO 371/2977	10 Sept 1917	Report of removal of Imperial Family to Tobolsk from Tsarskoe Selo between 14 and 19 August. (FO file 811/176585)
FO 371/2977	27 Sept 1917	Report on the Imperial Family at Tobolsk: their suite and guard. (FO file 811/187501)
FO 371/3329	3 May 1918	Report of King's concern on hearing of conditions of Imperial Family at Tobolsk. (FO file 78031)
FO 371/3329	27 May 1918	Letter from Lady Milford Haven to Balfour concerning Empress Alexandra Feodorovna and report that Imperial Family moved to Ekaterinburg. (FO file 78031/93852)
FO 371/3325	13 Sept 1918	Report describing arrival of Tsar and daughter in Ekaterinburg. (FO file 53740/156685)

Possibility of Tsar & Family Travelling to England

FO 371/2995	18 March 1917	Report suggesting future of Tsar. (FO file 811/57927)
FO 371/2995	20 March 1917	Miliukhov's enquiry as to the possibility of the Tsar going to England. (FO file 811/58700)

FO 371/2998	21 March 1917	Telegram concerning the advisability of the removal of the Tsar from Russia, and the feasibility of him travelling to England. (FO file 3743/59540)
FO 371/2998	21 March 1917	Telegram conveying the King's offer of asylum to the Tsar. (FO file 3743/60234)
CAB 23/40(2)	22 March 1917	Minutes of War Cabinet decision to issue invitation to Tsar to come to England for the duration of the war. Item 5.
FO 371/3008	23 March 1917	Telegram concerning the provisional invitation to the Tsar to come to England. (FO file 61920/61920)
FO 371/2998	23 March 1917	Report concerning offer of asylum to Tsar. (FO file 3743/61184)
FO 371/2998	24 March 1917	Telegram concerning request to Russian government to give Tsar safe conduct to Port Romanoff for departure to England. (FO file 3743/62911)
FO 371/2998	26 March 1917	Report that King's telegram not delivered to Tsar through fear of misinterpretation. (FO file 3743/63163)
FO 371/2998	28 March 1917	Thanks conveyed from Russian Minister of Foreign Affairs at being asked to cancel King's telegram. (FO file 3743/65073)
FO 800/205	30 March 1917	Letter expressing the King's personal friendship for the Tsar, but doubting the advisability of the Imperial Family coming to England. (FO file 63)
FO 800/205	2 April 1917	History of proposal that Tsar come to England. (FO file 65)
FO 800/205	13 April 1917	Report that public opinion against Tsar coming to England, and against the King for supporting him. Suggests Tsar go elsewhere. (FO file 88)
FO 800/205	15 April 1917	Telegram expressing agreement with view that Tsar should not come to England if any danger of anti-monarchist movement. (FO file 90)
FO 800/205	17 April 1917	Letter stating that the King, while devoted to the Tsar, was now held to be anxious that the invitation not be taken up, due to public opinion. (FO file 73)

FO 800/205	22 April 1917	Letter expressing relief that British invitation dropped, and opinion that the Imperial Family would not be welcome in France because of the Tsarina's German birth and leanings. (FO file 89)
FO 800/205	23 April 1917	Suggestion that Tsar could go to France for duration of the war. (FO file 105)
FO 371/2998	28 April 1917	Parliamentary Question concerning the future domicile of the Tsar. (FO file 3743/86955)
FO 370/273	1928	Correspondence between the Foreign Office and Sir Alfred Knox MP, occasioned by the publication of Kerensky's view of the asylum question.

The Supposed Assassination of the Tsar

FO 371/3977A and FO 371/3977B		Parts 1 and 2 Reports on fate of Russian Imperial Family, with photographs. Includes a report by N. Sokolov in Russian with English translation received by the Foreign Office 1958 April from an official source.
FO 371/3339	16 July 1918	Copy of *Izvestia* reporting the decree approving the Tsar's execution and the decree confiscating Imperial property. In Russian. (FO file 141879/141879)
FO 371/3335	27 July 1918	Parliamentary Question as to whether government received any official information about the fate of the Tsar – reply in the negative. (FO file 128730/130817)
FO 371/3335	28 July 1918	Prince Max of Baden informs that Tsar shot on 16 July as a military execution. (FO file 128730/128731)
FO 371/3335	29 July 1918	Telegram reporting that Tsar shot on 16 July by order of Ekaterinburg Soviet, in view of his possible capture by Czechs. (FO file 128730/131060)
FO 371/3335	29 July 1918	Report from Danish minister at Petrograd suggesting responsibility and motivation for execution of Tsar. (FO file 128730/131067)

FO 371/3329	31 July 1918	Telegram concerning proposed negotiations by Spanish government for the release of Tsarina and daughters. (FO file 78031/132818)
FO 371/3335	10 August 1918	Enquiry by Russian chargé d'affaires about confirmation of death of Tsar – negative reply. (FO file 128730/138376)
WO 33/962	28 August 1918	GOC Archangel to Director of Military Intelligence, War Office reporting eye-witness account of perpetrators of shooting.
CAB 23/7	4 Sept 1918	Rumour that the family had been killed reached the Cabinet.
FO 371/3329	18 Sept 1918	Mr Preston's report on death of Tsar. (FO file 78031/158859)
FO 371/3329	30 Sept 1918	Report of Dowager Empress's refusal to believe Tsar dead. (FO file 78025/164848)
FO 371/3329	8 Oct 1918	(FO file 78031/168981)
FO 371/3335	16 Oct 1918	Out-of-date wireless report from Mr Preston on the shooting of the Tsar. (FO file 128730/173020)
FO 371/3329	25 Oct 1918	Reports on conflicting rumours about the Tsarina's assassination. (FO file 78031/178431)
FO 371/3330	2 Dec 1918	Report of opinion held by Ekataterinburg officials that Tsarina and children were murdered near there at the same time as Tsar. (FO file 86748/198075)
FO 538/1		Various Archives of the Allied High Commission at Vladivostock. Correspondence regarding the murder of the Tsar. Includes reports by Sir Charles Eliot, the Tsarevich's tutor Sydney Gibbes, Thomas Preston, and the investigators Sergeyev and Sokolov.

Aftermath of Alleged Assassination of Tsar
Rumours of Survival of Imperial Family

FO 371/3338	4 Aug 1918	Report that steps taken for removal of Imperial Family to Spain. (FO file 134862/134862)
FO 371/3325	29 Aug 1918	Report that Tsarina and children believed to be at Verkhotur in Urals, then held by Bolsheviks. (FO file 53740/148881)
FO 371/3335	13 Sept 1918	Report of rumour that Tsar still alive, at a monastery between Perm and Ekaterinburg. (FO file 128730/156419)
FO 371/3338	19 Sept 1918	Report on appearance of a number of 'doubles' of Tsar in Russia. (FO file 136965/159277)
FO 371/3335	11 Oct 1918	Report from Ekaterinburg on possibility of members of Imperial Family being still alive, a statement by the Bolsheviks being the only proof that Tsar was shot. (FO file 128730/170999)
FO 371/3335	29 Nov 1918	Report that Count Tatischeff was shot instead of Tsar. (FO file 128730/196849)

Memorial Services for the Tsar

FO 371/3335	24 July 1918	Enquiry as to whether the King should be represented at the memorial service in Paris. (FO file 128730/128730)
FO 371/3335	25 July 1918	Note that a Secretary to represent the British Embassy at memorial service in Paris. (FO file 128730/129426)
FO 371/3335	29 July 1918	Description of memorial service in Paris. (FO file 128730/131500)
FO 371/3335	5 Aug 1918	Description of Requiem service at Russian Church in Rome. (FO file 128730/135349)
FO 371/3335	6 Aug 1918	Description of memorial service for Tsar at The Hague. (FO file 128730/135797)
FO 371/3335	15 Aug 1918	Report of Requiem service in Stockholm. (FO file 128730/141152)

Miscellaneous Opinions Regarding the Affair

FO 371/3320	5 March 1918	Telegram giving French press comments on Sir G. Buchanan's tribute to Tsar. Refers to letter from Tsar to French President dated 13 May 1916 expressing determination to fight to the finish. (FO file 40433/40433)
FO 371/3320	7 March 1918	Extract of article in *Gaulois* of 3 March, giving text of Tsar's letter to M. Poincaré. (FO file 40433/42602)
FO 371/3320	9 March 1918	Question in French chamber respecting publication of letter from Tsar. (FO file 40433/43461)
FO 371/3320	19 March 1918	Parliamentary Question as to whether the British government were consulted about publication of the Tsar's letter. (FO file 40433/49901)
FO 371/3335	27 July 1918	Letter from Royal Martyr Church Union to Secretary of State for Foreign Affairs, expressing condemnation of shooting of Tsar. (FO file 128730/131020)
FO 371/3335	3 Aug 1918	Article from Vienna press placing responsibility for murder of Tsar with England. (FO file 128730/134358)
WO 32/5721	1919 and 1920	Letters to and from War Office concerning enquiry into the murder of the Tsar and other members of the Imperial Family, especially regarding allegations of Jewish complicity. Includes Report by Procurer of the High Court of Kazan, and report of Bolshevik trial of those accused of the murder.

Fate of Others Connected with the Imperial Family

FO 371/2998	23 March 1917	Report on difficulty of Grand Duke Nicholas retaining chief command of the Russian army. (FO file 3743/61190)
FO 371/3316	4 Feb 1918	Telegram enquiring as to welfare of the Grand Duchess Cyril. (FO file 22111/22111)
FO 371/3317	9 Feb 1918	Telegram reporting announcement of death of Grand Duke Nicholas Constantinovich. (FO file 24918/24918)

FO 371/3323	18 March 1918	Letter from Royal Martyrs Church Union enquiring as to circumstances of Dowager Empress. (FO file 49238/49238)
FO 371/3330	16 May 1918	Report that Grand Duchess Elizabeth Feodorovna, widow of Grand Duke Serge Alexandrovich, was removed from her nunnery and sent to Ekaterinburg. (FO file 86748/86748)
FO 371/3330	22 Oct 1918	Report to effect that Grand Duchess Elizabeth Feodorovna was taken to Alapaievsk in the Urals in May 1918, and interned together with four of the Grand Dukes. (FO file 86748/86748)
FO 371/3330	31 Oct 1918	Report of memorandum received from former tutor of Tsarevich stating that all those confined at Alapaievsk believed killed. (FO file 86748/180970)
FO 371/3330	5 Nov 1918	Message from consul at Ekaterinburg to effect that bodies of Grand Duchess Elizabeth and others found at Alapaievsk. Wife of Prince Johan believed to be at Perm. (FO file 86748/183677)
ADM 137/953	23 Nov 1918	Admiralty telegram number 747 describing the visit of two naval officers to the Dowager Empress in the Crimea. She declined the King's invitation to convey her to safety.
FO 371/3330	18 Dec 1918	Serbian Princess Hélène reported killed by Bolsheviks at Perm on 17 November. (FO file 86748/207583)
FO 371/3330	28 Dec 1918	Report from United States consul at Ekaterinburg that Princess Hélène at Stockholm. (FO file 86748/212764)
ADM 53/485587	April 1919	Entries in the log of HMS *Marlborough* concerning the evacuation of the Dowager Empress from Yalta on 7 April and her arrival in Malta on 20 April.
ADM 53/47287	29 April 1919	Entry in the log of HMS *Lord Nelson* remarking the embarkation of the Dowager Empress in Malta, on her way to England.
HO 45/11549/ 380030	May 1919	List of the Dowager Empress's party, and arrangements for her onward journey from Malta to Portsmouth on HMS *Lord Nelson*. (HO file 380030/3)

| FO 749/13 | 1928–1930 | Estate of the late Dowager Empress in Denmark. |

Claims to the Throne

| CO 730/153/9 | 1930 | Sworn statement to police in Iraq by a young Russian who arrived there on foot from Persia late in 1929, claiming to be the Tsarevich. |
| CO 372/7160 | 1952 | Letter in French from Portugal by a lady claiming to be Olga Romanov. |

Other Items

| FO 371/4047 | 1919 | Correspondence concerning papers and remains collected by Sokolov, and taken out from Siberia to China. |
| FO 371/16336 | 1932 | Foreign Office official report on the matter. |

Bibliography

Abraham, Richard, *Alexander Kerensky: The First Love of the Revolution*, New York, Columbia University Press, 1987

Alexandrov, Victor, *The End of the Romanovs*, New York, Little Brown, 1966

Andrews, Christopher, *Secret Service*, Heinemann, 1985

Aucleres, Dominique, *Anastasia, qui etes-vous?* Paris, Hachette, 1962

Baden, Michael, *Dead Reckoning*, New York, Simon & Schuster, 2001

Bariatinsky, Princess Anatole, *My Russian Life*, London, Hutchinson, 1923

Benckendorff, Count Paul, *Last days at Tsarskoe Selo*, London, Heinemann, 1927

Benvenuti, Francesco, *The Bolsheviks and the Red Army*, 1918–1922, Cambridge, CUP, 1988

Bergamini, John, *The Tragic Dynasty*, New York, Putnam, 1969

Bing, Edward J. (editor), *The Secret Letters of the Last Tsar*, London, Longmans, 1938

Bobrick, Benson, *East of the Sun: The Epic Conquest and Tragic History of Siberia*, New York, Poseidon, 1992

Botkin, Gleb, *The Real Romanovs*, Revell, 1933

Botkin, Peter, *Les Morts sans Tombes*. Paris, Louis Conard, 1921

Botkin, Tatiana, *Au Temps des Tsars*, Paris, Grasset, 1980

Brinkley, George, *The Volunteer Army and Allied Intervention in South Russia, 1917–1921*, University of Notre Dame Press, 1966

Bromage, Bernard, *Man of Terror: Dzherzhinskii*, London, Peter Owen, 1933

Brook-Shepherd, Gordon, *Iron Maze*, London, Macmillan, 1998

Buchanan, Sir George, *My Mission to Russia Vol I & II*, London, Cassell & Co, 1923)

Bulygin, Paul, and Alexander Kerensky, *The Murder of the Romanovs*, London, Hutchinson, 1935

Bury, Herbert, Right Reverend, D D, *Russian Life Today*, London, Mowbray, 1915

Chamberlain, William Henry, *The Russian Revolution*, London, Hutchinson, 1935

Charques, Richard, *The Twilight of Imperial Russia*, London, OUP, 1958

Chernow, Ron, *The Warburgs*, New York, Random House, 1993

Bibliography

Clarke, William, *The Lost Fortune of the Tsars*, London, Weidenfeld & Nicolson, 1994

Cockfield, Jamie, *White Crow: The Life and Times of Grand Duke Nicholas Mikhailovich of Russia, 1859–1919*, Westport, 2002

Cohn, Norman, *Warrant for Genocide: The Myth of the Jewish World Conspiracy and the Protocols of the Elders of Zion*, New York, Viking, 1967

Cook, Andrew, *To Kill Rasputin*, Tempus, 2005

Cowles, Virginia, *The Russian Dagger: Cold War in the Days of the Czars*, New York, Harper & Row, 1969

Crankshaw, Edward, *The Shadow of the Winter Palace: Russia's Drift to Revolution*, New York, Viking, 1976

Crawford, Rosemary, *The Life and Love of the Last Tsar of Russia*, London, Weidenfeld & Nicolson, 1997

Cross, Colin (editor), *Life with Lloyd George; The Diary of A.J. Sylvester 1931/45*, London, Macmillan, 1975

De Basily, Nicholas, *The Abdication of Emperor Nicholas II of Russia*, Princeton, NJ, Princeton University Press, 1984

Dehan, Lili, *The Real Tsarina*, London, Thornton Butterworth, 1922

Dorr, Rheta Childe, *Inside the Russian Revolution*, New York, Macmillan, 1918

Essad-Bey, Mohammed, *Nicholas II: Prisoner of the Purple*, London, Hutchinson, 1936

Figes, Orlando, *A People's Tragedy: The Russian Revolution 1891–1924*, London, Random House, 1996

Fleming, Robert, *The Fate of Admiral Kolchak*, London, Rupert Hart-Davis, 1963

Florinsky, Michael T., *The End of the Russian Empire*, New York, Collier, 1961

Fogelsong, David S., *America's Secret War against Boshevism: U.S. Intervention in the Russian Civil War 1917–1920*, University of North Carolina Press, 1995

Fraser, John Foster, *The Real Siberia*, London, Cassell, 1902

Freund, G., *Unholy Alliance: Russian-German Relations from the Treaty of Brest-Litovsk to the Treaty of Berlin*, London, Chatto & Windus, 1957

Fry, Michael G., *Lloyd George and Foreign Policy, Vol I*, Queen's University Press, 1977

Fulop-Miller, Rene, *Rasputin, The Holy Devil*, New York, Doubleday, 1928

Fyodorovna, Alexandra, *The Letters of the Tsar to the Tsarina, 1914–1917*, London, Duckworth, 1923

Gill, P., & P.L. Ivanov et al., 'Identification of the remains of the Romanov family by DNA analysis', *Nature Genetics Vol 6*, February 1994

Gilliard, Pierre, *Thirteen Years at the Russian Court*, London, Hutchinson, 1921

Graves, Major General William S., *America's Siberian Adventure, 1918–1920*, New York, Jonathan Cape, 1931

Hall, Coryne, *Little Mother of Russia*, London, Shepheard-Walwyn, 1999

Hanbury-Williams, Major General Sir John, *The Emperor Nicholas II as I Knew Him*, London, Arthur L Humphreys, 1922

Harcave, Sidney, *Years of the Golden Cockerel: The Last Romanov Tsars 1814–1917*, New York, Macmillan, 1968

Holmes, Richard, *The Western Front*, London, BBC, 1999

Iliodor (Sergei Trufanov), *The Mad Monk of Russia*, Century, 1928

Johnson, Paul, *A History of the Jews*, New York, Harper & Row, 1987

Judd, Alan, *The Quest for C*, London, Harper Collins, 1999

Kerensky, Alexander F., *The Catastrophe*, New York, Appleton, 1927

Kettle, Michael, *The Allies and the Russian Collapse*, London, André Deutsch, 1981

Kettle, Michael, *The Road to Intervention*, London, Routledge, 1988

King, Greg & Penny Wilson, *The Fate of the Romanovs*, John Wiley & Sons, 2003

Klier, John, *The Quest for Anastasia*, Smith Gryphon, 1995

Knox, Alfred, *With the Russian Army*, London, Dutton, 1921

Lloyd George, David, *The War Memoirs of David Lloyd George*, London, Vol. I & II Odhams, 1938

Lockhart, Robert Bruce, *Diaries 1915–1938*, London, Macmillan, 1973

MacDonogh, Giles, *The Last Kaiser*, London, Weidenfeld & Nicolson, 2000

Magnus, Philip, *King Edward the Seventh*, New York, E.P. Dutton & Co. , 1964

Massie, Robert K., *Nicholas and Alexandra*, New York, Atheneum, 1967

Mayre, George Thomas, *Nearing the End in Imperial Russia*, London, Dorrance, 1929

Mikhailovich, Alexander Grand Duke of Russia, *Once a Grand Duke*, New York, Farrar & Rinehart, 1932

Morrow, Ann, *Cousins Divided*, Stroud, Sutton Publishing, 2006

Nicolson, Harold, *King George V*, London, Constable & Co., 1952

Radzinski, Edvard, *The Last Tsar*, London, Doubleday, 1992

Reed, John, *Ten Days That Shook the World*, Stroud, Sutton, 1997 edition

Rose, Kenneth, *King George V*, New York, Alfred A. Knopf, 1984

Service, Robert, *Lenin*, London, Macmillan, 2000

Slater, Wendy, *The many deaths of Tsar Nicolas II*, Studies in the History of Russia and Eastern Europe, 2007

Spiridovich, A., *Les dernières années de la cour de Tsarskoié-Sélo*, in two volumes, Paris, Payot, 1928

Stopford, Hon. Albert, *The Russian Diary of an Englishman*, Heinemann, 1919

Trotsky, Leon, *The Russian Revolution*, London, Victor Gollancz, 1934

Vassilyev, A.T., *The Ochrana*, London, Harrup, 1930

Wood, Anthony, *Europe 1815-1945*, London, Longman, 1965

Yusupov, Prince Felix (translated Oswald Rayner), *Rasputin*, London, Cape, 1927

Yusupov, Prince Felix, *Lost Splendour*, London, Jonathan Cape Ltd, 1953

Zhivotovsky, Lev, 'Recognition of the remains of Tsar Nicolas II and his family: a case of premature identification?' *Annals of Human Biology*, vol 26, 1994

List of Illustrations

35. Portrait of Alexei, 1917.
36. Alexei with companions the Markov brothers, Mogilev, 1916.
37. Alexei by the fountain, Eupatoria, 1915.
38. Olga and Tatiana at Tsarskoe Selo, 1917.
39. Alexei at Tsarskoe Selo, 1917.
40. Nicolas and Alexei at Tobolsk, 1918.
41. A signed portrait of Nicolas and Alexandra, 1917.
42. A signed portrait of Olga and Tatiana serving as nurses during the war, 1916.
43. British Agent Major Stephen Alley.
44. A cartoon of Alexandra, Nicolas and Rasputin.
45. A cartoon of Alexandra and Rasputin.
46. British Ambassador Sir George Buchanan.
47. The Ural Regional Soviet who condemned the Imperial family to death along with other Romanov relatives they held captive.
48. Grigory Rasputin, the mystic holy man.
49. The corpse of Grand Duke Ioann, executed the day after the Imperial family on the orders of the Ural Regional Soviet.
50. The corpse of Alexandra's elder sister, Grand Duchess Elizabeth, executed by the Ural Regional Soviet the day after her sister.
51. The Ipatiev House, Ekaterinburg.
52. Chekist Yakov Yurovsky, leader of the execution squad and murderer of Nicolas II.
53. The skull of Nicolas II, identified after his exhumation.
54. The skull of Grand Duchess Anastasia, identified after her exhumation.
55. Koptyaki Forest, location of the Romanov graves.

Illustrations 1–42: State Archive of the Russian Federation (GARF), Moscow
Illustrations 44, 45, 47: The Museum of Political History, St Petersburg
Illustrations 43, 46, 48, 49, 50, 51, 52, 53, 54, 55: Author's Collection

Also available from Amberley Publishing

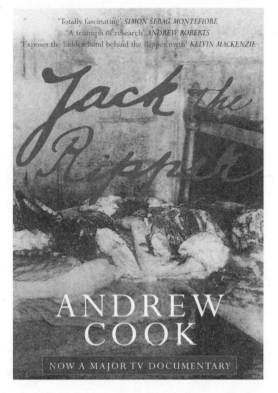

Finally lays to rest the mystery of who Jack the Ripper was

'Totally fascinating' SIMON SEBAG MONTEFIORE
'A triumph of research' ANDREW ROBERTS
'Exposes the hidden hand behind the Jack the Ripper myth' KELVIN MACKENZIE

The most famous serial killer in history. A sadistic stalker of seedy Victorian backstreets. A master criminal. The man who got away with murder – over and over again. But while literally hundreds of books have been published, trying to pin Jack's crimes on an endless list of suspects, no-one has considered the much more likely explanation for Jack's getting away with it... He never existed.

£9.99 Paperback
53 illustrations and 47 figures
256 pages
978-1-84868-522-2

Available from all good bookshops or to order direct
Please call **01285-760-030**
www.amberleybooks.com

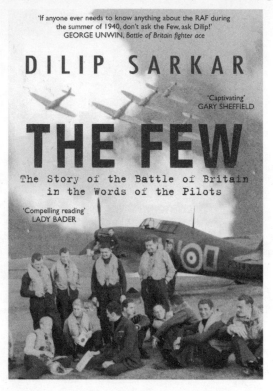

Also available from Amberley Publishing

The identity of Robin Hood is one of the great historical mysteries of English history – until now

'Impeccably researched and highly original... David Baldwin is a brilliant historical detective'
PHILIPPA GREGORY

David Baldwin sets out to find the real Robin Hood, looking for clues in the earliest ballads and in official and legal documents of the thirteenth and fourteenth centuries. His search takes him to the troubled reign of King Henry III, his conclusions turn history on it's head and David Baldwin reveals the name of the man who inspired the tales of Robin Hood.

£9.99 Paperback
76 illustrations (40 colour)
288 pages
978-1-4456-0281-3

Available from all good bookshops or to order direct
Please call **01285-760-030**
www.amberleybooks.com

Also available from Amberley Publishing

A major new history of the disaster that weaves into the narrative the first-hand accounts of those who survived

It was twenty minutes to midnight on Sunday 14 April, when Jack Thayer felt the Titanic lurch to port, a motion followed by the slightest of shocks. Seven-year old Eva Hart barely noticed anything was wrong. For Stoker Fred Barrett, shovelling coal down below, it was somewhat different; the side of the ship where he was working caved in.

For the next nine hours, Jack, Eva and Fred faced death and survived. They lived, along with just over 700 others picked up by 08.30 the next morning. Over 1600 people did not. This is the story told through the eyes of Jack, Eva, Fred and over a hundred others of those who survived and either wrote their experiences down or appeared before the major inquiries held subsequently.

£20 Hardback
40 illustrations
448 pages
978-1-84868-422-5

Available from all good bookshops or to order direct
Please call **01285-760-030**
www.amberleybooks.com

Also available from Amberley Publishing

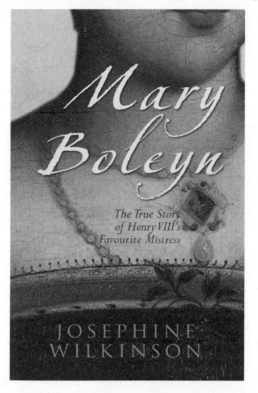

The scandalous true story of Mary Boleyn, infamous sister of Anne, and mistress of Henry VIII

Mary Boleyn, 'the infamous other Boleyn girl', began her court career as the mistress of the king of France. François I of France would later call her 'The Great Prostitute' and the slur stuck. The bête-noir of her family, Mary was married off to a minor courtier but it was not long before she caught the eye of Henry VIII and a new affair began.

Mary would emerge the sole survivor of a family torn apart by lust and ambition, and it is in Mary and her progeny that the Boleyn legacy rests.

£9.99 Paperback
22 illustrations (10 colour)
224 pages
978-1-84868-525-3

Available from all good bookshops or to order direct
Please call **01285-760-030**
www.amberleybooks.com

Index